Tired of Sunday-only faith? Do y
This book reveals how your wor.
how it affects the workplace. Then, discover the step-by-step process for bringing the power of the gospel to where we spend the majority of our time—at work.

DR. MICHAEL KELLER, senior pastor, Redeemer Lincoln Square

Missy Wallace and Lauren Gill offer, in *Faith & Work: Galvanizing Your Church for Everyday Impact*, a rich vision of church life that extends outward from Sunday gatherings into the workplaces of all its members. They encourage church leaders to imagine a Christian discipleship in which daily work plays an integral role and offer a well-tested pathway through which churches can navigate this shift. This book will radically transform how churches understand themselves and how they bear witness to the gospel of Jesus.

C. CHRISTOPHER SMITH, senior editor, *The Englewood Review of Books*; author, *How the Body of Christ Talks*

Churches that are gospel-centered and mission-driven know that the everyday work of the congregation is a crucial context for frontline ministry. But how can churches better equip their people to live out this calling? With a pastoral heart and an implementation mindset, Wallace and Gill combine solid theology and wise, practical guidance for churches that want to empower the scattered congregation for missional impact. Read this book and share it with your leaders.

MATT RUSTEN, president, Made to Flourish

This book should be required reading for every church leader who believes the people of God are called to live out their faith in every sphere of life—including their work.

MICHAELA O'DONNELL, PHD, MDIV, director, the Max De Pree Center for Leadership; assistant professor, Marketplace Leadership; lead professor, Redemptive Imagination in the Marketplace, Fuller Theological Seminary; coauthor, *Life in Flux*; author, *Make Work Matter*

Faith & Work: Galvanizing Your Church for Everyday Impact is an essential guide for any church looking to equip believers to see their daily jobs as a meaningful part of God's mission. With rich biblical insight and practical steps, this book shows how integrating faith and work can transform not just individuals but also entire communities. It's a must-read for those eager to make an eternal impact right where God has placed them. I can't wait to share this with my pastor!

JORDAN RAYNOR, best-selling author, *The Sacredness of Secular Work* and *Redeeming Your Time*

The prospect of starting a ministry for faith and work in a local church can feel daunting for many busy pastors and church leaders. I know because I was one for nearly twenty years! The overwhelm for leaders ranges from not knowing how to integrate faith and work in their theology or ministry philosophy to struggling to envision what it might look like in their church to being unsure about the difference it would make in their city or broader community.

Remarkably, Missy Wallace and Lauren Gill have managed to demystify the full range of these concerns in a single, theologically rich yet unwaveringly practical volume. They have distilled several decades of on-the-ground, hands-on experience—both in their own career journeys and through their work with churches in cities across the globe through Redeemer City to City—into the book you now hold in your hands. Every sentence, every framework, every tool and case study are the hard-won fruit of decades of ministry-tested, cross-cultural, cross-sector work, reflection, and distillation. There is not a word in here that is wasted.

Whether you are a local pastor, a Christian leader in your industry, or a city leader seeking the gospel renewal of your city, this is an indispensable guide for you. Cities will not be renewed by the gospel on the weekends. It will require the collective work of every Christian in every sector of society. *Faith & Work: Galvanizing Your Church for Everyday Impact* gets us closer to that reality.

REV. ABRAHAM CHO, vice president, Thought Leadership, Redeemer City to City

This book is destined to become a classic. It is a comprehensive manual for operationalizing faith at work through the local church. The development process emphasizes assessment so that every action step reflects the context of conditions on the ground. Wallace and Gill have provided effective tools that are accessible for immediate implementation. The format is user-friendly, both for reading as an overview and for ready reference at any time. With a resource like this, the local church is now much better positioned to become a catalyst for redemptive impact worldwide!

CHUCK PROUDFIT, founder and president, At Work on Purpose; author, *Citywide Workplace Ministry in a Box* and *Vocation Transformation*; coauthor, *BIZNISTRY*

Pastors, if you want to see your members, leaders, church, and city transformed, then read this book! Wallace and Gill provide a clear and proven roadmap that will help you unlock and unleash the latent kingdom potential that resides within your church. Through practical tools and real-life examples, this book will help all those God has called you to lead and disciple to bridge the Sunday-to-Monday divide while breaking down the sacred-secular divide, leading them to live more integrated, Spirit-led, and mission-focused lives.

ROB KELLY, founder and CEO, For Charlotte Network; cofounder and CEO, City Leaders Collective; coauthor, *Metanoia*

How can the local church have a gospel impact throughout the entire city? Tested by years of leadership experience in the trenches, Wallace and Gill offer pastors a practical roadmap for discipling workers and catalyzing marketplace renewal. This book is a real gift.

REV. DR. MATTHEW KAEMINGK, Richard John Mouw Associate Professor of Faith and Public Life, Fuller Theological Seminary; founder, Worship for Workers; author, *Work and Worship*

If you're a pastor or church planter seeking to empower your congregation to live out their faith in their daily work, this book is your roadmap. It combines deep theological insight with practical, actionable steps to help you build a church where faith and work are seamlessly integrated. The "Getting Started Guide" at the end offers clear, hands-on strategies to embed this vision into your church's DNA. Through this book, Wallace and Gill—whose extensive experience in faith and work spans diverse cultures—equip city pastors to inspire leaders, transform congregations, and ignite gospel renewal in the most strategic place: the workplace. A must-read for pastors ready to see their cities transformed.

GUNA RAMAN, CEO, City to City Asia Pacific

A clear, concise, accessible, yet brilliant "work" book for every church's lay leaders and pastors. Wallace and Gill address the brokenness and goodness of communities, the larger world, and our lives while challenging church leaders to deep reflection as well as action. Through a biblically based analysis, they identify key boosters and blockers to the impact for change that integrating faith and work can make when the church lives faithfully and fruitfully in the world. This book should be required reading for every Christian who wants to be salt and light in a world of decay and darkness. The seventeen appendices alone are worth the price of the book!

DR. L. GREGORY JONES, president, Belmont University; **SUSAN PENDLETON JONES**, senior fellow, Christ-Centered Visioning, Belmont University

Today's pastors recognize that equipping their church members for the workplace is essential for fulfilling their fundamental mission, maybe even for filling their pews. But the task is daunting. Missy Wallace and Lauren Gill break it down into achievable steps. Each step yields a small win that builds the congregation and makes the next step easier. Their real-world experience working with hundreds of pastors and churches really shows. Any pastor and church can get started with this guide and make a big difference in their people's commitment to the church, witness to the community, and service to the world.

WILLIAM MESSENGER, executive editor, Theology of Work Project

Applying faith-and-work theology and principles to your church has finally been practically spelled out. Moving from ideas to action, from principles to praxis, and from reading to doing—everything you need is here to renew and rework your ministry, your congregation, your community, and your city. There are now thousands of faith-and-work books in print, but this is the one for pastors who are ready to move beyond theory and theology and want or need examples, frameworks for understanding, practical tools, and references.

C. JEFFREY WRIGHT, CEO, Urban Ministries, Inc., Chicago, IL; business and ministry leader; attorney; contributing author, *Nonprofit Leadership in a For Profit World* and *Chasing Paper*

Many books on faith and work focus on individual believers—but *Faith and Work: Galvanizing Your Church for Everyday Impact* flips the script. Wallace and Gill offer a pastor-friendly guide to equipping congregants for real, gospel-driven impact in their daily work—without piling another exhausting program onto your plate. Drawing from their experience training hundreds of pastors in over forty countries, they provide real-world examples and practical tools that work in churches of all sizes. If you're ready to move beyond the usual "just volunteer more" message and mobilize your people for real change—in the places where they spend most of their time—this book is a must-read.

DENISE DANIELS, PHD, Hudson T. Harrison Professor, Entrepreneurship, Wheaton College; author, *Working in the Presence of God*, *Religion in a Changing Workplace*, and *Working for Better*

Faith & Work: Galvanizing Your Church for Everyday Impact offers a comprehensive and strategic guide for pastors to implement faith-and-work integration in both their churches and cities. Missy Wallace and Lauren Gill masterfully combine theological insight with practical frameworks, offering clear steps from defining your destination to becoming an integrated leader and church. If you're ready to equip your congregation to live out the gospel in their everyday work, this book is an indispensable resource.

PAUL SOHN, director, Center for Faith & Work

This long-awaited book is a game changer for the church leader looking to help their congregants connect faith to their daily work. From two trusted and tested leaders, it provides a needed roadmap for integrating faith and work into various aspects of church life. This book is a must-read for anyone seeking to mobilize a powerful pathway for church health, city impact, and individual heart transformation.

REV. DR. DAVID KIM, CEO, Goldenwood

While we celebrate the continued growth in resources for Christians looking to integrate faith and work, I am most excited to celebrate, recommend, and advocate for this one-of-a-kind book for church leaders. It will become required reading for pastoral training at seminaries around the world. Wallace and Gill's unique leadership experience and expertise in working with church leaders globally to see faith and work as a context—not an initiative or fad—led them to create this practical, theologically rooted guide for the health, impact, and relevance of the church. The workplaces of our time are the church's most strategic opportunity to show what heaven on earth looks like. Finally, capable leaders have pulled the best of their own and others' learnings to offer the right book for the right time to form and mobilize the church at work for the reconciliation of all things.

ROSS CHAPMAN, DMIN, CEO, Denver Institute for Faith & Work; coauthor, *Faithful Work*

Biblical theology, when done well, should always transform us personally and our contexts practically. *Faith & Work: Galvanizing Your Church for Everyday Impact* strongly delivers an accessible theology of work applied first to the formation of church leaders, then to congregational discipleship, leading to missional impact in the city. Loaded with crystal-clear diagrams and concrete reflection tools, it reads like professional coaching for leaders bent toward equipping redemptive action in their congregations. The appendices alone are an invaluable tool kit that cannot go unused! We'll absolutely have church leaders in our faith-and-work accelerators read and apply these field-tested approaches for vocational discipleship and community impact.

BRIAN GRAY, vice president, Formation, Denver Institute for Faith & Work (DIFW); director, 5280 Fellowship, DIFW; catalyst, CityGate

Rooted in rich theology and focused on actionable strategies, this is the resource every church leader needs. Wallace and Gill's helpful discipleship framework and practical tools weave vocational discipleship into busy ministry leaders' existing goals—deeper discipleship in their people's lives and kingdom influence in their communities. Don't miss this valuable resource to help your congregation love God and serve others through their work.

JOANNA MEYER, executive director, Women, Work, & Calling

This book powerfully exposes the hidden ways we sabotage our own efforts to shape disciples of Jesus who joyously participate in God's redemptive purposes in this world. Whether you're well-versed in integrating faith and work or just beginning to explore it, you'll find the clear, practical, and transformative steps that church leaders have been craving.

GEOFFREY HSU, executive director, Flourish San Diego

I have had the honor of working closely with Missy Wallace and Lauren Gill and witnessing firsthand their integrity, wisdom, and commitment to equipping others for meaningful impact. Few are as uniquely qualified as they are to guide churches seeking to integrate faith and work. *Faith & Work: Galvanizing Your Church for Everyday Impact* is not just a book—it's a roadmap forged from extensive experience and vision to help churches become catalysts for city flourishing. I commend this work to any church leader seeking to empower their congregation to leave the world better than they found it.

    REV. SCOTT SAULS, author; founder/president, Healthy Leaders, Inc.

Churches often reduce spiritual formation to the development of devotional practices and disciplines, worship attendance, and attempts to verbally bear witness to Christ. However, if a church fails to help people conceive all of their lives as being lived unto and for Christ, it is a huge mistake. And it undermines the spiritual transformation process that God intends to effect in our lives. Wallace and Gill effectively erase the artificial barrier between the spheres of faith and work and demonstrate that every person's life can be lived unto and for Christ and thus experience the fullness of life that our Creator has intended for us. Every church needs to take its exhortations seriously to rethink how we can help our people fulfill their callings in life.

    AL BARTH, global catalyst/vice president, Redeemer City to City

I didn't know it was possible to write a book about faith and work that truly felt like the "easy yoke" and "light burden" of Jesus, but Wallace and Gill have done just that. They start with "why" but also lead the reader through the "how" and the "what" of integrating faith and work into the life of the church. They graciously guide the reader through the theological and practical ways of being the church for the world in any and all contexts. Also, chapter six is worth the price of the book for any pastor.

    ELLIOTT CHERRY, lead pastor, Midtown Fellowship 12 South, Nashville, TN

Daily work is the primary context in which we are shaped and formed (or malformed). And yet there remains a wide gap in how most local churches disciple their people considering this reality. People everywhere, especially young people, yearn for a faith that helps them make sense of all of life, including finding purpose and meaning in their work and occupations. Wallace and Gill have offered a world-class resource—theologically grounded and eminently practical—for pastors and churches to reimagine ministry in light of a world yearning for the truth of a gospel for all of life.

    LISA PRATT SLAYTON, consultant, coach; founder, Tamim Partners LLC; catalyst, CityGate; coauthor, *Life in Flux*

Faith and work is often seen as an oxymoron in today's society. Individualism wrapped in a cancel culture can truncate how we live out our faith. *Faith & Work: Galvanizing Your Church For Everyday Impact* is a book for pastors that provides a robust theology of faith and work combined with very practical methods on how to cultivate this in the life of your church. This primer will enhance your life and ministry.

           BOB BRADSHAW, CEO, McGowan Global Institute

There haven't been many "faith and work" books written directly to pastors in a way that is empathic rather than accusatory. This book has two benefits: an understanding of the difficult role of pastoring in meeting multiple needs of denominations and their congregations; and research from twenty years of direct consultation with a thousand pastors globally. Critically, it transforms an understanding of faith and work from just another program to a context for discipleship and church/kingdom impact. What has been produced is a much-needed resource that will heal the faith-work divide in the church and accelerate building for the kingdom.

       KARA MARTIN, adjunct professor, Gordon-Conwell Theological Seminary, Boston; author, *Workshop*; coauthor, *Keeping Faith*

FAITH & WORK

FAITH & WORK

Missy Wallace
& Lauren Gill

GALVANIZING YOUR CHURCH FOR EVERYDAY IMPACT

GLOBAL FAITH & WORK INITIATIVE
A MINISTRY OF REDEEMER CITY TO CITY

REDEEMER CITY to CITY

Published by Redeemer City to City
Copyright © 2025 by Lauren Gill & Melissa Wallace

All rights reserved. No portion of this book may be reproduced or transmitted in any form or by any means, electronic or mechanical, including photocopying, recording, or by any information storage and retrieval system, without permission in writing from the authors. The only exception is brief quotations in printed reviews.

The authors have no responsibility for the persistence or accuracy of URLs for external or third-party internet websites referred to in this book and do not guarantee that any content on such websites is, or will remain, accurate or appropriate.

Redeemer City to City
57 W. 57th Street
4th Floor
New York
NY 10019
United States

www.redeemercitytocity.com

All Scripture quotations, unless otherwise indicated, are taken from the Holy Bible, New International Version®, NIV®. Copyright © 1973, 1978, 1984, 2011 by Biblica, Inc.™ Used by permission of Zondervan. All rights reserved worldwide. www.zondervan.com. The "NIV" and "New International Version" are trademarks registered in the United States Patent and Trademark Office by Biblica, Inc.™

Scripture quotations marked KJV are from The Authorized (King James) Version. Rights in the Authorized Version in the United Kingdom are vested in the Crown. Reproduced by permission of the Crown's patentee, Cambridge University Press.

"Anthropose," © Jennifer Pirecki, used by permission.
"Your Labor is Not in Vain" © The Porter's Gate Worship Project, used by permission.

ISBN 979-8-218-61574-1 (print)
ISBN 979-8-218-61589-5 (eBook)

There are two strategies to reach the world. The first one is to recruit the people of God to use some of their leisure time to join the missionary initiatives of church-paid workers. And the second one is to equip the people of God for fruitful mission in all of their life.

MARK GREENE

CONTENTS

Foreword by Katherine Leary Alsdorf		xxvii
1	The Everyday Impact Your Church Could Have: An Introduction	1

SECTION ONE 13
A BIBLICAL FOUNDATION AND A DISCIPLESHIP MANDATE
The Role of Work in a Broken World

2	Why Does Work Matter to God?	15
3	Work as a Context	27
4	A Faith-and-Work Framework for Unleashing the Gospel	41

SECTION TWO 61
FAITH-AND-WORK-INTEGRATED LEADERS, CHURCHES, AND CITIES
A Journey Map for Implementation

5	Defining our Destinations	63
6	Becoming a Faith-and-Work-Integrated Leader	77
7	The Journey Map for Implementing Faith and Work in the Church and City	99
8	Becoming a Faith-and-Work-Integrated Church: An Overview	103
9	The Integrated Church: Step 1–Build Leadership	109
10	The Integrated Church: Step 2–Understand Needs	119
11	The Integrated Church: Step 3–Implement	135
12	The Integrated Church: Step 4–Assess	155
13	Becoming a Faith-and-Work-Integrated City	163
Conclusion		183
Acknowledgments		185
Getting Started Guide: Hacks to Incorporate Faith and Work Into Your Existing Church Activities		191

Appendix 1: Integrated Leadership Assessment	205
Appendix 2: Spiritual Attunement as a Tool for Integrated Leadership	207
Appendix 3: Integrated Leadership Team Assessment	209
Appendix 4: City-Based Learning Tool	211
Appendix 5: Congregation Work Survey	217
Appendix 6: Workplace Visit Guide	223
Appendix 7: From→To Chart	227
Appendix 8: Church Service Inclusion Tools	230
Appendix 9: Sermon Inclusion Tool	237
Appendix 10: Industry Prayer Examples	241
Appendix 11: Guide to Writing an Industry Prayer	245
Appendix 12: Industry Article Examples to Include in Communications	247
Appendix 13: Impact Assessment Tool	248
Appendix 14: Transformative Learning Experience Guide	255
Appendix 15: Transformative Learning Experience Sample Survey	258
Appendix 16: Church and City Journey Maps	262
Appendix 17: Recommended Faith-and-Work Organizations	265
About the Authors	267

FOREWORD

KATHERINE LEARY ALSDORF

During my teen years, I walked away from anything to do with religion because it seemed irrelevant, hypocritical, and boring. As an adult, my life became largely wrapped up in (and controlled by) my work. But I was hungry for something that would lighten the load and speak to the daily challenges I faced. This hunger for something more led me to Redeemer Presbyterian Church in New York City—where I discovered a gospel that changes lives.

The good news I got, and continue to get, from Redeemer's pulpit is that Jesus Christ ushered into the world a gospel that changes everything: It changes our individual hearts, it changes how we relate to others, and it is changing the world we live in. What I learned challenged my motivations for working. I saw hope for reconciling tenuous relationships at work. And, as a recently appointed CEO of a growing technology company, I was eager to know how to lead distinctively as a Christ-follower and how to align the mission of our company with God's purposes.

Tim Keller's gospel-centered teaching was phenomenally helpful. Even when I moved to Silicon Valley to lead another tech start-up, I listened to his sermons at night. Yet, I longed for others with whom to process these teachings and better apply them to my work life. I also bemoaned the fact that references to work, let alone specific teachings about work, were very uncommon in the churches near my new home. Instead, some congregants were creating their own groups and organizations, completely disconnected from their churches, to discuss the challenges of living out their faith at work. Often these groups centered on prayer, job-search optimization, or evangelism. In addition to drawing people away from church, the groups often suffered from a lack of depth, theological grounding, and spiritual formation.

In 2002, Redeemer invited me to move back to NYC to help them start a marketplace ministry. I accepted because the need was so great. I often say that in all my years in business, I never had a product or service with as much "pent-up demand" as the programs at Redeemer's Center for Faith & Work

(CFW). Congregants were eager to express their needs and volunteer to help. Twenty-two years later, I can report that this ministry effectively equipped people to integrate their faith and their work, transformed their hearts, changed the church, and brought hope, love, and justice into workplaces across the city that the church had never reached before.

Tim Keller and I attempted to articulate some of the theological foundations of CFW in our 2012 book *Every Good Endeavor: Connecting Your Work to God's Work*.[1] This resource has helped many individuals and churches relate the gospel to their work in the world through the lens of the biblical storyline: God's good plan for work beginning at creation, the problem with work because of the fall, and the new story for work because of the gospel. Subsequently—in response to a burgeoning need among global church planters to equip their congregations to be God's ambassadors in their workplaces—Redeemer's church-planting organization, City to City, created the Global Faith & Work Initiative.

The demand for theological foundations related to faith and work is great, and the resources are now available. But how to get started? How can pastors and ministry leaders guide their churches to become communities that spread the good news of God's kingdom through the daily work of every person in every part of the town or city? How might congregants be equipped to embody the mercy, justice, and love of God not just on Sundays but throughout their everyday lives?

Like most pastors, you might feel daunted, understandably, by the thought of yet another ministry. Instead, approach this as broadening and deepening the scope of your current discipleship in ways that makes the gospel relevant to the whole of people's lives, beyond just church and family life. It strengthens the outward face of your church—the way your church loves and serves the community in which you live. In all areas of church ministry—Sunday worship, small groups, children's ministry—you will be discipling people to *be* the church, not just when gathered for worship or teaching but in every endeavor of their lives. Along with your evangelism, mercy, and justice ministries, people equipped to live out their faith in and through their work will be an effective part of your outward face. Make faith and work part of your whole church vision.

---

[1] Timothy Keller with Katherine Leary Alsdorf, *Every Good Endeavor: Connecting Your Work to God's Work* (New York City, NY: Dutton, 2012).

Given the pressing need to equip your congregants, and in the face of the many demands on you as a pastor, how would I suggest you move forward? Frankly, there is no generic map because every church is unique; however, this book was written to help you create your own contextualized "journey map" that fits the people and places you are seeking to reach.

For the past ten years, I have worked closely with Missy Wallace and Lauren Gill, who founded the Global Faith & Work Initiative. I also collaborated with Missy as she formed the Nashville Institute for Faith and Work. I have witnessed—as a partner, coworker, advisor, and friend—how Lauren and Missy shape pastors and church planters around the globe to help them cast vision and build pathways for their congregants to see their everyday work as vital to God's mission. This book distills their expertise and hard-earned practical wisdom.

In part one of this book, you will explore why work matters to God, you will reimagine your view of work, and you will be introduced to a faith-and-work framework designed to unleash the power of the gospel in your midst. Part two unpacks the journey of becoming a faith-and-work-integrated leader and church through a tested step-by-step process. The appendices are a treasure trove of tools and materials that may be helpful along the way.

Leading change is hard, and perhaps there is no greater (or harder) change than gospel change. While the gospel changes everything, our hearts and our minds are often formed more by the cultural stories around us than the truths revealed in God's Word. And our congregants' work lives are more shaped by the idols of their industries and organizations than they often recognize. Actually, there's no harder change, for any of us, than turning from serving ourselves to loving others and serving God. Yet, by God's grace and mercy, the Holy Spirit is planted in our hearts, ready for the opportunity to refine, restore, and inspire us. There's no harder change, but there's also no more rewarding, God-glorifying change. Work can be the Refiner's fire. Work can be where the church becomes the hands and feet of Jesus. I encourage you to embrace this journey—along with Missy, Lauren, me … and so many others.

1

THE EVERYDAY IMPACT YOUR CHURCH COULD HAVE

AN INTRODUCTION

If it was not beneath the Son of God to work as an artisan, then surely it is beneath none of His children. Because He was no stranger to "the dust and sweat of toil," as the hymn asserts, "sons of labour are dear to Jesus," and He has imparted to a life of toil both dignity and nobility.

J. OSWALD SANDERS

Work is often the area of people's lives where they have received the most secular discipleship and the least biblical discipleship. They've gotten undergrads and master's degrees, they've studied for licensures, and gotten professional coaching, and all the while their church has been silent, perhaps even a little threatened by their expertise and ambition. This creates an implicit secularism in what is quantitatively the majority of people's waking hours. Equipping the church with a robust theology of faith and work is a clear antidote to this secularism and the meaninglessness which attends it. People catch fire when they realize that Paul wasn't kidding when he said their labor in the Lord is not in vain (1 Cor. 15:58).

JAMES RATHMANN

In a 2022 Lifeway Research study about "The Greatest Needs of Pastors,"[1] almost two in three interviewees said they were facing stress in ministry, and nearly half also pointed to discouragement and distraction as ministry challenges.

---

[1] "The Greatest Needs of Pastors: A Survey of American Protestant Pastors," Lifeway Research, 2022, accessed December 11, 2024, research.lifeway.com/wp-content/uploads/2022/01/The-Greatest-Needs-of-Pastors-Phase-2-Quantitative-Report-Release-1.pdf.

In our combined twenty years of working with pastors and their congregants across the globe, we have witnessed the extent of this exhaustion firsthand. Many pastors attend our training events feeling harried and discombobulated from juggling meetings, sermons, pastoral care, staff leadership, volunteer development, Bible studies, and finance meetings—leaving them with little mental, emotional, or time capacity.

We have rarely met an apathetic pastor; every leader we have encountered is interested in the hearts of their people more than anything else in their role. The same Lifeway Research report confirms our experience: Pastors care deeply about faith apathy, the ability to reach unchurched people, and developing leaders and volunteers.

Given all of this, it's perhaps not surprising that, according to Christian research organization Barna, 38 percent of pastors have considered leaving their role in recent years.[2] Perhaps you are one of them. It is partially this precise juxtaposition—the deep concern you have as a pastor and the overwhelming stress that comes with the role—that compelled us to write this book. We believe that if you can help your congregants understand how to integrate their love of Christ into their day-to-day work—where they spend a good proportion of their waking hours—it may accelerate some of your biggest hopes while alleviating several of your pressing problems.[3]

We appreciate that helping your congregants to integrate their faith and work may feel daunting, another thing to add to an already too-full plate. However, this book aims to equip you for the journey. As we have seen time and again—from pastors in the US, Latin America, the UK, and Southeast Asia—when congregants are empowered to connect their faith with their daily work, it catalyzes the work of the gospel in their own hearts and beyond. Church members are drawn closer to Christ as they begin to impact their cities through the overflowing of the fruit of the Spirit.

---

[2] "38% of U.S. Pastors Have Thought About Quitting Full-Time Ministry in the Past Year," Barna Group, November 16, 2021, https://www.barna.com/research/pastors-well-being/.

[3] "Average Working Hours (Statistical Data 2023)," Clockify, accessed July 26, 2024, https://clockify.me/working-hours.

WHAT IS "FAITH AND WORK," AND WHY IS IT IMPORTANT?

Many Christians have diverse interpretations of work and its connection to their faith. Although most people think of paid jobs when they hear the term "work," the concept is much broader. According to Merriam-Webster, to "work" is defined as "to exert oneself physically or mentally especially in sustained effort for a purpose."[4] In this book, we affirm that all purposeful effort is work. This encompasses paid work, such as that of financial managers, custodians, or waiters, as well as unpaid work, such as that of parents, volunteers, or caregivers. Although we will focus on paid work—because this is the area where most people find it challenging to integrate their faith—the concepts explored in this book are equally applicable to both paid and unpaid effort.

Using the above definition of work, faith-and-work integration can be described just as it sounds: *a holistic integration of the truths of the gospel applied into the parts of one's life that are work.*

When Christians think about applying the truths of the gospel, they sometimes focus primarily on individual salvation offered for the forgiveness of sins and less on the accompanying personal transformation. But our personal transformation should compel us to contribute to God's mission to mend the world. Timothy Keller notes, "God's plans for the world extend beyond our inner selves. They involve the coming of his kingdom. Over the last few decades, the evangelical world has rediscovered the importance of the biblical idea that God's kingdom will draw close."[5]

Jesus proclaimed and demonstrated the arrival of this kingdom, offering foretastes of its reality. This is the life he calls his disciples to, as we participate in the ongoing establishment of God's reign. This is evident in many places throughout the four Gospels, but none more noteworthy than in the Lord's Prayer where Jesus teaches us to pray, "Thy kingdom come. Thy will be done, on earth as *it is* in heaven" (Matt 6:10 KJV). As New Testament scholar N. T. Wright says, "[We] are not just to be a sign and foretaste of that ultimate 'salvation';

---

[4] Merriam-Webster, s.v. "Work," accessed August 26, 2024, https://www.merriam-webster.com/dictionary/work.

[5] Timothy Keller, *Gospel-Centered City Ministry: The City to City DNA*, 17, accessed July 26, 2024, https://redeemercitytocity.com/dna.

[we] are to be *part of the means by which* God makes this happen in both the present and the future."[6] Given most people in your congregation spend many of their waking hours in their occupations, their work is the primary sphere in which they do this.

Jesus understood the value of applying his message to the day-to-day work of his people. He routinely used work as a key context for teaching through everyday examples. In Jesus' roughly thirty-seven unique parables, thirty-two refer to work as part of the narrative, and in twenty-seven of those, work is the main point of the parable. Across all the parables, twenty-two different types of work are mentioned. So, "to convey spiritual concepts, [Jesus] incorporated work images and technical commercial terms familiar to his audience."[7] Although Jesus was likely well acquainted with the pains of work due to his years growing up in an agrarian community and participating in a trade, the frequency of using work metaphors as a teaching tool makes it evident that he saw the importance of work as a context to mold hearts.

Work is actually evident throughout the whole biblical narrative. The Bible is full of ordinary people, doing ordinary and extraordinary things amid their everyday workplace roles. As British pastor and leadership coach Kate Coleman notes in *Metamorph*,

> From Abraham to Deborah and Jesus to Paul, few were ... what we would consider ordained religious professionals today. Instead, many were ordinary people with regular jobs, playing typical roles within their respective communities....
>
> Abraham was a businessman, Deborah a prophetic civic leader, David a military man and songwriter, Isaiah a politician, Amos a shepherd, Nehemiah a civil servant, Peter a commercial fisherman, and even Jesus was a carpenter.... Paul too was a religious scholar and a tentmaker.
>
> Each exercised profound spiritual leadership wherever they were in life, and each knew how to pray, influence, and bless their respective communities. We too are called to influence our environments by serving as spiritual leaders

---

[6] N. T. Wright, *Surprised by Hope* (London, UK: SPCK, 2007), 213 (emphasis original).

[7] Klaus Issler, "Exploring the Pervasive References to Work in Jesus' Parables," *Journal of the Evangelical Theological Society*, vol. 57, no. 2, 2014: 323–339, https://etsjets.org/wp-content/uploads/2014/06/files_JETS-PDFs_57_57-2_JETS_57-2_323-39_Issler.pdf.

within God's community and contributing positively to wider society.... Any position can enable us to influence the lives of others for good, be it within our family, community, church, business, or other sphere, and to fulfill some crucial leadership role.[8]

GALVANIZING THE CHURCH THROUGH FAITH AND WORK

Peter Ong, a pastor and movement leader in New York City, once described the importance of integrating faith and work in such a way that it not only transforms the worker and the city but also the church:

> For congregants and leaders alike, faith and work is the cornerstone of gospel formation. As a movement and church leader, I've seen firsthand how there is a deep desire among individuals to express a holistic, faithful presence in every area of their lives. This longing extends to the workplace, where they strive for excellence and to outwardly reflect a rich gospel perspective on the theology of faithful presence. Seeing the gospel take root and grow in this daily practice of integrating faith and work is such a grace.
>
> I've seen the transformative power of this integration by encouraging congregants to discern their professional calling as a locus of ministry and witnessed how God has met them in their profound desire to be Christ-formed in their work. I have seen them transform into servant workers who embody a new way of seeing people, inspiring them to pray for others. Their work becomes an extension of their worship, offering a powerful witness to the world. This integration fosters a depth of seeing work as redemptive and strengthens connections within a broader Christian community, creating a ripple effect that collectively builds up the church.[9]

Of the roughly one thousand pastors we have trained in faith-and-work integration, most arrive with an open mind to learn but a hesitant commitment to action. Pastors have varying ideas about what this buzz phrase "faith and work" means and a healthy suspicion about whether it is just a passing fad.

---

[8] Kate Coleman, *Metamorph: Transforming Your Life and Leadership: Inspired Wisdom from the Ordinary, Extraordinary People of the Bible* (Richmond, VA: 100 Movements Publishing, 2024), 171–72.

[9] From personal correspondence with Peter Ong. Used by permission.

However, our work with pastor cohorts around the world has given us story after story of how churches are changed when their attendees finally understand what the death, resurrection, and ascension of Jesus mean in the context of their work. When faith and work are fully integrated, it ignites a flame in a Christian that changes not only their church behaviors (attendance, Bible study, volunteering, and more[10]) but also, and more importantly, the way they personally commune with Jesus and engage their community, organization, and industry on a day-to-day basis. Individuals with their hearts transformed by Jesus can change every sphere of work. And, as these arenas are transformed, others attribute the positive changes to the work of Christians, leading to the spread of the gospel and the growth of the church.

Take a moment and imagine the many industries your church family interacts with every week: As they drive or take public transportation to work, school, and church, they use the transportation industry. As they log into their email at work or use their map to navigate to a meeting, they intersect with the technology industry. As they take out loans for college and mortgages and save for retirement, they engage with the finance industry. And as they head to dinner to celebrate a birthday, they touch hospitality. And so on and so on. Each of them intersects with hundreds of industries over the course of a week. What might it look like for members of your congregation employed in each of those fields to be looking for opportunities to love others in and through their work—for God to be using all his disciples in every sphere of society to be part of ushering in the kingdom on earth as it is in heaven?

Now imagine your church equipping and empowering people in each of these industries to tackle the broken systems of your city and work toward renewal and flourishing in the community. We acknowledge this vision can feel daunting, regardless of your church size—from tiny startup churches to well-resourced megachurches. You're likely already operating at maximum capacity, as are those you serve in your congregations. Some in your church family are juggling demanding jobs, families, and their faith. For others, finding work seems impossible and the very concept feels hopeless. Whether employed or not, work significantly impacts their time, mental health, and stress levels.

---

[10] See Barna *Christians at Work* study referred to in footnotes fourteen and fifteen, chapter three.

WHY THIS BOOK?

The purpose of this book is to help you as a pastor or lay leader to catch a vision for the importance of equipping your church members to integrate their faith with their work—discipling them to live with Christ every minute of every day. And more importantly, to create a roadmap to help you realize that no matter how big or small your church, you can make significant progress without too much effort.

If you want your church to be relevant to the day-to-day lives of your congregants and those in your city who don't yet know Christ, addressing faith and work is essential. We strongly believe you can't afford *not* to do this. Work is a key mechanism for discipleship because so much of who we are is intertwined with the work we do, and work is part of God's unfolding story to redeem the world.

All of that said, this book is for you if you are:

- looking to learn more about faith and work and its benefits,
- confused about what faith and work even is,
- cynical about faith and work and its priority in the church,
- interested in faith and work but overwhelmed with other priorities,
- curious about a long-term vision for faith and work,
- looking for examples of faith and work in other contexts, or
- needing instruction on how to implement faith and work in your context.

OUR FAITH-AND-WORK STORIES

My (Lauren's) first interaction with work was on my family farm in Kentucky, picking red bell peppers and stripping tobacco. However, after high school, I moved to New York City to go to college to study acting and journalism. While there, I attended a seminar given by Tim Keller to actors, in which he spoke about why God needed us as actors to help tell stories that communicated both the fallenness and glory in his creation. I was amazed. The unintentional message of my Christian upbringing had been that the only way to integrate my faith and work was to be a missionary, pastor, or youth group leader. As someone deeply passionate about the arts from a very young age, that inherently felt wrong—although I could not articulate why. My time participating in a program called the Gotham Fellowship at Redeemer Presbyterian Church's Center for Faith & Work (CFW) gave me the theological foundation I needed to internalize that belief—that all work had value for God and could be used for his purposes. I began working at CFW and was deeply moved by the ways professionals from all walks of life wanted to use their work for God's glory in New York City. Journalists, financiers, artists, healthcare professionals, lawyers, educators, those in marketing and in nonprofits, were all asking the same question: How can God use my hands for his glory in this city?

At the same time I was working at CFW, I got a master's degree in counseling and worked for seven years at Redeemer Counseling Services where I heard over and over the day-to-day pain and suffering of those who were working in deeply broken situations or seeking God's wisdom for how he wanted to use them. These two experiences went hand in hand for me, showing me both the importance of making sure our personal relationship with God is aligned with the larger vision for how the work of each person contributes to the glorious tapestry of the work of all of God's people in a city. In 2018, I moved to Redeemer City to City's Global Faith & Work Initiative. Missy and I began working with pastors, ministry leaders, and marketplace leaders around the world who wanted to build faith and work into their cities in more meaningful ways. By God's grace and with the help of our global faith-and-work catalysts, we have built an ecosystem that has trained more than one thousand pastors in over forty countries.

My (Missy's) relationship with work has been a journey marked by both passion and uncertainty, shaped by experiences that continually redefine its meaning in the context of the death, resurrection, and ascension of Jesus Christ. Over the past thirty-five years since college, whether navigating various professional roles or parenting our three (now grown) children with my husband, Paul, my understanding of work has evolved significantly.

For the first decade of my career, I was fully immersed in the hardcore business world in Charlotte, Chicago, Singapore, Bangkok, and New York, driven by ambition and success, with no real sense of how my faith intersected my work. The sacred/secular was not just a divide in my life; it was a wall. Work was intellectually stimulating and was mostly a means to an end—a source of meaningful relationships, achievement, and self-actualization—but little more.

Then, in a spur-of-the-moment decision, I left the corporate grind to join a startup education endeavor where I stayed for another decade. I believed that moving into a "helping" profession would be better for the world and thus would bring more meaning to my life. And while I don't regret that decision (it was one of my life's great honors), I later realized that the decision was based on flawed theology. I thought I was being a better person simply by working in a more altruistic industry, but I was still missing the deeper connection between my work and Jesus—which could be possible in any type of work. I was also missing the truth that my identity is *fully* rooted in being a daughter of Jesus, not in my professional accomplishments.

Everything changed a few years into the school endeavor when our oldest child was struck by a mysterious and dire illness. The doctors offered little hope and sent her home with instructions for hospice. In an instant, my work took on a new form; for three years, I became a full-time caregiver, online neurological disease researcher, and medical advocate for my daughter. My previously thin theology, which viewed Jesus more like a self-help tool than the Lord of Life, crumbled under the weight of this crisis. But it was during these dark years that I began studying theology, which ignited a transformation in me. The teachings of Tim Keller led me to some seminary classes, where my heart was set aflame for Jesus in new and profound ways as I studied faith and work. I realized I had missed so much; my work had always been about self-fulfillment (even through doing good), but now I saw its true purpose in the broader narrative of God's kingdom.

As our daughter miraculously recovered (a tale for another day), my vocation took a new direction. A seminary class about missional strategies indirectly led me to the founding of the Nashville Institute for Faith and Work, which I went on to lead for five years. Those years were deeply rewarding, as I sojourned with others on our joint journeys of integrating faith and work. Unexpectedly, God called me away from that role, and I joined Redeemer City to City to help implement faith-and-work initiatives in churches around the world. There, Lauren and I had the joy of working together, and the pastors we have worked with globally have shaped this book.

Still, I am by no means finished with learning about faith and work.

Ironically, while leading a global faith-and-work initiative, I began to make work more than it should have been in my life, even as I was teaching others about its rightful place.

What I'm learning now, more than ever, is the importance of the One who guides our work and how we access his voice hour to hour. The most crucial chapter of this book may well be the one about the faith-and work-integrated leader (chapter six). I'm in yet a new phase of surrendering my work to Jesus Christ, the Lord of Life. I call this surrender 57.0. Even now, in real time, I keep having to surrender more and more. My hope is that this book will draw you closer to God as you pursue your own journey of faith and work while leading others in theirs.

THE FLOW OF THIS BOOK

We have outlined this book to provide a clear understanding of faith-and-work integration, why it matters, and practical steps for implementation in your context.

This chapter introduces the book's key themes and objectives. Section one (chapters two through four) explain the "why" behind faith-and-work initiatives. Chapter two establishes the doctrinal foundation for the significance of work, delving into key aspects and themes of the biblical narrative. Chapter three challenges you to shift your perspective, recognizing work as a central context for your congregants' discipleship and mission rather than a program. It also addresses common obstacles you'll need to overcome to help integrate faith and work in the lives of your people. In chapter four, we introduce a key framework about work, which will empower you to equip your congregants with a comprehensive understanding of personal and system brokenness. This approach will help your church members to understand their role in addressing this brokenness through their daily work and to foster a holistic view of faith and work that extends beyond evangelism or social impact.

Section two (chapters five through thirteen) is the "how" portion of this book, providing practical guidance for implementing the principles explored in section one.

In chapter five we outline the three levels where faith-and-work integration takes place—the individual *leader* level (both you and those you serve), the *church* level, and the *city* level. We explore the interconnected nature of these levels and detail the ideal destination for each—a vision of what full faith-and-work integration could look like.

Chapter six challenges you to embody the journey of faith-and-work integration and to equip others to do the same so that you and those you lead have a strong and cohesive understanding of how the gospel impacts you at the *heart* level in your relationship with God, at the *community* level in how you interact with others, and at the *world* level in how you operate within your work industry, city, and beyond. We explore a framework and provide exercises that will help you cultivate an integration for yourself and your leaders—focusing on work as the context in which both you and they are formed.

Chapters seven through thirteen provide a map and practical steps to help you begin your implementation journey, initially focusing on the faith-and-work-integrated church and subsequently the faith-and-work-integrated city. The journey map is intended as a launching pad—to stimulate learning and action rather than prescribe a rigid process.

At the end of the book, we include a Getting Started Guide that offers practical steps to quickly incorporate faith and work in your existing church activities. If you can only do one small thing, we advise you to start with the sermon incorporation described in the guide. However, we strongly recommend you review the whole process highlighted in the journey map because it will help you to envision the integration as well as create more sustainable and impactful first steps that can lead to greater momentum.

Finally, in the appendices, we provide numerous supplementary materials to equip you as you seek to build out faith-and-work initiatives in your context.

Most importantly, we want this book to show how integrating faith and work can mobilize those you lead to commune more closely with God and glorify him by living out Christ's love for us in the world. Intentional integration of faith and work will galvanize your church for everyday impact by not only transforming individual lives but also revitalizing your ministry and city.

SECTION ONE

A BIBLICAL FOUNDATION AND A DISCIPLESHIP MANDATE

THE ROLE OF WORK IN A BROKEN WORLD

2

WHY DOES WORK MATTER TO GOD?

Everyone will be forgotten, nothing we do will make any difference, and all good endeavors, even the best, will come to naught. Unless there is God. If the God of the Bible exists, and there is a True Reality beneath and behind this one, and this life is not the only life, then every good endeavor, even the simplest ones, pursued in response to God's calling, can matter forever.

TIMOTHY KELLER AND KATHERINE LEARY ALSDORF

[Of] many diverse callings, many diverse vocations ... the common thread is that the purpose of all of them is service. [Messiah alumni] are stewarding their vocational power to advance the virtues of the Kingdom. They are deploying their gifts for the common good. ... And living this way has required intentionality. It has required faithfulness. Living this way requires creativity and imagination and risk and prayer and perseverance.

AMY SHERMAN, COMMENCEMENT ADDRESS, MESSIAH COLLEGE, MAY 2011

For more than a decade, Teena Dare worked in the hospitality industry as a bartender and server. As a Christian, she longed for a "godlier" vocation, something aligned with her faith, something that really mattered. Over time, Teena's perspective began to shift. Rather than searching for more "meaningful" work, Teena discovered a surprising calling amid appetizers and cocktails. It was there that she envisioned transforming the hospitality industry into a reflection and foretaste of God's kingdom.

However, as Teena surveyed her restaurant and others, she noticed a pervasive brokenness. She recognized that the powerful and privileged in her industry relied on a marginalized workforce—the undocumented, the poor, and the formerly incarcerated. These individuals were the invisible backbone, laboring in the kitchen's "back of house," far from the public eye. Further, in Teena's training, she had been taught to treat those who would give bigger tips differently from those who would not. This custom—framed as good business practice and to her benefit—fueled her awareness of the inherent biases within the system.

Witnessing these inequities and brokenness within her industry, Teena felt compelled to embody an alternative way, one that reflected God's restorative love and presence. She committed herself to offering the same quality of service regardless of the potential tip. For many patrons, this meant they were being treated with a level of respect and kindness they rarely experienced elsewhere. Teena realized this new vision for her restaurant wasn't just for the customers she was serving; it also extended to helping her coworkers view their work as sacred and meaningful. One of the ways Teena sought to do this was through creative writing. She started a blog and, in it, she attempted to capture the goodness and beauty of her restaurant and the work within it. Her writing even resonated with non-Christians. Some of her coworkers printed out her words and displayed them in the restaurant—a constant reminder to themselves of the dignity inherent in their everyday tasks.

After a decade of faithful service, Teena became convinced that God's redemptive mission to reconcile all things in heaven and on earth isn't just confined to churches, nonprofits, and traditional mission fields. It's unfolding in the everyday restaurants and bars scattered across our cities, in the bustling kitchen as much as in the dining areas ... one small act at a time, one customer at a time.

We have seen other Christians choosing to express love in the hospitality industry through acts of care, whether it be prioritizing the highest quality and sustainability of ingredients or offering employment opportunities to those facing barriers, such as those reintegrating into society from prison. We can all consider what it means to foreshadow the heavenly eternal reality in our own contexts.[1]

---

[1] Thank you to Teena Dare for allowing us to share her story and to Charlie Meo for helping us craft it.

THE BIBLICAL NARRATIVE THROUGH THE LENS OF WORK

Teena's testimony is one of countless stories we've heard over the years. It reveals some key principles found in the biblical narrative—the reality of God's good creation, the effects of the fall, God's desire to redeem all things through his great love for us and the power of the cross, and the ultimate restoration where creation will be completely redeemed in the new heaven and new earth. Yet, rarely does the average Christian learn how to make these connections.

As you consider a faith-and-work journey in your context, it is important to remember what the biblical narrative reveals about work. As Christians, we interact daily with many narratives that compete with the gospel in shaping our views on work. The most common Western story tells us that work is about hustle; about gaining financial success, power, or fame; and that the "good" end justifies the means by which we get there. And once we are there, we can focus on rest and leisure. Another common narrative tells us that work is a necessary evil; something we endure so we can earn money solely to survive. A further competing story positions work as the means to becoming the savior for those who "need" our help—in professions such as medicine and childcare—where individuals become the hero by "saving" children or healing the sick.

In North America in particular, hit songs focus on these narratives (you may know of "Everybody's Working for the Weekend" by Loverboy), retirement brochures featuring golf courses and swimming pools portray idyllic visions of life without work, and countless movies idealize the success of fame and power. These stories either make too much or too little of work, and even our churches inadvertently repeat them. Often the subconscious message our churches communicate is that the only work that matters is that of ministers, missionaries, and helping professions, and that the only contribution Christians outside of those spheres can make is to earn money to tithe to the church. Only the narrative of God's unfolding story puts work in its proper place. The biblical narrative gives us the framework to see work as foundational to God's redemptive mission in the world. Understanding the significance of work is critical if we are to build a faith-and-work initiative on the right foundations.

Abraham Cho, vice president for Thought Leadership at Redeemer City to City, says,

> It is no mistake that the story of the Bible begins in a garden in Genesis but ends in a city in Revelation, and that all of human history is in between. The history of human civilization is part of God's work in moving his creation forward toward the ultimate desired end. When we situate ourselves within that story, we see that our creative story fits into the narrative arc of the history of the entire world. We are able to put ourselves into the larger mosaic of what God is doing.[2]

The biblical narrative can be considered in four acts:

Act 1: Creation
Act 2: Fall
Act 3: Redemption
Act 4: Restoration

Without this narrative, work can be viewed as both much more and much less than God intends. The biblical narrative helps us understand work as one of God's greatest gifts, allowing us to participate in his redemptive mission and help others to do the same.

ACT 1: CREATION

> Then God said, "Let us make mankind in our image, in our likeness".... So God created mankind in his own image, in the image of God he created them; male and female he created them. God blessed them and said to them, "Be fruitful and increase in number; fill the earth and subdue it. Rule over the fish in the sea and the birds in the sky and over every living creature that moves on the ground."
>
> GENESIS 1:26–28

---

[2] Redeemer City to City, *"Why Your Work Matters: Work as Cultivation,"* accessed July 30, 2024, https://learn.redeemercitytocity.com/library/why-your-work-matters-43482/88399/path/.

> The LORD God took the man and put him in the Garden of Eden to work it and take care of it.
>
> GENESIS 2:15

Let's start at the beginning. In the very first sentence on the very first page of Scripture and throughout Genesis 1 and 2, we see God working by *creating*, calling it "good." Then on the sixth day, he creates humans in his image and calls them "very good." At the pinnacle of creation, he brings humans into the picture and entrusts them with specific tasks: naming the creatures (Gen. 2:19–20), being fruitful, (Gen. 1:28) and taking dominion over the earth (Gen 1:28). Though he could do everything and anything without them, God allows humans to work alongside him. Said otherwise, he asks humans to go out and create flourishing. In its description of Genesis, *The Theology of Work Bible Commentary* points out,

> God could have created everything imaginable and filled the earth himself. But he chose to create humanity to work alongside him to actualize the universe's potential, to participate in God's own work. It is remarkable that God trusts us to carry out this amazing task of building on the good earth he has given us. Through our work God brings forth food and drink, products and services, knowledge and beauty, organizations and communities, growth and health, and praise and glory to himself.[3]

God created from the very beginning. *For five days he brought structure out of chaos, form to the formless.* And then, he brought more structure out of chaos by forming us in his image—the image of a Worker.

Today, there is barely a job in the world that does not follow God's model of bringing structure out of chaos with the aim of calling it good. Your congregants might be creating a spreadsheet that helps turn a mess of financial data into a clear and organized format, allowing analysts to make a more informed judgment about a company's true value. Or they might be sweeping the floors at a restaurant, turning chaos into structure by removing germs and dirt to create a hygienic eating environment. Or perhaps they are organizing professional

---

[3] "Fruitfulness/Growth (Genesis 1:28; 2:15, 19–20)," Theology of Work Project, accessed July 26, 2024, https://www.theologyofwork.org/old-testament/genesis-1-11-and-work/god-creates-and-equips-people-to-work-genesis-126-225/fruitfulness-growth-genesis-128-215-19-20/.

sports leagues, turning the chaos of men or women running around a field into structure with rules and objectives, and bringing a community together to cheer toward a common goal while appreciating human athleticism.[4]

Many Christians think of work as the result of the fall or sin entering the world—as merely a necessary evil or a way of bringing glory to self. However, helping others to see that work existed *before* the fall shifts their paradigms as they realize that all of us are *created* to work in the image of the greatest Creator of all. Although this may be obvious to those of us in ministry, we have seen time and again that this perspective—that we are actually created to work—is revolutionary for many in our congregations. This concept is foundational, yet it is the complete antithesis of our worldly narratives.

God calls humans to bring flourishing to his creation with everything they do—whether that's driving a school bus to make sure students get to school on time, painting a mural, or cleaning a hospital so that surgeries take place in hygienic environments. In the earlier story, Teena brought flourishing to creation by bringing an excellent hospitality experience to everyone she served at her restaurant. God creates humans in his image, and then he gives them the task of drawing out the potential he has placed in his creation. Although we may not be tending a literal garden, our work contributes to the ongoing cultivation of what God first planted.

ACT 2: FALL

We know that after creation came the fall (Gen. 3). Most of us think of the fall as being about human sin, yet in reality, the fall affects not only individuals but also every system and element of creation, including work. Genesis 3:17–19 reads,

> "Cursed is the ground because of you;
>   through painful toil you will eat food from it
>   all the days of your life.
> It will produce thorns and thistles for you,
>   and you will eat the plants of the field.
> By the sweat of your brow

---

[4] Missy Wallace, "From Chaos to Goodness—Step by Step, Industry by Industry," Eventide Center for Faith & Investing, November 9, 2017, https://www.faithandinvesting.com/journal/from-chaos-to-goodness/.

> you will eat your food
> until you return to the ground,
> > since from it you were taken;
> for dust you are
> and to dust you will return."

One of the consequences of a fallen world is that work will now be "painful toil." The effort we put into our work will no longer equate to the output of our work because creation is impacted by brokenness in individuals and systems. Your congregants will feel the toil of work in many ways: They may choose serving self over others; relationships with their coworkers and bosses may be fractured; they may work in unsafe conditions; or they may contribute actively or passively to broken systems that hurt others. Pride. Jealousy. Greed. Exploitation. It is all sin. All of us interact with people and systems in ways that don't reflect our Creator. We seek control, influence, acclaim, and financial stability more often than we seek God. We contribute to unjust systems in conscious and unconscious ways. Every industry, system, and structure has areas of brokenness that have been impacted by the fall. For example, we saw in Teena's story the temptation to exploit marginalized workers and give greater focus to those who were more likely to give better tips.

But this brokenness does not change the reality that God created us to work, imperfect as we are and broken as the systems we have created are. God will not abandon his creation even though the ugliness of sin impacts every part of it. He is working to redeem it.

ACT 3: REDEMPTION

Christ entered into the brokenness to redeem all things through his sacrifice on the cross. This incredible miracle impacts all of creation as God seeks to reconcile all things to himself through Christ—and this includes the realm of work.

> The Son is the image of the invisible God, the firstborn over all creation. *For in him all things were created*: things in heaven and on earth, visible and invisible, whether thrones or powers or rulers or authorities; all things have been

created through him and for him. He is before all things, and in him all things hold together. And he is the head of the body, the church; he is the beginning and the firstborn from among the dead, so that in everything he might have the supremacy. For God was pleased to have all his fullness dwell in him, and *through him to reconcile to himself all things,* whether things on earth or things in heaven, by making peace through his blood, shed on the cross.

COLOSSIANS 1:15–20, emphasis ours

God's desire for restoration is comprehensive. He seeks to bring redemption not just to his people but to all of creation. As God works to reconcile creation to himself, he invites us as his image-bearers to participate in that process; and part of your role as a pastor is nurturing those you lead to respond to that invitation. He beckons us to bring order out of chaos in all systems and spaces around us just as he sends us out into the world to bring flourishing to his creation. Through their relationship with Christ, your congregants can address their own brokenness, reconcile relationships at work, seek to fix broken systems and processes, and work for justice in inequitable situations. For example, Teena actively worked to address the fallen areas of her field. She publicly blogged about the inherent dignity of the hospitality industry and shared the posts with her coworkers. She sought to reverse the industry norm of prioritizing those who might give greater tips and instead provided an excellent hospitality experience to everyone. All of our work allows us an opportunity to serve as redemptive agents for God's work, no matter our industry.[5]

The gift of redemption is that we live on earth in what is often called an "already-but-not-yet" period of time, in which Christ's lordship has begun but is not complete. Through the work of Jesus, the kingdom of God is already present in a limited way, but the full realization of the kingdom—with all its glory—is yet to come (see 1 Cor. 15:23–28).

As an ambassador for Christ, each member of your church is invited to walk with him, identifying broken places that have been impacted by sin, and pointing people toward Jesus by pushing against the brokenness and loving them. Whenever your congregants pray, "Thy kingdom come. Thy will be

---

[5] That said, there are some business categories that one would be hard pressed to view as redemptive, for example, prostitution, pornography, and illegal drugs.

done, on earth as it is in heaven" (Matt. 6:10 KJV)—they are part of that plan. "Reframing work this way allows us to connect our hearts more deeply with our role with Christ in this already/not yet interval between his ascension and return. Rarely is an industry secular only—almost all of them reflect something of God's goodness. Thus, the challenge is finding the redemptive edge."[6] And work in almost all industries is a primary context for those in your congregation to express this, as they encounter people, workplaces, and industries longing for redemption.

ACT 4: RESTORATION

The final act of the biblical narrative is restoration, where we see creation completely redeemed in the new heaven and new earth.

> Then I saw "a new heaven and a new earth," for the first heaven and the first earth had passed away, and there was no longer any sea. I saw the Holy City, the new Jerusalem, coming down out of heaven from God, prepared as a bride beautifully dressed for her husband. And I heard a loud voice from the throne saying, "Look! God's dwelling place is now among the people, and he will dwell with them. They will be his people, and God himself will be with them and be their God. 'He will wipe every tear from their eyes. There will be no more death' or mourning or crying or pain, for the old order of things has passed away."
>
> . . .
>
> I did not see a temple in the city, because the Lord God Almighty and the Lamb are its temple. The city does not need the sun or the moon to shine on it, for the glory of God gives it light, and the Lamb is its lamp. The nations will walk by its light, and the kings of the earth will bring their splendor into it. On no day will its gates ever be shut, for there will be no night there. The glory and honor of the nations will be brought into it. Nothing impure will ever enter it, nor will anyone who does what is shameful or deceitful, but only those whose names are written in the Lamb's book of life.
>
> REVELATION 21:1–4, 22–27

---

[6] Wallace, "From Chaos to Goodness."

These verses reveal a foretaste of the new heaven and the new earth. Finally, God will dwell with humanity in a fully redeemed world of the new heaven and earth where there will be no more death, mourning, crying, or pain.

How will work be redefined in the new creation? In his book *When the Saints Go Marching In*, Richard Mouw highlights passages in Isaiah that suggest the possibility of a flourishing society with diverse industries. For instance, the ships of Tarshish appear in the vision of New Jerusalem despite their being an earlier symbol of the evils of commerce (Isaiah 2 and 60).[7] Therefore, it is possible that many of the industries in which your congregants participate will exist in redeemed and restored ways in the next act of the narrative. Imagine how the Holy City might look if all the work taking place within it has been redeemed. Have you considered what the industries of your church family would be like if each was a perfect version of work? Envision the buildings. Imagine the perfection of the food and the exquisiteness of the art. What would a redeemed public transportation experience be like? If the financial institutions were always equitable and just, what would be different?

Revelation provides hope and encouragement for what is to come. It gives Christians a reason to imagine the creational goodness of all work and the motivation to work to mend the world. Until that is a reality, disciples of Jesus work toward "on earth as it is in heaven," and you can inspire your church family to have an imagination for a redeemed version of their industry or job now.

Somehow, although the specifics remain veiled, the work of every person in your congregation can be infused with hope, knowing that there is continuity between what they create now and what lasts into the new creation. N. T. Wright, in his book *Surprised by Hope*, exhorts us with a similar message:

> What you *do* in the present—by painting, preaching, singing, sewing, praying, teaching, building hospitals, digging wells, campaigning for justice, writing poems, caring for the needy, loving your neighbour as yourself—all these things *will last into God's future*. They are not simply ways of making the present life a little less beastly, a little more bearable, until the day when we

---

[7] Richard J. Mouw, *When the Kings Come Marching In: Isaiah and the New Jerusalem* (Grand Rapids, MI: Eerdmans Publishing Company, 2002), 41–54.

leave it behind altogether.... They are part of what we may call *building for God's kingdom*.[8]

Think back again to our story of Teena. Although she may not have fully grasped the impact of her kindness, she glimpsed a glorious, fully restored future when she wrote about how important hospitality is to God and shared it with her coworkers. One day she will fully understand how her work in the present contributed to God's kingdom. Perhaps her hospitality inspired others to be more welcoming and inclusive. Maybe it helped others to serve with more joy. By imagining a restaurant in heaven—exquisite food, divine flavors, loving service, high-quality drink, meaningful conversation, and inclusivity—Teena can imagine what her present-day work might look like fully perfected. The same is true for you and those you lead. God allows his followers the privilege of working alongside him to build toward the new heaven and the new earth.

The four-act biblical narrative provides a powerful framework for reimagining work, reminding us that, through Christ, we can all—whether a pastor, a church worker, or a member—approach our vocational callings with purpose, joy, and overflowing abundance, while also expecting brokenness. Enable your congregants to envision their work or industry in its intended state and uncorrupted by sin (creation), so they can appreciate its true potential. Teach them to soberly assess the impact of sin (fall) but also to recognize God's ongoing work of renewal in their professions (redemption). Finally, equip them to imagine a future where their work is fully perfected in the new heaven and new earth (restoration). Doing this provides you with an incredible opportunity to encourage and enable your congregation to actively seek God's face and participate in his unfolding story for the world through the many hours they spend in their work.

REFLECTION QUESTIONS

- What part or parts of the biblical narrative do you think your community would most identify with in relation to their work?

---

[8] Wright, *Surprised by Hope*, 205 (emphasis original).

- What drives those in your community to work? How might a vision of being "called to cultivate creation" alongside God influence their motivation?
- Can you identify any work that does not follow the creation pattern of bringing structure out of chaos?
- How do your congregants perceive God moving in their work? Where do they see signs of redemption taking place?
- How can you point your congregants toward a broader vision of their work contributing to God's kingdom?
- Are there particular industries or professions that seem impossible to redeem, even with God?

3

WORK AS A CONTEXT

If it falls to your lot to be a street sweeper, sweep streets like Michelangelo painted pictures, sweep streets like Beethoven composed music, sweep streets like Leontyne Price sang before the Metropolitan Opera. Sweep streets like Shakespeare wrote poetry. Sweep streets so well that all the hosts of heaven and earth will have to pause and say: Here lived a great sweeper who swept his job well.

MARTIN LUTHER KING JR.

If we see that human history and the unfolding of culture and society are integral to creation and its development, that they are not outside God's plans for the cosmos, despite the sinful aberrations, but rather were built in from the beginning, were part of the blueprint that we never understood before, then we will be much more open to the positive possibilities for service to God in such areas as politics and the film arts, computer technology and business administration, developmental economics and skydiving.

ALBERT M. WOLTERS

Through exploring the biblical narrative, you've hopefully gained a greater appreciation that work matters to God. However, even with this understanding, it's crucial to examine a few key perspectives that ensure you don't minimize the importance of faith and work in those you lead. Adopting a biblical perspective on the significance of work and its relevance to the new heaven and new earth will motivate you and your congregants to prioritize it now rather than postponing it for a later time. This story from Pastor Andres Garza (Monterrey, Mexico) expresses this shift.

When I saw a man's business mindset transformed in a Bible study about faith and work, it helped me to understand Ephesians 4:12 more deeply. This verse talks about "[equipping God's] people for works of service, so that the body of Christ may be built up."

As a pastor, I felt called to equip people to serve within and beyond the church walls. Initially, I found it difficult to understand that work outside of the church was as important as "ministry" work. I had been educated to believe that ministry work held greater meaning for God than "secular" work.

After a year of meeting once a week with a businessman in Monterrey, he surprised me by saying that he now saw his business as God's work, and therefore his goals and motivations had been completely changed. "It is impossible for me to speak to my team without referencing the business as the business of God," he told me.

His testimony helped me to realize that my core calling as a pastor was to equip men and women to view their entire being—who they are, what they do, and how they think—through the lens of their relationship with and faith in Jesus Christ. Within two years, more businesspeople started coming to our Bible study, and finally, in 2013, we decided to start a new church with this kind of discipleship focus. Since then, I cannot separate discipleship from the connection between faith and work.[1]

MAJOR PARADIGM SHIFT: WORK AS A CONTEXT

Andres underwent a powerful realization: Discipleship is inextricably linked to faith and work because work is the *environment* in which congregants can process all that God is teaching and asking of them. Thus, work is the *context* God uses in their lives for his work in and around them. Viewing work in this way is crucial if you are to appreciate the significance of your congregants' work. Instead of viewing faith and work as a program or a checklist from the lens of a current church model, work needs to be embraced as a fundamental *context* for living out faith. Pastors spend a great deal of time thinking about how to contextualize services and environment. If you begin to include the work lives of your

---

[1] From personal correspondence with Andres Garza. Used by permission.

congregants into your contextualization, you will quickly become relevant and meet their needs.

Adopting this view and integrating faith and work into your church may feel overwhelming, making it easy to delay addressing this need. Yet, when you view your congregants' work as the main context of their daily lives, it can be understood as a key to penetrating their hearts with gospel truths. Their work is the primary arena where they interact with others, navigate challenges, and contribute their unique talents for the flourishing of God's creation. When work is viewed this way, it becomes a powerful means through which your church family can experience the transformative power of the gospel. Empowered by this understanding, your church can begin to see their work not just as a job but as place to serve alongside God. So, whether your congregants are truck drivers or bankers, artists or stay-at-home parents, they can unleash the power of loving God and loving neighbor in their everyday lives. This will ripple outward, creating a positive impact in their families, communities, workplaces, industries, and cities. Ultimately, this shift unlocks the transformative potential in your congregation and subsequently your city. By viewing work as *the primary context* for faith impact, you can begin to equip your members to become agents for change in every sphere of their lives.

The context of work is important to the lives of those you lead and your city because

- work is a conduit for the *heart change* you long to see in your congregants;
- work is a catalyst for the *impact* you hope to make in your city;
- work is an area of life that *answers* your congregants' *questions*; and
- work is a way to *strengthen* the local church.

WORK AS A CONTEXT FOR HEART CHANGE

Since the average worker spends a minimum of 40 percent of their waking hours in some type of work, it is important to explore its meaning to those in your church.[2] In a worldwide survey of more than 150 countries entitled "The World

---

[2] "Average Working Hours (Statistical Data 2023)," Clockify.

Poll,"[3] analytics and advisory company Gallup uncovered what they describe as one of the "most important discoveries Gallup has ever made."[4] Gallup's CEO Jim Clifton states,

> Humans used to desire love, money, food, shelter, safety, peace, and freedom more than anything else. The last 30 years have changed us. Now people want to have a good job, and they want their children to have a good job. This changes everything for world leaders. Everything they do—from waging war to building societies—will need to be carried out within the new context of the need for a good job.[5]

Clifton's application is for "world leaders," but the implication for you as a church leader is just as important. According to this data, work trumps nearly everything else in people's lives, regardless of their cultural, geographic, or socioeconomic context. Work is more important than love, money, food, and shelter! This widespread sentiment, though driven by varying reasons, is impossible to ignore if you care about what people care about. If work occupies such a central place in most people's lives—surpassing even *love*, according to the data—then it must become a critical context for discipleship. And because having a good job is so important to your congregants, talking about work provides a unique opportunity to address one of the core desires of their hearts. The root cause of this desire varies. For those who are deeply marginalized by poverty, the need may be fueled by survival. For those who long for self-actualization, it may be more about purpose. Whatever the reason—regardless of geographic, socioeconomic, or cultural context—work matters deeply. So, work is the ultimate sphere you must penetrate in order to call your people to a deeper relationship with God. Without a focus on work, it will be almost impossible for those in your church family to experience holistic heart transformation.

---

[3] The World Poll began in 2005, and Gallup have committed to continuing it for one hundred years. Gallup's discovery that "what everyone wants is a good job" was made six years into their global data collection. See Jim Clifton, *The Coming Job Wars* (New York, NY: Gallup Press, 2001), 8–10; and "How Does the Gallup World Poll Work?" Gallup, accessed November 5, 2024, https://www.gallup.com/178667/gallup-world-poll-work.aspx).

[4] Clifton, *The Coming Jobs War*, 10.

[5] Clifton, *The Coming Jobs War*, 11.

Given the value people place on work, perhaps it's not surprising that it is also a significant source of strain. In 2017 in the US, over 85 percent of people reported work-related stress, and only 30 percent of people worldwide considered themselves fully engaged at their job.[6] A recent *New York Times* article on wealth and happiness cites a study that concludes "work is the second-most miserable activity; of 40 activities, only being sick in bed makes people less happy than working."[7]

Work is therefore not only a central longing but also a source of pain. This disconnect calls for the gospel to become relevant to the very arena where people spend so much of their time and energy. They need help integrating what the Bible says about work with their day-to-day lived experience. With its inherent challenges and triumphs, work is the very platform where God meets and shapes your congregants, sanctifying them amid all the ups and downs.

As your church members work—whether it be in construction sites, banks, schools, businesses, or any other profession—they will experience significant pains, joys, conflicts, and confusion. You can help them view their work as a context to press into their relationship with Christ, as an opportunity to improve or alleviate broken systems, and as a way to examine their relationships and engagement with colleagues, coworkers, and competitors.

WORK AS A CONTEXT FOR CITY IMPACT

In addition to being an on-ramp to heart change, focusing on faith-and-work integration can help catalyze Christians to impact their communities and cities throughout the week.

No doubt you desire those in your church to impact your city. It can be incredibly frustrating to labor week after week on sermons and teaching only to realize that your congregants' lives are unchanged in their day-to-day. Work is a place of focus for city change. While workers spend about two thousand hours a year at work, they only spend about fifty hours a year at church and around

---

[6] "State of the Global Workplace 2017," Gallup, May 14, 2019, https://www.gallup.com/workplace/349484/state-of-the-global-workplace.aspx.

[7] Seth Stephens-Davidowitz, "The Rich Are Not Who We Think They Are. And Happiness Is Not What We Think It Is, Either," *The New York Times*, May 14, 2022, https://www.nytimes.com/2022/05/14/opinion/sunday/rich-happiness-big-data.html.

fifty-two hours per year volunteering in churches and other nonprofits.[8] Yet when most churches plan projects and programs to impact the city, they are often focused on volunteer work and/or partnerships with nonprofit organizations. Imagine the leverage if the other 1,948 hours per month were unleashed for Christ through the daily work of your congregants. In their book *Work and Worship*, Matthew Kaemingk and Cory B. Wilson state,

> The city will be renewed not by five church planters and five nonprofit leaders; it will be renewed by the complex callings and careers of the five hundred other people sitting in the pews.... The mission of the local church is not limited to a single outreach program. It is not limited to a single missionary. It is pluriform, complex, and all-inclusive. The church's mission is embodied in the diverse work of all the people all over the city.[9]

If your church wants to truly impact your city and fight against the sin and brokenness in the community, it can't rely solely on a few hours of contribution from congregants, who, after work and family, have little time to spare. Trying to change a community with only volunteer hours creates an unnecessary burden on both you and your congregants. But if you equip your church family to integrate their faith into their work, imagine the possible ripple effect in your city. When you encourage them to work for renewal in government, finance, education, healthcare, the arts, manufacturing, media, technology, and transportation, your church may become a powerful catalyst for citywide renewal and impact.

WORK AS A CONTEXT FOR ANSWERING CONGREGANTS' QUESTIONS

There is much data to suggest that people are sorely longing to integrate their faith and work, especially the younger generation. In 2019, Barna and World Vision did a global study of eighteen- to thirty-five-year-olds. This study, called "The Connected Generation," highlights that churches are not helping

---

[8] "Volunteering Statistics for 2024: How Charitable Are We?" Team Stage, accessed December 11, 2024, https://teamstage.io/volunteering-statistics/. Based on 2023 data in the United States.
[9] Matt Kaemingk and Cory B. Wilson, *Work and Worship: Reconnecting Our Labor and Liturgy* (Eugene, OR: Cascade Books, 2020), 50.

millennials find answers to their key questions about day-to-day life.[10] And since this generation longs to make a difference and needs the church to help, silence in this area is driving people away. According to the study, "Those who have left the faith are particularly inclined to find flaws or gaps in its teachings, which they believe cannot address their questions, their day-to-day life or real issues in society." And "one of the clear imperatives of this [global study] is to offer more holistic forms of leadership development and vocational training and to mobilize a generation already inspired toward justice."[11] Further, a different Gallup poll about church attendance reveals that "a full seventy-five percent of respondents indicated that, of all the offerings from their places of worship, they cared most about sermons, preferring those which taught scripture and were relevant to their lives."[12] What this is really saying is that they want teachings that highlight how *work* is relevant to their lives since, as noted earlier through the Gallup data, work is one of the most important areas of concern.

Yet despite clear data that work-and-life-relevant sermons matter greatly to people, most churches struggle to embed such work relevance into their liturgy and discipleship. The themes of work, its accompanying toil, and the opportunity to love God and others in and through it, are often absent. To take just one example, a review of five years of talks and sermons from a church on the east coast of the United States revealed that work was only mentioned once or possibly two times.[13] Is it any wonder that young people feel that our messages are irrelevant if we are not addressing the core concerns of their lives?

WORK AS A CONTEXT FOR STRENGTHENING THE LOCAL CHURCH

You may be concerned that if you emphasize the importance of work, it will reduce the amount of focus, energy, and time that a congregant gives to the

---

[10] "The Connected Generation," Barna (with World Vision), accessed July 26, 2024, https://theconnectedgeneration.com/.
[11] "The Connected Generation," Barna.
[12] Casey Cep, "What American Christians Hear at Church," *The New Yorker*, October 7, 2021, https://www.newyorker.com/news/on-religion/what-american-christians-hear-at-church.
[13] Doug Sherman and William Hendricks, *Your Work Matters to God* (Colorado Springs, CO: NavPress, 1987), 16.

church and to spiritual formation. However, Barna's study, "Christians at Work," reveals an association that suggests just the opposite. The study shows that congregants who understand how faith connects to work are more engaged in their churches in the ways most pastors desire. Specifically, the study shows that people who understand faith-and-work integration read their Bible more, attend church more, pray more, and volunteer more than Christians who are not equipped in this way.[14] Although causation cannot be assumed, it is clear that churches that emphasize the integration of faith and work have high levels of behaviors that would suggest stronger churches.

Activities Associated with a Strong Local Church
Personal Activities of Christians Who Integrate Faith and Work Versus All

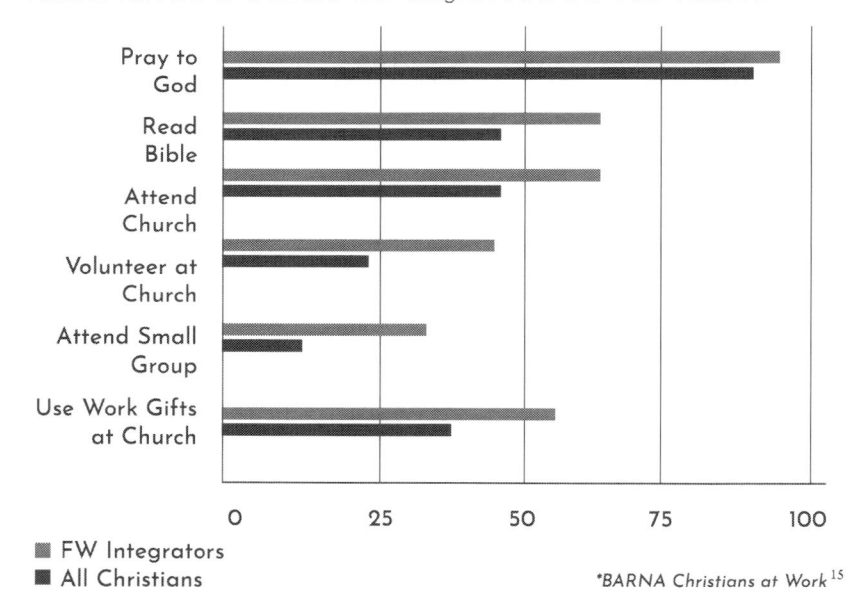

Activity	FW Integrators	All Christians
Pray to God	~95	~90
Read Bible	~62	~45
Attend Church	~62	~45
Volunteer at Church	~45	~25
Attend Small Group	~32	~12
Use Work Gifts at Church	~55	~38

■ FW Integrators
■ All Christians

*BARNA Christians at Work[15]

---

[14] Barna scored faith and work integration based on four statements: 1) "I can clearly see how the work that I am doing is serving God or a higher purpose." 2) "I find purpose and meaning in the work I do." 3) "I am looking to make a difference in the world." 4) "As a Christian, I believe it is important to mold the culture of my workplace." Christians who agreed strongly with these statements are defined by Barna as integrators of faith and work. Barna, *Christians at Work: Examining the Intersection of Calling & Career* (Barna Group, 2018), 50.

[15] Image created from data in Barna, *Christians at Work*, 79.

OVERCOMING THE HURDLES

Even if you are beginning to appreciate the importance of the integration of faith and work, we know that there are a few other hurdles you will need to overcome. In our interactions with pastors—whether through one-on-one coffees, weeklong learning intensives, short webinars, or consulting projects—the message we consistently hear both directly and indirectly is, "I cannot get to this right now." These words usually imply one or more of the following issues, which we refer to as "defeaters":

- "I don't have time."
- "I don't have the budget."
- "I don't have the staff or volunteers."
- "I have higher priorities/problems/opportunities."
- "I am not an expert in the types of work my people do, so I am not equipped to do this."
- "I have not seen it effectively implemented anywhere."
- "I'm not sure I believe that all work matters to God."

At their heart, these defeaters can be distilled into four main categories:

- Competing priorities
- Feeling ill-equipped
- Being misinformed about the effort required
- Holding a false dichotomy between sacred and secular work

We understand all these defeaters, and we also appreciate that as a pastor, you have a real desire to lead a thriving church that points people toward Jesus—so we want to directly address these issues. We believe that overcoming them will enable you to better support your congregants to integrate their faith with their work.

DEFEATER #1: COMPETING PRIORITIES

One afternoon we were having coffee with a pastor who had been encouraged to talk to us about faith and work. About halfway through our time, he confided something along the lines of, "Can I level with you? I'm here because I was asked to be here by an elder, but I just can't do one more thing right now. Prayer is currently our priority, plus we need to refresh our youth program to be more effective, and our people are not attending church enough. My plate is full."

This encounter mirrors hundreds we have had, and you may feel exactly the same way. The most frequent defeater voiced around the faith-and-work contextualized ministry is its assumed unimportance compared to other priorities. We appreciate that faith-and-work integration feels like just "one more thing" amidst a myriad of new ideas, programs, and priorities for focus.

If you are unsure whether to prioritize the integration of faith and work, remember:

- When faith and work is viewed as a critical context of your laity's lives rather than as a program, it may actually inform your highest priorities and solve some of your pressing concerns (e.g., attendance).
- Integrating faith and work is not a checklist item to "get to later" any more than thinking about your context is something for later. Faith-and-work integration is a high priority that has potential to draw congregants deeper toward Christ and impact your city.

DEFEATER #2: FEELING ILL-EQUIPPED

Perhaps you feel unqualified to understand the work of those you lead, or maybe you even *avoid* talking about work so as not to appear unprepared or ignorant. You may have limited experience in industries outside of formal vocational ministry, even if you are a bi-vocational pastor. Seminaries rarely teach much about the intersection of faith and work, and it's unlikely that your mentors gave you examples of faith-and-work integration.

If you went to seminary, no doubt you were formed to be *the expert* in your flock on theological matters and tending to congregant-care concerns; but you are probably not an expert on work industries, and so you may feel ill-equipped to talk about work. But who could be an expert on every industry, every work trend, every philosophical worldview underlying work? It's impossible! However, remember, you *are* an expert on the human heart and its longings. You *are* an expert on the biblical narrative and the truth of the gospel as it applies to the pains and joys of work. And issues at work are rarely related to finance or marketing; they are usually matters of the heart—fear, idolatry, conflict, arrogance, pride, or survival. Congregants deeply need your voice on these issues.

If you are feeling ill-equipped to provide expertise around work, remember:

- You do not *need* to be an expert on all the trends, particulars and types of work. Merely sharing that all work matters to God and to the leadership of the church is a significant encouragement.
- You *are* an expert around the truths of the Bible which apply to work. Enabling those you lead to see work through the lens of creation, fall, redemption and restoration (see chapter two) can be a helpful starting point for almost any work conversation, and thus industry expertise is not required.
- Whether congregants are experiencing extreme pain or great joy in their work or whether they make too much of it or not enough, pastors are experts at asking questions about joy and possibilities, about pain and brokenness, and sharing biblical truths.
- Your church is full of people who long for their work to matter and will gladly give you time if you need help understanding their industry. And there are many free resources that can help you learn about industries and their relevance to the Christian faith and vice versa. (You can find links to many of these resources in the Getting Started Guide at the back of this book and appendix seventeen.)

DEFEATER #3: BEING MISINFORMED ABOUT THE EFFORT REQUIRED

Perhaps you have been exposed to examples of faith-and-work programs or initiatives that have been underway for years, and the maturity and depth of these programs seem impossible in your own context. It may be tempting to view well-developed and highly resourced faith-and-work efforts, both inside and outside the church, as benchmarks. With the intensity of your already full workload and tight budget, it's easy to see why the idea of starting a new initiative may seem daunting.

If you feel overwhelmed about the effort required, bear in mind that:

- Faith and work is a *context*, not a program.
- Encouraging faith-and-work integration can happen with very small steps that require almost no time or money yet can create immediate impact.

DEFEATER #4: HOLDING A FALSE DICHOTOMY BETWEEN SACRED AND SECULAR WORK

A couple of years ago, we were on a video call with a pastor who was clearly exhausted from the everyday demands of ministry, which were compounded by some significant personal and family challenges. Like any of us in vocational pain, he reframed his sense of calling to comfort himself in his distress: "At least I know *my* work is for God's kingdom." In his reframe, he revealed what is perhaps the biggest defeater for pastors trying to implement faith-and-work initiatives. Although of course his assertion is true, further discussion showed us that what he meant was this: "I am out late night after night missing time with my family, and I could work a whole lot less and make a whole lot more money in a different career. However, I am okay because this is work for God, and I was called by him. *But* that other, higher paying work might not be." By comforting himself with "at least I work for God," he was inadvertently reinforcing a hierarchy of work, which implies that work outside of formal vocational ministry (i.e., nearly all other work) is in fact *not* for God. This view is rooted in a false dichotomy between the "sacred" and the "secular." Mark Greene, former executive director of the London Institute for Contemporary Christianity, calls this "the great divide":

> The great divide is the all-too-common belief that some parts of our life are sacred and really important to God—prayer, Sunday services, church-based activities—but that others are secular and irrelevant to God—work, school, university, sport, the arts, music, rest, sleep, hobbies. It's a lie that distorts God's character and severely limits our everyday enjoyment of him. Tragically, it also severely limits our understanding of our everyday role in God's purposes.[16]

---

[16] Mark Greene, "The Great Divide," The London Institute for Contemporary Christianity, accessed May 29, 2024, https://licc.org.uk/resources/the-great-divide/.

Many of us succumb to a similar mentality, even though we may not be consciously aware of it. After ten years in banking and management consulting, and another ten in secondary education, I (Missy) too had fallen prey to accepting a faulty hierarchy of work. In my mind, there was an A team of workers for God, which included pastors and missionaries; a B team, which included all the helping professions like doctors and teachers; and a C team, which was everyone else except for the D team, which included management consultants, corporate attorneys, and private equity and hedge fund investors. My husband and I were both squarely on the D team. And, as my faith grew, I could not find a model to help me process this. In fact, I did not even realize I was looking for one.

As a result, in a quick decision in 2003, I left corporate life to help one of my clients start a school. I am hugely thankful for that formative decade of work. But I must confess that my main impetus for the change was that I thought I would be moving from the D team to the B team, and thus doing something God would consider more valuable. The reality is that *all* my work has mattered to God.

If you are unconsciously missing opportunities to see the spiritual value in all types of work, consider the following:

- Although the Bible shares that your role as a pastor is a special calling that necessitates incredible respect (1 Tim. 3:1–7, 5:17; Titus 1:5–9), the Bible is also quite clear that every good endeavor can be done for his glory (Gen. 1:28, 2:15; Ps. 50:23; 1 Cor. 10:31, 15:58; Col. 3:23). Sometimes we are not even aware of the hierarchal view we hold in relation to work and its value.
- If you do not believe that the work of your people matters to God, it will be difficult to implement faith-and-work efforts in a meaningful or permanent way. Commune with God about your beliefs around the hierarchy of work that could impact your view of others' work.

We have yet to meet a pastor in any context—large or small church, US- or internationally-based—who does not feel busy. This dedication is undoubtedly fueled by a deep love of God, real demands on time, and the sacrifice modeled by Jesus. However, this constant busyness can also hinder the ability to connect with God to identify what truly matters and what he calls you to do. In our view, the defeaters outlined above may prevent you from fully integrating faith and work into your ministry—meaning that your church, your people, and your city are not impacted in the ways that they could be. We hope that, by reflecting on each of these challenges in prayer, you will be inspired to see how the integration of faith and work as a context can not only empower your congregants but also address your most pressing issues.

REFLECTION QUESTIONS

- In what ways do you think the congregants in your church perceive the significance of their work in relation to God's plan?
- How often do you incorporate the context of work into your preaching and teaching?
- To what extent do you view your congregants' work as a sphere to unleash change in your neighborhoods and cities?
- How much does your church focus on volunteer efforts rather than equipping members for a Christ-centered life in all aspects of life, including their occupations?
- What evidence do you see in your setting that young people are clamoring for church to address the questions of their everyday lives?
- How do you perceive the spiritual significance of ministry work compared to work that is considered secular? Are there any unconscious biases or assumptions that might hinder a holistic understanding of God's purposes in all occupations?
- What things do you regularly say that could be implicitly devaluing the day-to-day work of your congregants?
- Where in the Bible do you see ordinary people bringing the kingdom on earth as it is in heaven?
- What percentage of people in your church do you think really understand how their Christian faith impacts their work?

4

A FAITH-AND-WORK FRAMEWORK FOR UNLEASHING THE GOSPEL

The two ideas, justice and vocation, are inseparable.... It is by way of the practice of vocation that sanctity and reverence enter into the human economy. It was thus possible for traditional cultures to conceive that "to work is to pray."
WENDELL BERRY

*Cultivation happens in your vocation and the workers are few.
You can be called, but first, the caller must change you....
Cultivation happens in your vocation and the harvest is plenty,
You don't need to be an architect to build a better city.*
SHO BARAKA

If you and your congregants are to grasp a holistic view of faith-and-work integration, it's important to become more deeply aware of brokenness in its various forms and how it impacts work. Brokenness affects our experience of work, and understanding brokenness reveals opportunities for personal sanctification as well as ways to love others. We've developed a model called the Faith-and-Work Framework for Unleashing the Gospel that focuses on what the Bible calls us to, daily, as disciples of Jesus. It reveals how understanding brokenness is a key to unlocking our fullness in Christ. This model can help empower your congregation by equipping them to express the biblical mandates in and through their work, and by helping them understand how brokenness manifests in that process. Most of all, it will help them commune more deeply with Christ.

Many Christians have different understandings of how the gospel applies to their work. Most often, people have a view that is not wrong but is truncated by a mostly singular focus on either evangelism *or* social impact, neither of which is a full expression of the gospel. This framework offers a more holistic view of faith-and-work integration by highlighting brokenness in its various forms. In particular, this 2x2 grid can help your congregants appreciate that a full view of brokenness—both personally and in systems—is essential if they are to fully embrace their roles as disciples of Jesus in their workplaces and spheres of influence. This nuanced awareness of brokenness can help unleash the power of the gospel in the way they love people, places, and things in their workplaces, communities, and cities.

The Faith-and-Work Framework for Unleashing the Gospel

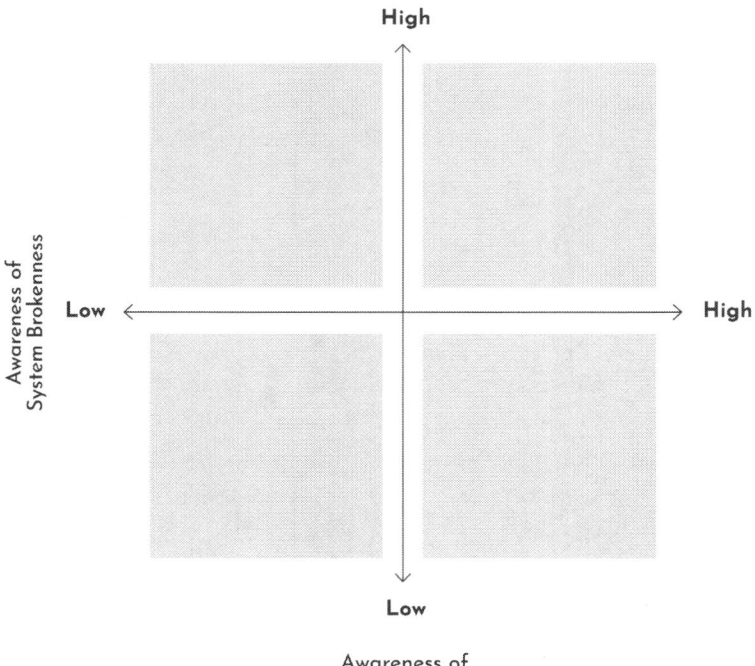

Y-axis: Awareness of System Brokenness (Low to High)
X-axis: Awareness of Personal Brokenness (Low to High)

Most of your congregants likely have a good understanding of *personal* brokenness—the existence and power of sin in all people. In the workplace, sin can be as overt as embezzlement or as subtle as jealousy in one's heart.

Fewer in your congregation will have an appreciation of the fall's impact on *systems*. Understanding brokenness in systems involves realizing that sin affects all of creation, including organizations, structures, and processes. Even when people intuitively grasp the brokenness of work in their day-to-day lives, they may not link it to the fall. Those who have been in oppressed or persecuted environments are often more familiar with the concept of broken systems, which can range from fractures in vast economic structures such as capitalism all the way down to a dysfunctional process in healthcare or the hidden biases that disadvantage job candidates in an interview room. Brokenness in systems can be as explicit as the use of sexuality to sell products in Western consumer culture or as subtle as pay inequity.

In our model, the vertical axis represents the range of awareness one can have of personal brokenness, and the horizontal axis represents the range of awareness one can have of broken systems.

In the following paragraphs, each quadrant will be reviewed through the lens of work and the opportunity to unleash workers toward fulfilling biblical mandates.

QUADRANT 1—SELF FOCUS/NOMINAL CHRISTIANITY

The bottom-left quadrant is representative of an individual in your church family who has *low awareness of personal brokenness* and *low awareness of broken systems*.

Persons in this quadrant are likely not Christians since understanding personal brokenness is key to accepting Jesus as Lord and Savior; however, it may represent persons who call themselves Christians due to cultural context or who made a childhood confession of faith but lack an understanding of the depth and prevalence of sin in every human, including themselves. Individuals in this quadrant may view people as inherently good, believing people make occasional mistakes of minimal consequence, and they may not see the need for a savior. Since they also display a low awareness of system brokenness, they may be blind to how the fall has impacted their organizational structure and the systems around them.

The Faith-and-Work Framework for Unleashing the Gospel

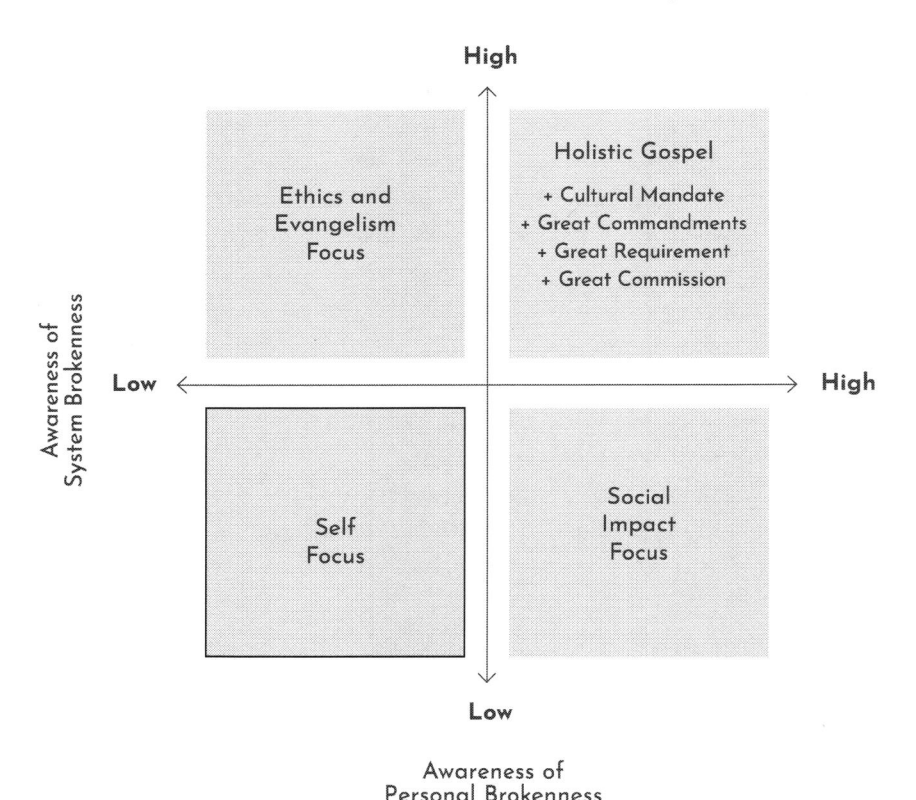

```
                              High
                               ↑
        ┌─────────────────┐   │   ┌─────────────────────────┐
        │                 │   │   │    Holistic Gospel      │
        │   Ethics and    │   │   │                         │
        │   Evangelism    │   │   │   + Cultural Mandate    │
        │     Focus       │   │   │   + Great Commandments  │
        │                 │   │   │   + Great Requirement   │
        │                 │   │   │   + Great Commission    │
        │                 │   │   │                         │
        └─────────────────┘   │   └─────────────────────────┘
  Low ←─────────────────────────────────────────────────→ High
        ┌─────────────────┐   │   ┌─────────────────────────┐
        │                 │   │   │                         │
        │                 │   │   │       Social            │
        │      Self       │   │   │       Impact            │
        │      Focus      │   │   │       Focus             │
        │                 │   │   │                         │
        │                 │   │   │                         │
        └─────────────────┘   │   └─────────────────────────┘
                               ↓
                              Low
```

Awareness of System Brokenness (y-axis)

Awareness of Personal Brokenness (x-axis)

An individual in this quadrant is most likely highly focused on self-progress and not interested in integrating their faith into their work. They may be unmotivated to help others or to fix broken areas at work unless it is for self or organizational gain. If a person in this quadrant calls themselves a Christian, they likely see Jesus as a self-help tool and a moral teacher rather than as their Lord and Savior.

QUADRANT 2–ETHICS AND EVANGELISM FOCUS

A member of your church family who is in the upper-left quadrant of the model has a *high awareness of personal brokenness* (and the depth of sin's impact on an individual) but has a *low awareness of broken systems*.

The Faith-and-Work Framework for Unleashing the Gospel

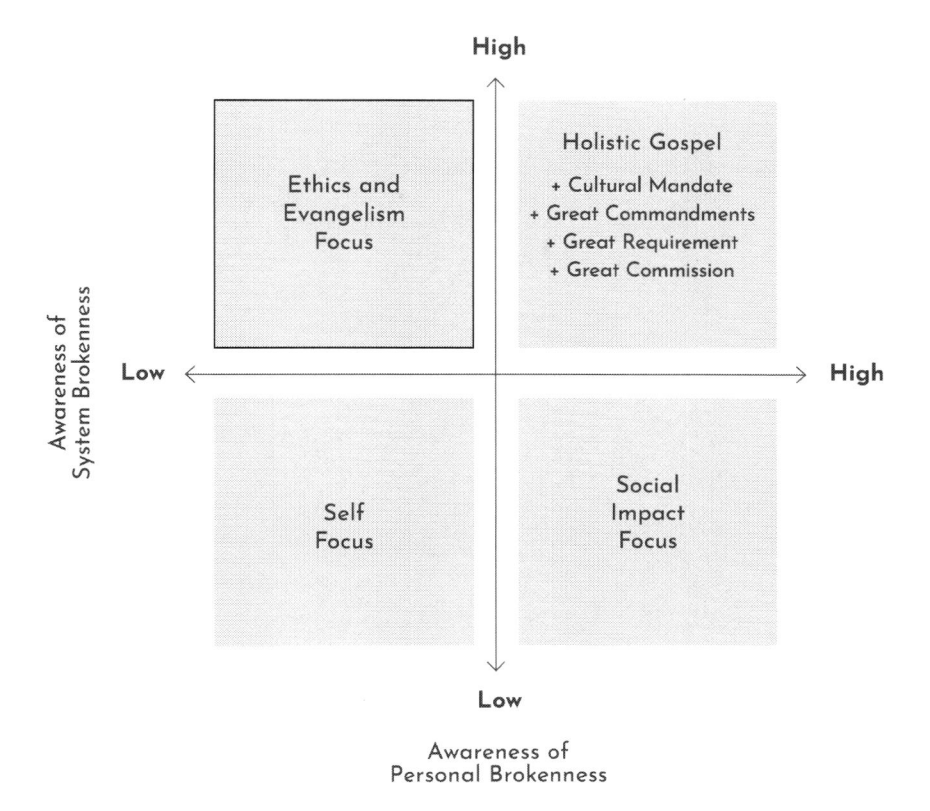

```
                              High
                               ↑
        ┌─────────────┐    ┌──────────────────────┐
        │             │    │  Holistic Gospel     │
        │  Ethics and │    │  + Cultural Mandate  │
        │  Evangelism │    │  + Great Commandments│
        │    Focus    │    │  + Great Requirement │
        │             │    │  + Great Commission  │
        └─────────────┘    └──────────────────────┘
Low ←                                               → High
        ┌─────────────┐    ┌──────────────────────┐
        │             │    │                      │
        │             │    │    Social            │
        │    Self     │    │    Impact            │
        │    Focus    │    │    Focus             │
        │             │    │                      │
        └─────────────┘    └──────────────────────┘
                               ↓
                              Low
                         Awareness of
                      Personal Brokenness
```

(Y-axis label: Awareness of System Brokenness)

These persons are likely aware of their own sin and thankful for the saving grace of Christ. They try to avoid sin themselves and help others see the reality of personal sin. Thus, they want to share Christ with their coworkers or customers and are working (hopefully through the Holy Spirit) to address personal sin.

As such, they tend toward evangelism in the workplace either overtly through conversations or subtly through actions such as having religious items on their desks, walls, accessories (e.g., a cross necklace), or clothing. Further, since they desire to reduce sin in their own lives, these persons might prioritize ethical behavior, aligning their work practices with their Christian values.

Since they have limited awareness of broken systems, an individual in this quadrant may overlook potential biases or distortions. They rarely push against structural problems at work unless the change is part of their job description or the problem is blocking their personal success. As a result, they lose the gospel opportunity to more proactively engage in alleviating the pain and suffering caused by broken systems. For those struggling in these systems, the outward evangelistic and ethical expression of Christianity by a worker in this quadrant may appear superficial or hypocritical since they are not addressing harmful systems. These persons can come across as self-righteous and rigid.

QUADRANT 3—SOCIAL IMPACT FOCUS

A person in your church family who is in the bottom-right portion of the quadrant has a *high awareness of broken systems* around them but a *low awareness of their own personal brokenness.*

Because persons in this quadrant are so focused on the brokenness in systems, they may be less likely to see their own brokenness. While they may acknowledge the existence of personal sin at a high level, they do not focus on its detail. Instead, they tend to focus on the social impact of Christianity in their work through shaping and changing structures, communities, institutions, and industries.

A person in this quadrant may begin to subconsciously believe that they are the savior working to fix a system instead of understanding God's role as the One who ultimately brings renewal. This "savior syndrome" is particularly tempting to individuals who work in helping professions (such as teaching), as well as champions for social justice causes. Without a high awareness of personal brokenness, they lose the unifying truths of both the *imago Dei* ("image of God") and the reality of sin's grasp on all humanity. These persons may not extend grace for the failings of others who are operating within a given system, because they don't understand that they too are broken and in need of a

The Faith-and-Work Framework for Unleashing the Gospel

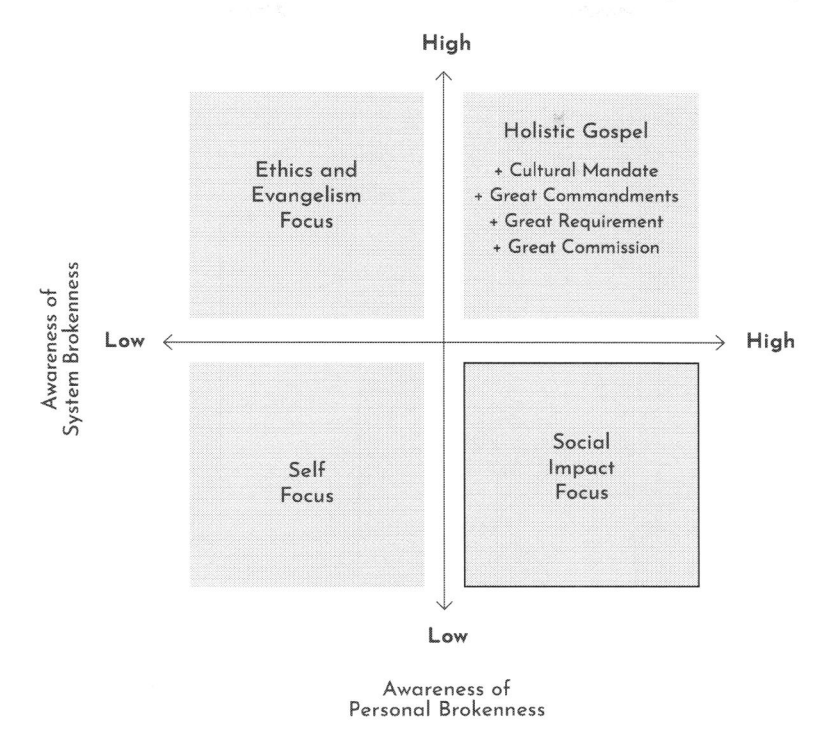

Awareness of System Brokenness

High / Low

- **Top-left (Low personal, High system):** Ethics and Evangelism Focus
- **Top-right (High personal, High system):** Holistic Gospel
  + Cultural Mandate
  + Great Commandments
  + Great Requirement
  + Great Commission
- **Bottom-left (Low personal, Low system):** Self Focus
- **Bottom-right (High personal, Low system):** Social Impact Focus

Awareness of Personal Brokenness (Low / High)

---

savior. They may accomplish amazing things; but without pointing to the need for Christ, they inadvertently make themselves or their work the savior instead of Jesus. Such individuals may also lose the ability to intimately commune with Christ through regular repentance and forgiveness. Consequently, they begin to see themselves as self-sufficient, forfeiting their reliance on God, losing their humility, and diminishing their ability to extend grace to others.

QUADRANT 4–HOLISTIC GOSPEL

To unleash the fullness of the gospel in the workplace requires a *high awareness of both personal and system brokenness,* characterized by individuals in the top-right quadrant. They are most likely to unleash the full power of Christ in their workplace because they not only see their own brokenness and the brokenness of others but also the deep fractures within the systems in which they operate. An encompassing awareness of brokenness can motivate them to fulfill the core tenets of discipleship as outlined in the Bible:

- The Cultural Mandate (Gen. 1:26–28)
- The Great Commandments (Matt. 22:36–40)
- The Great Commission (Matt. 28:19–20)
- The Great Requirement (Mic. 6:8)[1]

The Faith-and-Work Framework for Unleashing the Gospel

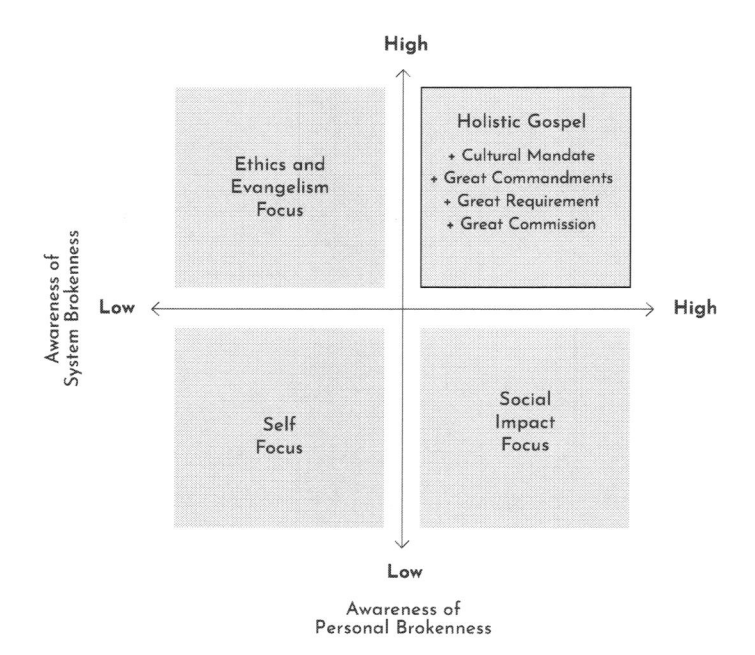

	Low Awareness of Personal Brokenness	High Awareness of Personal Brokenness
High Awareness of System Brokenness	Ethics and Evangelism Focus	Holistic Gospel + Cultural Mandate + Great Commandments + Great Requirement + Great Commission
Low Awareness of System Brokenness	Self Focus	Social Impact Focus

---

[1] We have ordered these four mandates in this way as they follow this progression: The Cultural Mandate establishes the foundational principle that humans were created to work and steward the earth. This mandate predates the fall of humanity and sin, demonstrating that work is a fundamental aspect of our existence. Following this, The Great Commandments to love God and others serve as the overarching principle governing all human relationships and activities. The Great Commission and The Great Requirement are specific manifestations of this love, emphasizing the importance of sharing the gospel and making disciples and practicing justice and mercy. We were introduced to Micah 6:8 being referred to as "The Great Requirement" by Abraham Cho, vice president for Thought Leadership at Redeemer City to City.

As a reminder, a holistic view of faith and work will include *all* these tenets and not just highlight one area of Scripture over the other. That being said, not all who are in this quadrant will be called to participate in each of them each day. But over time, all of these biblical concepts will be evident in their work as they walk closely with God and discern their steps each day, empowered by the Holy Spirit.

THE CULTURAL MANDATE

In Genesis 1:26–28, we read:

> Then God said, "Let us make mankind in our image, in our likeness, so that they may rule over the fish in the sea and the birds in the sky, over the livestock and all the wild animals, and over all the creatures that move along the ground."
>
> So God created mankind in his own image,
> in the image of God he created them;
> male and female he created them.
>
> God blessed them and said to them, "Be fruitful and increase in number; fill the earth and subdue it. Rule over the fish in the sea and the birds in the sky and over every living creature that moves on the ground."

As we discussed in chapter two, in the Cultural Mandate (sometimes called the Creation Mandate), God invites us to work alongside him to "be fruitful and increase in number" and to "fill the earth and subdue it." Some scholars say this can be paraphrased to "go out and create flourishing." Professor of Apologetics William Edgar notes that "the creation mandate is on-going and is not in competition with worshipping God; Christians are to care for this world even as we hope in the second coming of Christ."[2] If everyone in your church is to live out this mandate, it will involve actively contributing to the flourishing of their communities, teams, organizations, and industries. This work—done for the glory of God and in the power of the Holy Spirit—is rooted in an individual's deep understanding of their calling as a child of God, motivating them to

---

[2] William Edgar, "The Creation Mandate," The Gospel Coalition (U.S. Edition), accessed December 11, 2024, https://www.thegospelcoalition.org/essay/the-creation-mandate/.

identify areas of opportunity and to work toward the common good envisioned in the new heaven and earth. However, this requires a grateful acknowledgement of God's work in healing their own personal brokenness and to actively work to alleviate the broken systems around them.

THE GREAT COMMANDMENTS

In Matthew 22:36, Jesus was asked to identify the greatest commandment in the law. In response, he said: "'Love the Lord your God with all your heart and with all your soul and with all your mind.' This is the first and greatest commandment. And the second is like it: 'Love your neighbor as yourself.' All the Law and the Prophets hang on these two commandments" (Matt. 22:37–40).

The opportunity for your congregants to love their neighbors as themselves in and through their work is key to utilizing their work hours for God's glory.[3] But who exactly is a neighbor in a work context? The story of the Good Samaritan (Luke 10:25–37) expands the definition of neighbor to include all, even enemies. The parable in Luke comes directly after the account of the Great Commandments and is Jesus' response to a lawyer's question: "Who is my neighbor?" The Samaritan, like Jesus, gave of himself far more than was required. We too have the opportunity to display this costly love, but only through the fruit of the Spirit that comes from reckoning with the gift we did not deserve in Jesus himself.

> In the parable of the Good Samaritan, Jesus teaches that love is what God built us to do, that love is the essence of what it means to be human. In this story, we see that real love doesn't begin until you see that you can't really love—it doesn't begin until you see you're a sinner saved by grace alone. We also see that real love begins when you're stunned into silence by the love of Christ for paying your debt. Once you've experienced and been humbled by that kind of love, then you're capable of concrete and costly love toward others.[4]

---

[3] Note, the "love the Lord your God" aspect of this commandment is incorporated in the other mandates, so in this mandate, we are choosing to emphasize the "love your neighbour" aspect.

[4] Taken from summary sentence of a sermon preached by Timothy Keller, "The Good Samaritan: On Love," Gospel in Life and Redeemer City to City, preached August 2, 2008, https://podcast.gospelinlife.com/e/the-good-samaritan-on-love/.

Work is a key petri dish for extending costly love as it puts us alongside so many people whom we perhaps would not normally choose to associate with or befriend.

> At work we have many chances to be neighbors with co-workers, customers and others across ethnic or cultural divides. Being a Good Samaritan in the workplace means cultivating a specific awareness of the needs of the other. Are there people in your workplace who are being robbed in some way? Often specific ethnic groups are deprived of recognition or promotion. A conscientious Christian should be the one to say, "Are we giving this person a fair shake?"[5]

Loving our neighbor extends beyond ethnic and cultural differences; it includes those with opposing ideologies, those we have clashed with, and even those who have wronged us. Equipping your congregants to love their neighbors in and through their work requires encouraging them to embrace their own personal brokenness, to express gratitude for God's undeserved grace, and to discover how they can engage with individuals and broken systems where God has placed them, all through the power of the Holy Spirit. Author and artist Olive Chan describes how God used her work to form her in greater Christlikeness and to teach her how to love her neighbor:

> Modern-day enemies are often found in the workplace.... Maybe it's a boss that mistreats you. A colleague that is obnoxious. A supplier that is always making mistakes and creating extra work for you.
>
> For me, it was a customer that was both rude and demanding. In my first month of work, I made a mistake in some documentation that was given to a customer. Her name was Laura (not her real name) and she called me, lost her temper, and yelled at me for 10 minutes straight.... And for some reason, my boss assigned this customer to me—part of my job was to provide customer service to Laura. I hated it. She was so picky and rude and had anger problems, and I was always afraid she would blow up at me. She was my enemy. How do you know that someone is your enemy? My definition is that you do not wish

---

[5] "The Good Samaritan at Work—Loving Your Neighbor as Yourself (Luke 10:25–37)," Theology at Work Project, accessed December 11, 2024, https://www.theologyofwork.org/new-testament/luke/gods-provision-luke/the-good-samaritan-at-work-loving-your-neighbor-as-yourself-luke-1025-37/.

them well. I secretly hoped that her business would fail, so I wouldn't have to deal with her. But, her business survived.

Every week she called, and I would have to serve her, again and again. Book this shipment. Change this order. Give her this quotation. Week after week, month after month, year after year. The interesting thing is that after 2 years, I became quite fond of her. And she became quite reliant on me. Even after I switched roles at work, and my colleague took over my role, Laura would still call me to ask for things to get done. And when she did, I genuinely wanted to help her.

If it were my choice, I would never have interacted with Laura after that first experience. Instead of loving my enemy, I would have avoided my enemy. But because of my work, I had no choice but to serve her day in and day out, even though I really disliked her at first. And slowly, through the work of service, God formed and shaped my heart to learn to love my enemy.[6]

THE GREAT REQUIREMENT

In Micah 6:8, we are told:

> He has shown you, O mortal, what is good.
> And what does the LORD require of you?
> To act justly and to love mercy
> and to walk humbly with your God.

The Lord requires us to act justly, love mercy, and to walk in humility. If your congregants are to live this out in their work context, you will need to help them appreciate the deep interconnection of personal and system brokenness.

Walking in humility with God requires a high awareness of personal brokenness and the need for Christ as savior. And identifying ways to act justly and love mercy will mean your church will need help seeing the areas of personal and system injustice around them.

When you help those in your congregation apply this passage to work, their jobs will become vital contexts to pursue mercy and justice for God's

---

[6] Olive Chan, "The Meaning of Work (A Christian Perspective)," Tim and Olive's Blog, accessed December 11, 2024, https://timandolive.com/christian-meaning-of-work/.

glory. What kind of restorative presence might they be if they considered how work is a context to seek ways to help hurting and oppressed people? We learn in Psalm 33:5 that "[God] loves righteousness and justice; the earth is full of his unfailing love." What if your congregants viewed their workplaces as an opportunity to glorify God by actively noticing and pushing against the systems hurting the oppressed and seeking to embody God's love for righteousness and justice?[7]

THE GREAT COMMISSION

In Matthew 28:19–20, just before his post-resurrection ascension, Christ commanded, "Therefore go and make disciples of all nations, baptizing them in the name of the Father and of the Son and of the Holy Spirit, and teaching them to obey everything I have commanded you. And surely I am with you always, to the very end of the age."

How did Jesus suggest we accomplish the Great Commission? His last words, after heaping on his disciples such a large task ("make disciples of *all* nations"), was to remind them of his presence ("And surely I am with you always"). There is no strategic plan given for the evangelism mandate. Jesus' presence *is* the plan.[8] So, if the key to evangelism is seeking the face of Jesus, then it will be necessary to help those in your church to have a high awareness of their own and others' brokenness and sin, as well as deep gratitude for Christ's sacrifice and work on the cross. The more stupefied they are by how undeserving they are of God's grace, the more likely they are to express that gratitude and share the gift in their workplace. Thus, a high understanding of personal brokenness will drive members of your congregation toward the evangelism the Great Commission requires. They won't be able to contain the zeal of sharing his great work in their lives if they truly see the reality of his gift.

Engaging system brokenness will also help them to live out the Great Commission, albeit more passively. When coworkers, clients, customers,

---

[7] For a fuller discussion of justice in the Bible, we highly recommend "Justice in the Bible"—an article by Tim Keller (part of a four-part series), Gospel in Life, Fall 2020, https://gospelinlife.com/article/justice-in-the-bible/.

[8] Paraphrase from a sermon by Elliott Cherry, "The Great Commission," June 2, 2024, in *Midtown Fellowship 12 South Sermons* podcast, https://podcasts.apple.com/us/podcast/the-great-commission/id1149487769?i=1000657580588.

and colleagues see members of your congregation loving others the way Christ loved them, pushing against broken systems in their industry, and looking for opportunities to bring mercy and justice into the workplace, evangelism begins to take place meaningfully and organically. Over time, the work of the unleashed Christian—motivated by a holistic view of brokenness—will be distinctive from those around them who do not have Christ in their lives. Conflict resolution will be other-centered rather than self-serving as your church members seek to consider those perceived to be underdogs. Humility will be prioritized over success as they seek to push against broken individual-success narratives. Their response to failure will reflect the reality that Christ—not their work achievements—is their savior. The way they steward their personal resources and those of their organization will honor God. And these distinctions in the everyday witness of your individual congregants will create opportunities for each of them to winsomely enter conversations with their colleagues about why they do things differently, what motivates them in the difficult moments of their work lives, and how God cares about the work they are doing as a means of cultivating his creation. And in a full-circle manner, understanding their personal brokenness will allow members of your congregation to serve others in humility, recognizing their need for a savior because of their own sin and depravity.

This "Unleashing the Gospel" framework provides a powerful perspective on the intersection of personal and system brokenness, offering a holistic view of faith and work that leads to transformative action at both the individual and the system level. It reveals a way to live fully with Christ in daily work, empowering members of your congregation to

- create flourishing in their workplaces or industries (The Cultural Mandate);
- view their work as a place of service and love to the Lord and love for those they encounter in their professional lives (The Great Commandments);
- challenge areas of injustice and oppression and approach their work with humility (The Great Requirement), recognizing their own brokenness and need for salvation; and

- recognize that their salvation through Jesus gives them a unique perspective on work that can drive them to contribute to something greater. This can lead to increased visibility and natural evangelism opportunities in the everyday context of their work (The Great Commission).

PUTTING IT ALL TOGETHER

Though you may hope to empower your congregants in the plethora of ways that embody the top-right quadrant, it's also important to realize that not all environments offer every opportunity at all times. In addition, personal contexts and life experiences can blind those you lead to certain possibilities, driving them toward the bottom-right or top-left. These blind spots represent just one more area of brokenness that requires attention as we push toward the upper-right for ourselves and those we serve, all through the power of Christ, who has overcome both the brokenness in our lives and in the world as part of God's unfolding story. Praise be to Christ!

As you reflect on this quadrant analysis, consider the story below of a trucking-industry executive named Dustin.

> The trucking industry in the United States grossed almost one trillion dollars in revenue in 2022 alone.[9] The transportation of goods is central to a vibrant and working economy. In fact, many Americans finally recognized just how essential this industry was during the height of the global COVID-19 pandemic. In many ways, freight trucking is like electricity lines through our cities: often visible, yet rarely recognized for just how integral it is to our shared lives. But the real engine that drives this massive industry is not the pistons firing below the hood; it is the persons sitting behind the wheel: the drivers.
>
> Dustin had developed a successful career in the trucking industry. But as he spent more time leading companies in boardrooms, he began

---

[9] "Economics and Industry Data," *American Trucking Associations*, 2024, accessed December 11, 2024, https://www.trucking.org/economics-and-industry-data.

to notice a disconnect between company executives and the everyday truckers. He knew enough about the experience of truckers to know that the working conditions were likely poor, and the turnover rate of truckers showcased just how challenging the work was.

He wanted to bring about change to his industry through faithful presence and influence even when he knew he lacked the authority to have the final say on decisions. Through much prayer and consideration, he decided, in order to truly be an agent of change, he had to develop further proximity with the lived experiences of his drivers.

So he did just that. For three days and three nights, Dustin did a "ride-along" with a brand-new driver who had recently joined his company. This experience confirmed the suspicions Dustin had about the conditions and challenges every driver faced on the road.

First, Dustin observed that truck stops often were full of unhospitable practices: overpriced and poor-quality food options, expensive showers ($15 per shower), and a shortage of parking space for truckers to rest. He realized that because many of his drivers were already experiencing severe poverty, they would rarely pay for showers, and few had the funds to pay for three meals each day on the road. His own driver lacked the resources to pay for a regular shower and spent three days wearing the same clothes. On top of all of this, the trucking industry seemingly was designed to create situations that isolated drivers on long, lonely, arduous deliveries. Dustin wondered how an almost trillion-dollar industry was not able to provide access and funds for basic human needs: hygiene, healthy meals, rest, and community. As he wrestled with this reality, he came to the realization that his company, along with many others, was over-investing in new technology and under-investing in their human resources—their drivers.

But recognizing the problems was just the starting place for Dustin. His desire was to use his influence and position to be a restorative presence in his industry. One of the seemingly small, but very concrete, ways he started was by advocating for his company to

> provide showers for all drivers as part of their benefit package. This simple change took a long time to be implemented by the executives of his company, but it was a tangible step toward rehumanizing the primary workers of his industry and ultimately creating an environment for them to flourish in the process of delivering products for the good of their neighbors.
>
> Through Dustin's experience on the road, he now seeks to lead from a place of proximity to people directly impacted by his company's policies and urges others in higher levels of leadership to do the same. In fact, with his current company, he encourages every executive member to spend time at the company lodge where all new drivers prepare to set out on their first route.

When we look at Dustin's story, we can see how both a high view of personal brokenness and a high view of the broken systems of the trucking industry led him to want to love those in the industry with the love Jesus had shown to him. For Christians pondering the trucking industry, the question is: What will trucking look like in the city of New Jerusalem on streets of gold? Regardless of what it might entail, Dustin is convinced that every driver behind every vehicle will be granted incredible dignity and value as they round tight corners and usher in the goods of the kingdom.

REFLECTION QUESTIONS

- What personal blind spots were revealed to you by looking at the Faith-and-Work Framework for Unleashing the Gospel?
- Reflect on how you have personally encountered opportunities to focus on the following at work:
    - The Cultural Mandate
    - The Great Commandments
    - The Great Requirement
    - The Great Commission

- Where would you locate those in your congregation within the Faith-and-Work Framework for Unleashing the Gospel grid, based on the denomination and traditions of your church? Is there generally a high or low view of personal brokenness? What about broken systems?
- How might you begin to challenge your congregants to think about personal brokenness and broken systems more holistically?
- How might moving from one of the truncated quadrants to the top-right quadrant inform others' views of what renewal could look like in their future?
- How could you teach and preach about all four elements of the top-right quadrant of unleashing the gospel? How could you relate them to work?

SECTION TWO

FAITH-AND-WORK-INTEGRATED LEADERS, CHURCHES, AND CITIES

A JOURNEY MAP FOR IMPLEMENTATION

5

DEFINING OUR DESTINATIONS

Our recognition of what has occurred gives us reason to conduct our lives now with the knowledge that God has not abandoned but has begun to reclaim his creation. This recognition of God's commitment to his world ought to compel us to take our responsibility in this world with great seriousness; our work as one expression of the creation/cultural mandate remains.

VINCENT BACOTE

And the basic idea ... is that if we believe that God is present everywhere, then in your workplace, God is there and everywhere God is, is holy. And so as we walk into our workplace, how does that reorient our thinking? If God is in this place, what does that mean about the work that I am doing in this place?

DENISE DANIELS

Imagine a Bible study group at your church, including a nurse, a filmmaker, a teacher, a banker, and a coffee-shop worker.

Exhausted from a particularly challenging period at work, the nurse reflects on a conflict with one of the doctors at her hospital. The doctor's disapproving tone triggered the realization that her need for affirmation had become an idol. Recognizing this, she has become more prayerful, seeking God's face and asking about her work. As she looks for God's guidance, she asks him to reveal how he is active in the lives of her patients and how she can join him in this. Patients share not only their health concerns but also their emotional burdens, giving her the opportunity to comfort them with the compassion of Christ. She also realizes that the treatment rooms for pediatric cancer patients are sterile and depressing. So she petitions the pediatric advisory board to oversee the creation of child-centric playrooms on each floor so that the young cancer patients have some solace amid their treatment.

The filmmaker is looking for a story to produce. Her broadened understanding of the gospel's impact on her work life inspires her to use her art to reveal injustice by telling a story more redemptively. She discovers that irresponsible waste management practices of a local company have unfortunately caused high levels of illness near their disposal site. She researches extensively, interviews those impacted, and writes a script to highlight this issue. Her interviewees are deeply moved by the fact that someone is advocating for them through art and story. This commitment extends to her filmmaking process. She intentionally treats her crew with dignity and respect, giving them fair wages and adequate rest periods between shoots—a rarity in the often-exploitative industry.

The teacher in this Bible study is burned-out and exhausted and needs the gospel to speak into many areas of his life. After your church talked about integrating his faith and work, he realized that his mission field is the classroom, and those he needs to love well are his third-grade students. He entered this field because he believes in the importance of education, but now he realizes he cannot be his students' "savior." Instead, he endeavors to love them as well as he can and release the outcome of their lives to the Lord. He begins arriving at his classroom fifteen minutes early to pray over each child's desk before the students arrive. And as he goes through his day, the burden of teaching these children feels less heavy. By committing each child to the Lord, he finds he has more patience and grace for them. He also joins an advocacy group of teachers lobbying the city for equal arts opportunities across schools, since the more economically challenged schools receive fewer resources.

The banker—president of a small local branch—oversees around seventy-five employees, from loan officers to tellers to custodial staff. He realizes that all of these people, as well as the customers of the bank, are his mission. With this newfound perspective, he begins to consider how he can better love those around him without sacrificing the company's sustainability—and thus, bottom line. One employee suffers poor health and can no longer work as efficiently, so he seeks to accommodate her changing needs by shifting her role. Another employee is a single mother in her first job, and she needs coaching and grace in order to succeed, but she also needs help balancing the stressful realities of her life. He starts to see himself not just as a boss but also as someone who embodies the love of Jesus to his employees. The number of loans his bank rejects based solely on credit scores also troubles him. He wants more people to have responsible access to funds. As a result, he creates a new process where those who are unable to qualify for loans will be encouraged to apply for financial counseling from volunteers at a local nonprofit to improve their credit.

The final person in this group is a coffee shop worker. He has never imagined his job as anything more than a means to pay the rent, but now he recognizes that he has the power to model God's hospitality to those who walk through the doors of the café. He finds profound purpose in welcoming each person with love and kindness, which fosters a sense of community, offering regular interaction for those who might otherwise feel isolated in a lonely world. He tries to remember the orders of regular customers to make them feel seen, loved, and cared for. Furthermore, he proposes to the management that they use recyclable cups and source beans from places that do not extort farmers.

Each of these individuals, while personally seeking the face of Christ, touches hundreds of others in your city in any given year through their work. *Hundreds.* Imagine if even a small church of fifty congregants has *everyone* looking for opportunities to love God and love their neighbor in and through their work. Imagine if everyone sees the broken places of their given industry and looks for ways, large and small, to bring renewal. Can you grasp how impactful even a small church can be to a community—without any extra programs or volunteering? Imagine the exponential impact of a larger church. Simply adjusting the lens of mission to include the workplace as a primary context for God's work galvanizes people to live for Christ day to day. And eventually, the community will likely take notice as they start to see following Jesus as a common thread among the people loving and serving those around them. Over time, as more people in your church begin to live this way, your church will be changed—and, slowly, so will your city.

All this sounds ideal, but what are the steps needed to mobilize those in your church to live this way in their daily work? After covering the biblical foundation and theological frameworks for integrating faith and work, establishing its importance for those in your congregation, and confronting some key defeaters to implementation, we now want to explore how you can begin to apply these principles in your own life, in your leadership team, in your church, and eventually across your city.

First, we'll paint a picture of where we're going—the destinations—so we can see what it looks like to become a faith-and-work-integrated leader who is part of guiding a faith-and-work-integrated church, and who works toward a faith-and-work-integrated city.

Once we have established the ideal destinations for a leader, church, and city, we will provide maps, practical steps, and exercises to begin your implementation journey.

DEFINING THE DESTINATIONS: INTEGRATED LEADER, CHURCH, AND CITY

The integration of faith and work takes place at three levels: the individual *leader* level (both you and those you serve), the *church* level, and the *city* level.[1]

> **DEFINITIONS**
>
> - **Faith-and-work-integrated leader:** a Christian working in any industry who has holistically integrated their faith into their day-to-day work (both paid and unpaid), as an outpouring of a deeply rooted relationship with Father, Son, and Holy Spirit. This may include individuals in various roles, such as pastors, city leaders, and lay people.
> - **Faith-and-work-integrated church:** a church that embeds the integration of faith and work in its leadership, mission, and core church practices, so that the gospel can impact the hearts of all who are part of the church and equip them to lovingly serve and impact people, systems, organizations, and their city through their work.
> - **Faith-and-work-integrated city:** a city where organized efforts equip and mobilize individuals and churches to drive meaningful change for the common good.

---

[1] We would like to acknowledge Blake Schwarz and Damein Schitter for their input on the process laid out in the next two chapters. In particular, Blake helped us with the concept of the integrated leader being critical to integrated churches and cities. And in addition, Damein assisted us with the writing for the integrated leader and integrated church.

As you imagine the three levels of integrating faith and work—leader, church, and city—it's important to understand there is an intrinsic and synergistic relationship between these three levels. Each level requires and, in some way, reinforces the other levels. In other words, an integrated leader helps to cultivate and is sustained by an integrated church; and an integrated church is made up of integrated leaders sent week in and week out to cultivate an integrated city. Each level has an ideal destination—a vision of what full faith-and-work integration could look like. The destination for each level is interconnected with the others yet has its own distinct identity of integration.

IDEAL DESTINATION #1:
THE FAITH-AND-WORK-INTEGRATED *LEADER*

A leader who has integrated their faith and work has a strong and cohesive understanding of how the gospel impacts them at the *heart* level in their personal relationship with God, at the *community* level in how they interact with others, and at the *world* level in how they operate within their industry, city, and beyond.

At the *heart* level, a leader who has integrated faith and work

- hears God's voice and communes deeply with Christ;
- knows they are created to work;
- comprehends how their personal brokenness shows up at work;
- embraces the power of the Holy Spirit;
- is growing in expressions of the fruit of the Spirit; and
- believes in broken systems (i.e., understands that the fall impacts all of creation, not just people).

At the *community* level, a leader who has integrated faith and work

- comprehends that the image of God is in all people;
- realizes that the gospel changes how they interact with others in and through their work;
- embraces the idea of stewarding power;

- understands the concept of common grace and its abundance;[2] and
- seeks to love others in all areas of work as Christ first loved them.

At the *world* level, a leader who has integrated faith and work

- views their work as part of God's unfolding plan for the world;
- understands the innate goodness and brokenness in their industry and workplace;
- seeks opportunities to shine light on broken processes and systems at work;
- finds ways for their workplace and industry to best represent the goodness of God; and
- envisions creative new ways to bring goodness into the world.

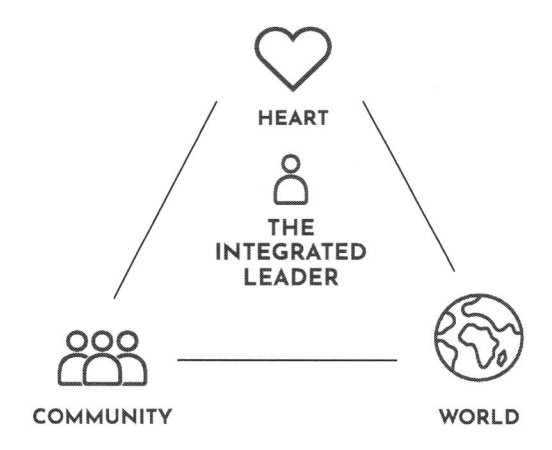

```
                    HEART
                      │
              THE INTEGRATED
                  LEADER
               /           \
         COMMUNITY ——————— WORLD
```

(See page 74 at the end of this chapter for an additional accompanying diagram.)

---

[2] The doctrine of *common grace* is widely acknowledged as a teaching of the Bible. The idea is that God bestows gifts of wisdom, moral insight, goodness, and beauty across the human race, regardless of religious belief. Isaiah 45:1 speaks of Cyrus, a pagan king, who God anoints and uses for world leadership. Isaiah 28:23–29 tells us that when a farmer is fruitful, it is God who has taught him to be so. Romans 1 and 2 confirm that there is a primordial knowledge of God that all human beings have. In Romans 2:14–15, Paul says that God's law is written on the heart of every human being—all people have an inward sense of morality, justice, love, the Golden Rule, and so on. All good and great artistic expressions, skillful farming, effective governments, scientific advances, etc., are God's gifts to the human race (James 1:17). These gifts, however, are "common" in that they do not save the soul, yet without them the world would be an intolerable place to live.

IDEAL DESTINATION #2:
THE FAITH-AND-WORK-INTEGRATED *CHURCH*

The destination for a church that fully integrates the context and concepts of faith and work into its identity and functioning will be characterized by three key elements: *mission, leadership team,* and *core church practices*.

A church that has integrated faith and work has a *mission* that

- views work as one of the primary contexts for spiritual formation, comprehending its significance for drawing people toward Christ and into heart renewal;
- overtly includes the role of work in their mission, viewing work as a primary context for congregants to impact their cities and communities, appreciating it as an essential conduit for mission; and
- incorporates the impact of its laity's everyday work into measurements of the church's vibrancy.

A church that has integrated faith and work is led by a *leadership team* that is

- equipped with a holistic understanding of faith-and-work theology and integrated at the heart, community, and world level (as outlined above);
- knowledgeable about the work lives of their congregants;
- committed to equipping the congregants with faith-and-work theology for heart change and city impact;
- partnered with lay leaders to execute a faith-and-work vision; and
- aware of broken systems as well as broken people (i.e., understands that the fall impacts creation, not just people).

A church that has integrated faith and work embeds faith and work into its *core church practices* by

- incorporating the concepts of faith and work into sermons;
- ensuring elements of the worship service emphasize work as a context;
- including a focus on work in its discipleship offerings, Bible studies, and community gatherings;

- viewing community service for the city through the jobs of its congregants; and
- promoting a culture of mutual respect and appreciation for all roles within the congregation.

MISSION ← → **LEADERSHIP TEAM**

THE INTEGRATED CHURCH

↓

CORE CHURCH PRACTICES

(See page 75 at the end of this chapter for an additional accompanying diagram.)

When a church has integrated faith and work in the areas of mission, leadership, and core church practices, the church will form integrated leaders who will

- embrace a holistic vision of work;
- view their work as a key area of mission; and
- live as an integrated leader (heart, community, world) in their work.

IDEAL DESTINATION #3:
THE FAITH-AND-WORK INTEGRATED *CITY*

When enough leaders and churches have integrated their faith and work, a faith-and-work-integrated city begins to emerge. As these leaders (and their congregants) are trained and sent out on mission into their communities, their work begins to impact the city positively. Inspired by this, leaders and churches with the capacity and calling to do so will establish *a leadership team* that begins to focus on addressing the city's complex challenges holistically, developing a city *vision, network,* and *initiatives* that surpass what any singular integrated leader or church could accomplish on their own. An integrated city's leadership team is dedicated to faith and work (most likely including integrated leaders from integrated churches).

A city that has integrated faith and work has a *leadership team* that

- comprises integrated leaders from a variety of integrated churches;
- represents the diversity of the city;
- includes cross-denominational members; and
- embraces a unified faith-and-work vision for the city.

A city that has integrated faith and work has a *vision* that

- focuses on the renewal and common good of the city through work; and
- views work as one of the primary contexts for Christians to impact their cities and communities, appreciating it as an essential conduit for mission.

A city that has integrated faith and work has *networks* that

- include robust relationships between faith-and-work-integrated leaders across industries and church denominations;
- seek to unify, connect, and multiply the work of individuals and churches across the city;

- reflect the socioeconomic, racial, and cultural diversity of the city; and
- understand the city's beauty and brokenness, including its economic drivers, its deepest wounds, and the struggles of those who are on the margins of society.

A city that has integrated faith and work has *initiatives* that

- include cross-denominational city-focused efforts with particular emphases in key industries, key city pain points, and entrepreneurism; and
- prioritize issues faced by the most marginalized communities, such as homelessness, unemployment, education gaps, and racism.

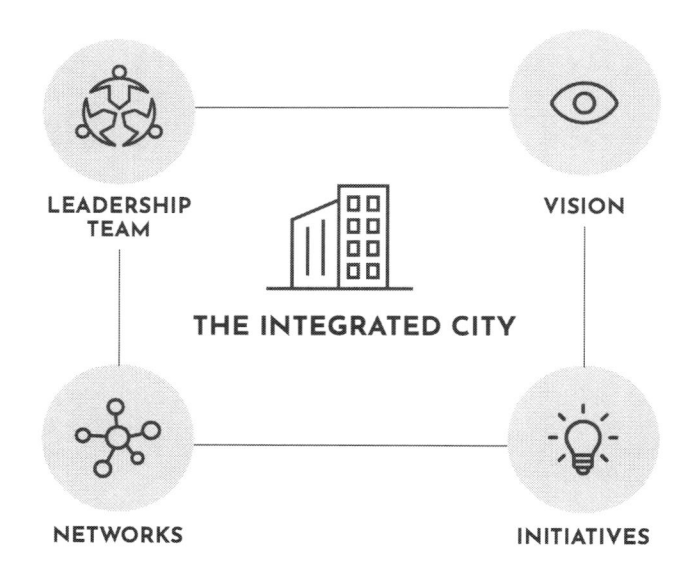

LEADERSHIP TEAM — **VISION**

THE INTEGRATED CITY

NETWORKS — **INITIATIVES**

(See page 76 at the end of this chapter for an additional accompanying diagram.)

THE POWER OF SYNERGY

As we alluded to when talking about the relationship between them, the integrated leader, church, and city form a powerful virtuous cycle. When any one of the three elements gains momentum, it will help the others. An integrated church forms leaders that impact a city. Likewise, an integrated leader pushes their church to integrate further. An integrated church and integrated leader form teams that integrate a city, and an integrated city goes on to form more integrated churches that equip integrated leaders—and so on, and so forth.

Full Faith-and-Work Integration

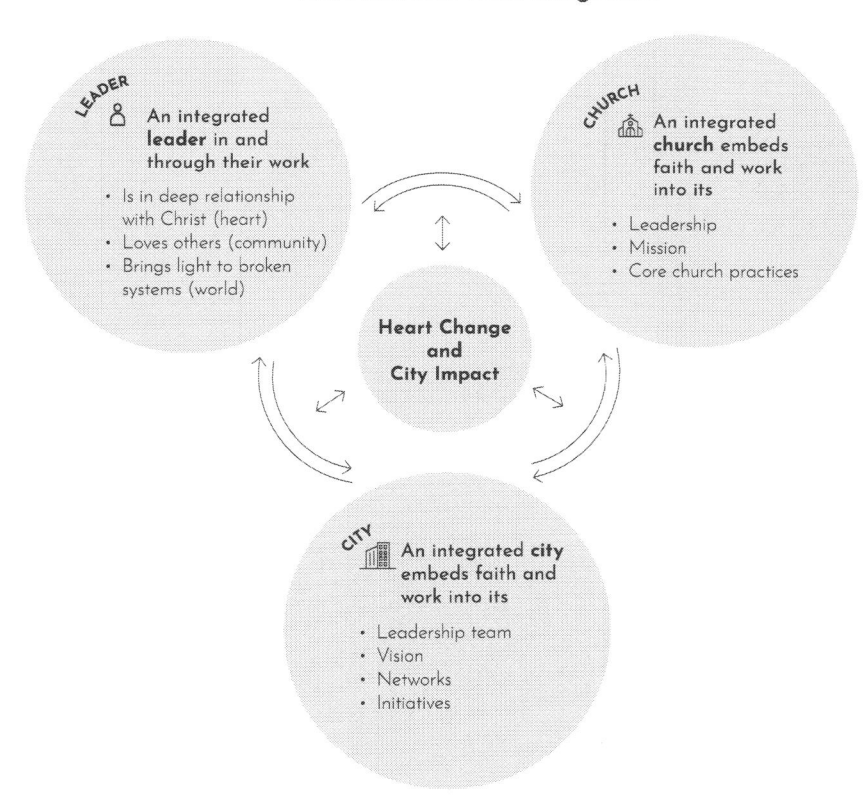

LEADER
An integrated **leader** in and through their work
- Is in deep relationship with Christ (heart)
- Loves others (community)
- Brings light to broken systems (world)

CHURCH
An integrated **church** embeds faith and work into its
- Leadership
- Mission
- Core church practices

Heart Change and City Impact

CITY
An integrated **city** embeds faith and work into its
- Leadership team
- Vision
- Networks
- Initiatives

REFLECTION QUESTIONS

- As you consider an integrated leader, what concepts are new for you?
- As you consider an integrated church, what is most surprising to you?
- Have you ever considered the concept of an integrated city? What is most noteworthy to you?

WORLD
A leader who has integrated faith and work at the world level

- Views their work as part of God's unfolding plan for the world
- Understands the innate goodness and brokenness in their industry and workplace
- Seeks opportunities to shine light on broken processes and systems at work
- Finds ways for their workplace and industry to best represent the goodness of God
- Envisions creative new ways to bring goodness into the world

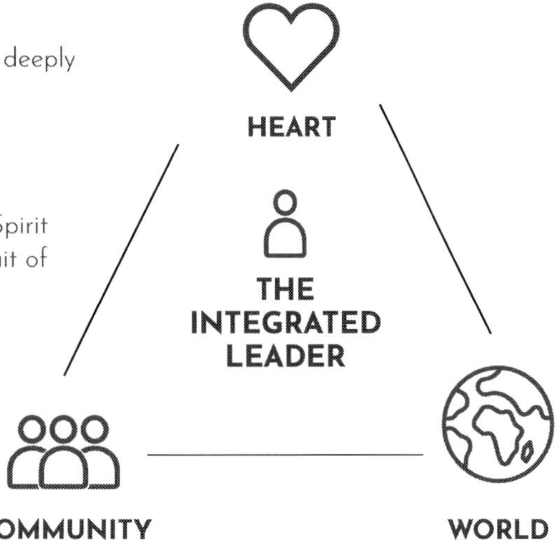

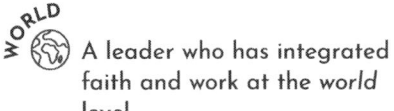

HEART
THE INTEGRATED LEADER
COMMUNITY
WORLD

HEART
A leader who has integrated faith and work at the heart level

- Hears God's voice and communes deeply with Christ
- Knows they are created to work
- Comprehends how their personal brokenness shows up at work
- Embraces the power of the Holy Spirit
- Is growing in expressions of the fruit of the Spirit
- Believes in broken systems (i.e., understands that the fall impacts all of creation, not just people)

COMMUNITY
A leader who has integrated faith and work at the community level

- Comprehends that the image of God is in all people
- Realizes that the gospel changes how they interact with others in and through their work
- Embraces the idea of stewarding power
- Understands the concept of common grace and its abundance
- Seeks to love others in all areas of work as Christ first loved them

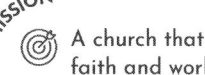

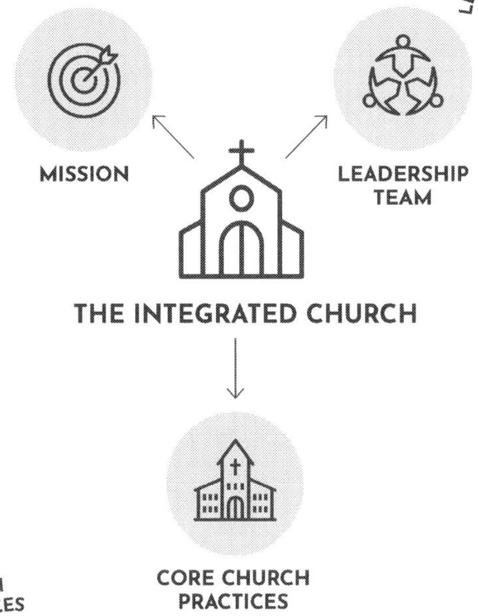

THE INTEGRATED CHURCH

MISSION

🎯 A church that has integrated faith and work has a *mission* that

- Views work as one of the primary contexts for spiritual formation, comprehending its significance for drawing people toward Christ and into heart renewal
- Overtly includes the role of work in their mission, viewing work as a primary context for congregants to impact their cities and communities, appreciating it as an essential conduit for mission
- Incorporates the impact of its laity's everyday work into measurements of the church's vibrancy

LEADERSHIP TEAM

A church that has integrated faith and work is led by a *leadership team* that is

- Equipped with a holistic understanding of faith-and-work theology, integrated at the heart, community, and world level
- Knowledgeable about the work lives of their congregants
- Committed to equipping the congregants with faith and work
- Partnered with lay leaders to execute a faith-and-work vision
- Aware of broken systems as well as broken people

CORE CHURCH PRACTICES

🏛 A church that has integrated faith and work embeds faith and work into its core *church practices* by

- Incorporating the concepts of faith and work into sermons
- Ensuring elements of the worship service emphasize work as a context
- Including a focus on work in its discipleship offerings, Bible studies, and community gatherings
- Viewing community service for the city through the jobs of its congregants
- Promoting a culture of mutual respect and appreciation for all roles within the congregation

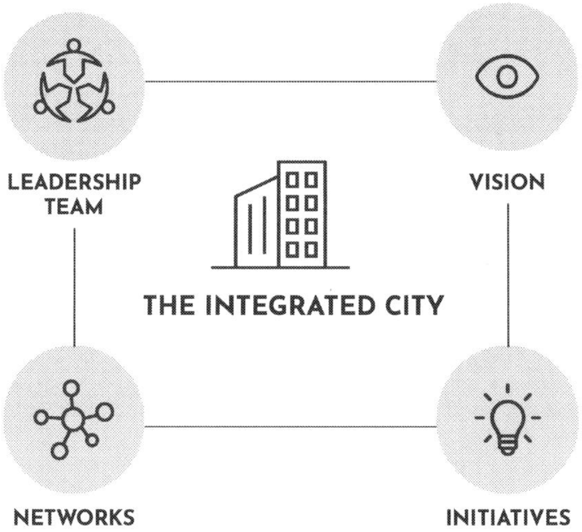

THE INTEGRATED CITY

VISION
A city that has integrated faith and work has a vision that
- Focuses on the renewal and common good of the city through work
- Views work as one of the primary contexts for Christians to impact their cities and communities, appreciating it as an essential conduit for mission

LEADERSHIP TEAM
A city that has integrated faith and work has a leadership team that
- Comprises integrated leaders from a variety of integrated churches
- Represents the diversity of the city
- Includes cross-denominational members
- Embraces a unified faith-and-work vision for the city

NETWORKS
A city that has integrated faith and work has networks that
- Include robust relationships between faith-and-work-integrated leaders across industries and church denominations
- Seek to unify, connect, and multiply the work of individuals and churches across the city
- Reflect the socioeconomic, racial, and cultural diversity of the city
- Understand the city's beauty and brokenness, including its economic drivers, its deepest wounds, and the struggles of those who are on the margins of society

INITIATIVES
A city that has integrated faith and work has initiatives that
- Include cross-denominational city-focused efforts with particular emphases in key industries, key city pain points, and entrepreneurism
- Prioritize issues faced by the most marginalized communities, such as homelessness, unemployment, education gaps, and racism

6

BECOMING A FAITH-AND-WORK-INTEGRATED LEADER

It comes the very moment you wake up each morning. All your wishes and hopes for the day rush at you like wild animals. And the first job each morning consists simply in shoving them all back; in listening to that other voice, taking that other point of view, letting that other larger, stronger, quieter life come flowing in. And so on, all day. Standing back from all your natural fussings and frettings; coming in out of the wind.

C. S. LEWIS

Becoming the Beloved means letting the truth of our Belovedness become enfleshed in everything we think, say, or do.... Becoming the Beloved is pulling the truth revealed to me from above down into the ordinariness of what I am, in fact, thinking of, talking about, and doing from hour to hour.

HENRI NOUWEN

Before you can lead others on a journey of faith and work, you'll need to begin embodying it yourself. The journey starts with you; you will need to become a role model for the integrated leaders in your church. This doesn't mean you need to be a perfect leader. It just means you are willing to deepen your own understanding and expression of what it means to be an integrated leader as outlined earlier—someone who has a strong and cohesive understanding of how the gospel impacts you at the *heart* level in your relationship with God, at the *community* level in how you interact with others, and at the *world* level in how you operate within your work sphere, city, and beyond. We will elaborate upon the Heart-Community-World framework below as we explore practices for cultivating faith-and-work integration for yourself and your leaders. As we do so, we will focus on work as the context in which both you and they are formed.[1]

This Heart-Community-World framework will repeatedly show up as you progress through the stages outlined in the remaining chapters because, as we noted earlier, the leader, church, and city levels are *interrelated, with the leader level as a necessary foundation for all.* The practices outlined in each of the segments below will clarify the growth you are seeking to embody in yourself as well as nurture in those you lead.

HEART, COMMUNITY, AND WORLD

The Heart-Community-World framework is a key tool for developing the integrated leader as it reveals how the gospel impacts everything: our hearts, our communities, and the systems and industries in our world. And, as we have already explored, work is a key context for impact. As you will see from the diagram below, the *heart* area focuses on our relationship with God, and out of that overflow we are able to impact our communities, industries, and cities.

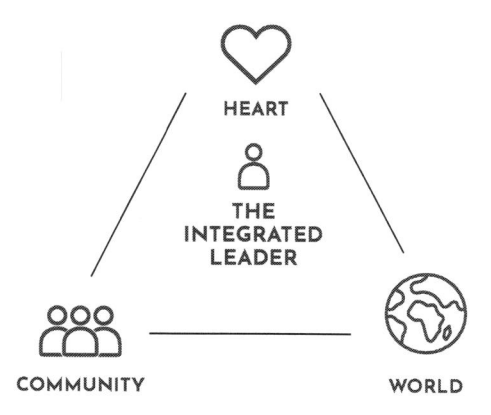

---

[1] The Heart-Community-World framework originated at Redeemer Presbyterian Church in a series of conferences in 2003 and 2004 with talks given by Timothy Keller and Tuck Bartholomew. (Heart: https://gospelinlife.com/series/the-gospel-and-the-heart-conference/; Community: https://gospelinlife.com/series/the-gospel-and-community-conference/; World: https://gospelinlife.com/series/the-gospel-and-the-world-conference/). The framework was then expanded by Katherine Leary Alsdorf, David H. Kim, and Amilee Watkins to apply to the faith-and-work space in their responsibilities at the Center for Faith & Work. It became a key framework of a licensed course called Gotham, originally published in 2008.

Below is an overview of each of these areas applied through the lens of work.

HEART

> Search me, O God, and know my heart;
>   test me and know my anxious thoughts.
> See if there be is any offensive way in me,
>   and lead me in the way everlasting.
>
> PSALM 139:23–24

The *heart* represents an individual's inner life and their relationship with Christ. A gospel-transformed heart creates the soil for transformed relationships, which leads to a transformed world.

Our relationship with God allows us to perceive both the beauty and brokenness in our work. We begin to understand that God has created us to co-labor with him and that we can commune with him not only about the types of work he has prepared for us but also in and through our endeavors, minute by minute.

Of course, as we have already discussed, we labor in a fallen world. Many areas of brokenness impact both yours and your congregants' work lives. The system brokenness in our workplaces, as well as our own personal brokenness, reveals the sin in our lives, which draws us to God in repentance and makes us more grateful and reliant on the saving grace of Christ.

As we toil in our tasks and commune with God about it, we begin to perceive the depths of our own sin in the workplace. Sometimes, deeper desires, affections, and hopes control us and our actions more than our love of God, and these failings often show up in work frustrations and sinful behaviors. These deeper desires are often "idols"—things we want more than we want a relationship with our loving God.

We can view these idols as our functional "saviors"—either consciously or subconsciously—and we pursue them because we believe they will ultimately not only satisfy us but also save us from our fears, insecurities, discomfort, and chaos. Idols can be good things that relate to the desires God has wired within us; but when these things become more important to us than Christ—when they absorb our hearts and imaginations more than God does—then we have looked to an idol to give us something that only God can provide. For example, a common idol at work is the desire for accolades or appreciation—a distorted reflection of our deep-seated longing for God's pleasure—and this applies in almost any industry, including ministry. How often have you been jealous if someone gets credit for your work? Or felt crushed if a project you care deeply about is failing? Or desperately need to hear someone say "good job" to keep you motivated? These longings lead to patterns of sin that could include spinning the truth; brooding with bitterness; or competing with, disrespecting, or hurting others. Another common idol at work is the desire for control. The need to be in charge can significantly impact the way you treat team members, particularly when a project is not going smoothly or when you disagree on vision. The impact of idols is pervasive, not only for you but also for every person in your church. To understand the true extent of our brokenness, we must uncover these idols.

In the context of work, there are many ways God can reveal our idolatry and ultimate need for him. One way we can think about idolatry is to consider what we feel we need beyond Jesus to be happy—any time when our hearts function with the equation, *Jesus + [X] = happiness*.[2] In other words, without the idol "X," we believe we cannot be happy, even if we have Jesus.

For instance, we may believe any or all of the following:

- Jesus + affirmation for my good work = happiness
- Jesus + impact at work = happiness
- Jesus + less work = happiness
- Jesus + more interesting work = happiness
- Jesus + nicer customers = happiness
- Jesus + more money = happiness
- Jesus + a promotion = happiness
- Jesus + a different job = happiness
- Jesus + a better boss = happiness
- Jesus + more stable work = happiness
- Jesus + a reputation of integrity = happiness

---

[2] Thanks to Patric Knaak of Serge Ministries for this diagnostic tool, which we have applied to various work scenarios.

In each of these scenarios, we have concluded that Jesus is not enough. We blame the circumstances of our jobs for the sinful roots that are embedded in our hearts. Work is therefore a key context for Jesus to reveal our sin and make us more reliant on him. As a pastor, it's essential to view your job—and to help your church members view their jobs—as a way to partner with God, cultivating his creation and glorifying him rather than viewing work as a means to fulfill needs that only Jesus can meet.

You have likely had many opportunities to evaluate the successes and failures of your church or ministry as it related to being faithful to the call of the gospel. Careful reflection can help determine whether your identity is derived from your own efforts, programs, or number of congregants—or if it is rooted in who God says you are as his beloved child. You may have felt anxious about aspects of your work. Are there enough people in the seats? Baptisms? Volunteers in the nursery? Dollars in the offertory plate? Will the work God has given you meet your needs or pay your bills? Are you getting enough affirmation for how hard you work? Will the fruit of your labor equal its input? Most of these are things your congregants are also dealing with—whether they are working in the home, custodial work, education, finance, the arts, transportation, or any other industries in your city. For some, work plays too significant a role in their lives, and their identities are tied to the success of their work. But for others, work can be devalued—viewed merely as a necessary evil to achieve material sustenance. Some perceive their work as lacking dignity; others may prioritize leisure over labor. Regardless of their viewpoint, every person in your congregation will wrestle with desires that can become idols. However, only understanding work in light of the gospel brings true fulfillment. Recognizing the insidious nature of our idols helps us appreciate Jesus' sacrifice for our sin more deeply, inspiring gratitude and increasing our dependency on him for our work.

Imagine a congregation deeply connected to Father, Son, and Holy Spirit, finding purpose and divine mission in and through their work. Through this lens, they recognize their own brokenness at work, fostering gratitude for their salvation and more dependence on Jesus, out of which more fruit of the Spirit unfolds (Gal. 5:22–23). We must embody this ourselves and then teach these principles to our congregants. Leading them through a variety of exercises to see their sin/brokenness at work and cultivate hearing God's voice are great first steps to help people deepen their relationship with Christ in and through their work. *Only through a deeper relationship with Christ will we see changed relationships, workplaces, and cities.*

A FAITH-AND-WORK-INTEGRATED LEADER'S HEART

A leader who integrates their faith and work understands that their work is part of what God created them to do. They recognize that their vocation not only glorifies God but also sanctifies them in their journey with God. They know God has given them gifts and opportunities to make concrete contributions to the world, and they welcome these opportunities, both paid and unpaid. They also recognize how their personal brokenness can be evident in their work. This means they understand the specific ways they are tempted to seek their identity and worth through their professions, and they actively embrace the power of the Holy Spirit to free them from this.

An integrated leader relies on the power and wisdom of the Holy Spirit to help them discern their vocational motivations and cultivate a personal relationship with Jesus, leading to increasing Christlike character. Empowered by the Spirit, they faithfully serve their neighbors through their work. This holistic integration is the fruit of abiding in Christ (John 15)—walking closely with Jesus on a lifelong journey that transforms their motivations and desires, aligning them with God's purposes for his kingdom.

They also recognize the fall's impact on all of creation—resulting in broken systems in every sphere and institution. These leaders understand that such systems are often corrupted by self-serving and sinful pursuits, most of which are able to be redeemed.

> At the *heart* level, an integrated leader works in a way that
> - hears God's voice and communes deeply with Christ;
> - knows they are created to work;
> - comprehends how their personal brokenness shows up at work;
> - embraces the power of the Holy Spirit;
> - is growing in expressions of the fruit of the Spirit; and
> - believes in broken systems (i.e., understands that the fall impacts all of creation, not just people).

PRACTICES FOR FORMING A FAITH-AND-WORK-INTEGRATED LEADER'S HEART

To establish a baseline for assessing where you need to focus your leadership development to more seamlessly integrate your faith and work, use the Integrated Leadership Assessment in appendix one.

You can use the practice below for your own personal heart growth as well as to disciple a faith-and-work leadership team. Eventually, you can use this practice more widely across your congregation.

THE HEART INVENTORY

Take a moment and use this *heart* inventory to bring the following question before God: *What idols prevent me from being a restorative presence at work?*

Part 1: Prayer
Start your time by praying this Scripture slowly:

> Search me, God, and know my heart;
>> test me and know my anxious thoughts.
>
> See if there is any offensive way in me,
>> and lead me in the way everlasting.
>
> PSALM 139:23–24

Now, prayerfully ask God to search you and reveal any area that might be keeping you from being a restorative presence in your industry. Spend some time in silence, meditating on this Scripture.

Part 2: Reflection
Reflect on a recent time when you behaved or held a posture that was sinful in your work. Perhaps you were in a work conflict. Maybe you were jealous, territorial, or aggressive. Perhaps you experienced

a significant injustice. Think deeply in prayer about this, considering what you most wanted. Based on the following bullet points, which of the four key idols—comfort, approval, control, and power—was most evident in your life?[3]

- Are there ways your need for *comfort* kept you from making a right choice in your work? From reaching out to those who are different? From sharing the gospel with others? From giving away influence? From avoiding helping with a project so you could have more leisure?
- How did your need for *approval* impact you? Did you prioritize receiving credit from influential people over helping others? Did you hesitate to advocate for someone or a group because you feared disapproval or judgment? Did you seek approval from coworkers or superiors by engaging in negative behaviors such as gossip, slander, or other activities that don't glorify God? Did constructive criticism hurt you or make you defensive?
- Are there ways in which a desire for *control* hindered your openness to what God was doing in your work? Did you cling to a project without seeking collaboration? Did you become overly stressed when circumstances changed? Were you able to view changes in circumstances through the lens of God's sovereignty? Did you exclude others with different perspectives because of your need for control?
- How did a desire for *power* impact your work? Did a fear of losing influence prevent you from giving authority and agency to others? Did you use your power to demonstrate your expertise or control outcomes? Did you prioritize your own interests over the needs of others when using your power?

---

[3] These four idols are more deeply explored in Timothy Keller, *Counterfeit Gods: The Empty Promises of Money, Sex, and Power, and the Only Hope That Matters* (New York, NY: Riverhead Books, 2009).

Part 3: What Does the Gospel Say?

Once you have identified an idol, ask the question, *What does the gospel say about this issue?* When our idols are revealed, it shows us where our hearts are us-centered rather than God-centered. It reveals to us the ways our desires are not aligned with what brings glory to Christ.

With the idol identified above in mind, consider these questions:

- When that idol arose, in whom and in what were you trusting?
- What were you doubting about God's nature and promises that had you placing your trust in this idol? What were you fearing?
- What does Scripture have to say about this misplaced trust or fear?
- How would you respond differently in this area if you were trusting in Christ and his gracious provision in your life?

Part 4: Moving Toward Christ

Return to prayer. Spend some time in repentance, confessing how your worship of this particular idol has kept you from loving others. Thank God for what he has revealed about your brokenness, recognizing it as an opportunity for a deeper experience of his grace. Meditate on the truth that Christ died for this sin, and all our sins, and how he voluntarily gave up comfort, approval, control, and power on the cross out of love for you.

Considering each idol, pray about what your response should be, based on truth. For example,

- *Comfort*: Christ is my comforter and has suffered a servant's death. Everlasting life with him is my end.
- *Approval*: I am approved and fully adopted as a child of my Father. My brokenness is covered by the sacrifice of Christ. I need no further approval through my work.
- *Control*: The Lord God is sovereign and my provider. Everlasting life with him is my end.
- *Power*: All the power and glory and honor is his. The way of the kingdom is upside-down.

> Commit to allowing the love of Christ to shape your identity and desires. As you do this, you are inviting his love to renew and restore your heart through the power of the Holy Spirit.
>
> **Part 5: Moving Toward a Friend**
> As you complete this practice, reach out to someone to share what God is graciously revealing to you about the ways you work, and ask them to pray with you for the renewal of your heart and deeper alignment with God's love for you.

Attuning Your Heart to His

Part of the *heart* journey is learning to discern God's voice more clearly—not only day-to-day but hour-to-hour, even in the most challenging work moments. Can you take a breath in the middle of a difficult negotiation and tap into hearing what God may want you to know, hear, or say? Can you seek God in the middle of a conflict with a boss or colleague?

The prayer practices that have deeply impacted us personally—as well as pastors we have worked with—engage both the right (intuitive) and left (logical) brain. God is omnipresent, and the Holy Spirit continues to reside with us; and although we might not always be able to hear him, he delights when we try. We highly recommend the work of Attune, an organization with a vision to help teams become healthy and adaptive by tuning into God together.[4] Their diverse listening exercises strengthen the ability to recognize God's voice and nearness, enabling us to align our lives with God and draw closer to him all day, every day. The ongoing pursuit of hearing God's voice is ultimately part of the long journey of being a disciple. For more information about the work of Attune, as well as a link to several attunement exercises, see appendix two.

---

[4] https://attunetogrow.org/.

COMMUNITY

> Do nothing out of selfish ambition or vain conceit. Rather, in humility value others above yourselves, not looking to your own interests but each of you to the interests of the others.
>
> PHILIPPIANS 2:3-4

Community represents the relationships in our day-to-day work. Thus, when applied to the context of work, community is the "work neighborhood" that God gives us to love well.

Most Christians know that Jesus calls us to love our neighbor—but how often do we consider our coworkers, our suppliers, our customers, and even our competitors as neighbors? All our interactions and work relationships are opportunities that God gives us to express the love of Christ; to be a presence working toward "heaven on earth" for his glory. The amount of love required of us of can seem limitless, and most of us tend not to love our neighbor enough. Very few of us give too much. The attunement work mentioned earlier is helpful in learning how to abide with Christ and listen to his voice in ways that help us discern how and when he is guiding us to love.

Katherine Leary Alsdorf emphasizes the practical ways we can love our neighbors:

> It may be helpful to reflect on your day and the different tasks you've performed that have been acts of love toward someone else. Did you clean up the kitchen? Take out the trash? Complete your expense report on time? Close a sale? Help a co-worker learn a new skill?.... The community of people with whom we work, along with the work itself, has God-ordained purpose and meaning. Whether that community includes fellow believers of the gospel or not, the experience of working together toward a common goal can be one that offers glimpses of God's purposes and love.[5]

When our hearts have been changed by God's grace, the way we treat people at work will be different. This difference could be as small as having extra

---

[5] Katherine Leary Alsdorf, "Loving Your Neighbor at Work," in Why Your Work Matters (online course) Redeemer City to City, 2019, accessed December 11, 2024, https://learn.redeemercitytocity.com/library/why-your-work-matters-43482/about/.

patience with a coworker whose habits are annoying or as broad as increasing the lowest wage across your company. It could include more transparency with customers, changing payment terms to assist suppliers through a crunch, amending human resource policies to avoid biases, or keeping break rooms tidy and welcoming.

It can be easy to assume that loving our neighbor at work will mean compromising on excellence or the requirements of our job. We may fear that focusing too much on relationships could affect profitability, efficiency, deadlines, or targets. If the work environment is highly competitive, it may even seem disadvantageous to love our neighbor. But, although love itself should be the motivation, research shows that being supportive of colleagues can lead to a more positive and collaborative work environment, potentially boosting productivity and bringing with it greater excellence.[6] Achieving excellence at work is another way we can love our neighbors, as a sustainable workplace keeps people employed. When it comes to profits themselves, Jeff Van Duzer, author of *Why Business Matters to God*, says that business exists primarily for two main reasons:

1. ***To provide goods and services that enable communities to flourish.*** Van Duzer emphasizes that businesses play a crucial role in society by creating products and services that meet the needs of people and enhance their quality of life. By doing so, businesses contribute to the overall well-being and flourishing of communities.
2. ***To provide opportunities for people to express their God-given talents in meaningful and creative work.*** Van Duzer believes that businesses should be platforms where individuals can use their unique skills and talents in ways that are fulfilling and meaningful. This perspective underscores the importance of work as a form of stewardship and a means through which people can contribute to the common good.[7]

---

[6] Val Dobrushkin, "Caring for Others Boosts Work Performance and Beyond," LinkedIn, March 10, 2014, https://www.linkedin.com/pulse/20140310145258-16759399-caring-for-others-boosts-work-performance-and-beyond/.

[7] See Jeff Van Duzer, *Why Business Matters to God: (And What Still Needs to Be Fixed)* (Downers Grove, IL: IVP Academic, 2010), 38–41.

These principles are rooted in Van Duzer's theological and ethical perspective on business, which views economic activity not merely as a pursuit of profit but also as a means to serve the greater good and honor human dignity—in other words, loving our neighbor. Further, he purports that profits are essential for the sustainability and growth of a business, but they should always be directed toward the higher purposes of serving communities and providing meaningful work opportunities.

Once we understand that workplaces are a context to love and serve our neighbors, we look for opportunities for God to use us to bless coworkers, colleagues, customers, and even competitors in and through our work.

A FAITH-AND-WORK-INTEGRATED LEADER'S COMMUNITY

A leader who has integrated faith and work is one who realizes the gospel changes how they interact with others through their work. They no longer passively measure others as better or worse than themselves. Rooted in a profound understanding of Christ's selfless and sacrificial love, this leader prioritizes the well-being of their colleagues over personal advancement. Consistent with this, the faith-and-work-integrated leader embraces the concept of stewarding power for those who have very little, recognizing they have been given a position of influence and authority not for their own benefit but for the benefit of others. This stewardship extends to all people, not solely Christians. For this leader to faithfully relate to any community of people, they must understand all individuals are created in the image of God, regardless of their background or circumstances. This understanding produces a recognition of the intrinsic worth and dignity inherent in every individual, as bestowed by God. Certainly, this is a challenging journey while also stewarding organizational excellence.

Faith-and-work-integrated Christians appreciate that God reveals his divine attributes, preserves what is good, restrains what is evil, and instills a capacity for truth, goodness, and beauty in all image-bearers, regardless of their beliefs. (This is the non-salvific work of the Holy Spirit that is common to all, known as "common grace."[8]) Common grace abounds, and God's goodness

---

[8] See footnote two in chapter five.

and mercy are evident throughout the world, even outside of the church or the explicitly religious sphere. In fact, we should expect to see God's common grace at work in our communities, alongside the distortions caused by sin. When we comprehend this reality, it produces a commitment to consider how all aspects of work either serve or harm other image-bearers.

> At the *community* level, a faith-and-work-integrated leader works in a way that
>
> - comprehends that the image of God is in all people;
> - realizes that the gospel changes how they interact with others in and through their work;
> - embraces the idea of stewarding power;
> - understands the concept of common grace and its abundance; and
> - seeks to love others in all areas of work as Christ first loved them.

A PRACTICE FOR FORMING A FAITH-AND-WORK-INTEGRATED LEADER'S FOCUS ON COMMUNITY

You can use the practice below for your own personal growth in the *community* aspect, as well as to disciple a faith-and-work leadership team. Eventually, you can use it more widely across your congregation.

> ### THE RELATIONSHIP INVENTORY
>
> This inventory is designed to help you understand relational dynamics within your workplace and to take steps toward building stronger relationships with those you interact with. Reflect on the following items:

- Create a list of all individuals and groups you interact with at work (customers, suppliers, managers, direct reports, custodians, etc.).
- Who in your workplace or industry holds the most power? Who holds the least? Who does the unseen work in your place of work (e.g., maintenance or cleaning)?
- Do you have relationships with those who are often overlooked or undervalued in your workplace?
- Do you have relationships with those who are directly affected by your work, such as your customers or those in your supply chain?
- What would it look like to create genuine relationships in work settings, where there is mutual giving and receiving?
- Is there someone in your workplace who might benefit from your encouragement and who might be open to discussing the Christian faith?
- In what ways does your organization create pain points for others (customers, suppliers, etc.)? How could relationship efforts change that?
- What could you do this week to pursue deeper friendship with an unlikely person in your workplace or industry?

Prayerfully consider the individuals you thought of in your answers. Refer to the Attune process in appendix two if helpful. Who do you sense God is guiding you to connect with more deeply in the coming weeks? What can you change to reduce the pain for others? How does God's love for you empower you to seek out opportunities to love others in the workplace?

WORLD

> Then I saw "a new heaven and a new earth," for the first heaven and the first earth had passed away, and there was no longer any sea. I saw the Holy City, the new Jerusalem, coming down out of heaven from God, prepared as a bride beautifully dressed for her husband. And I heard a loud voice from the throne saying, "Look! God's dwelling place is now among the people, and he will dwell with them. They will be his people, and God himself will be with them and be their God. 'He will wipe every tear from their eyes. There will be no more death' or mourning or crying or pain, for the old order of things has passed away."
>
> He who was seated on the throne said, "I am making everything new!" Then he said, "Write this down, for these words are trustworthy and true."
>
> REVELATION 21:1–5

In the context of work, *world* represents an individual's relationship with their workplace, industry, and its broader systems. Thus, *world* reflects how a leader understands and interacts with the gospel's relevance to an industry, system, or even city or region.

Imagining life in the new heaven and new earth gives us a glimpse of why caring now about our industries matters. Although most pastors we have trained have a clear understanding of the goodness of ministry, mission work, and those in helping professions (e.g., nurses), they have rarely considered why God might care about banking or advertising, for example. Few can envision what art or real estate might look like in the new heaven and new earth. But it is precisely this eternal thinking that can help congregants understand why their work matters to God, and how God might be using that industry to renew his entire creation.

The biblical narrative (explored in chapter two) helps us understand that most industries have a purpose in the world based on God's creation mandate and desire for humans to create flourishing communities. For instance, consider the evolution of currency and banking. People used to barter with goods and services; but as community complexity increased, money emerged, and banking systems were developed to bring structure out of chaos. Can you imagine still bartering by trading goats for fabric? Can you see how banking has brought structure out of chaos in an attempt to bring goodness for all? Yet it is also distorted by greed and other areas of brokenness. Economic systems continue to evolve today, as decentralized digital currencies such as bitcoin develop.

Thus, understanding both the creational goodness and system brokenness of all good work, and helping congregants to do so, can be a game changer. In other words, we want to ask why God would want a given industry in the world, and what sin has done to distort it. This informs what the industry can one day be.

To exegete the role of any industry, we can apply a creation-fall-redemption-restoration lens (explored in the biblical narrative in chapter two) to our industries:

- *The Creation lens*—We can first ask what God's original creational intent might have been. How does this industry bring structure out of chaos? What good can it bring about? How does it help flourishing?
- *The Fall lens*—Once we have a positive view of the role an industry can play, we can investigate how sin has tarnished it. What is broken about an industry? How has personal and system brokenness impacted the way this industry operates in the world?
- *The Redemption lens*—How did Christ in his work on the cross begin to redeem this creation so that Christians who work in this industry might help push against the sin and brokenness to recapture some of its creational goodness? How can you encourage your laity to join with Christ to bring renewal to these industries?
- *The Restoration lens*—What would this industry look like in the new heaven and new earth? How can you help your laity imagine a perfected version of their industry and work toward making it function "on earth as it is in heaven"? (Note, some industries exist to help with brokenness on earth and thus may in fact not be in the new heaven and earth [e.g., foster care and physicians].)

Below is an example of the creation-fall-redemption-restoration lens applied to the work of a custodian:

Creation—Humanity's mandate in Genesis was to steward God's good creation so that all might flourish. The role of the custodian is to steward a space for others to use where they can flourish. They do this by mopping floors, tending to trash, replenishing toilet paper in bathrooms, solving problems or fixing broken things. They bring structure out of chaos, just like God in the Genesis account.

Fall—The creation God made has been marred by sin, sickness and disease. Within this industry, custodians are often given the task of responding to the consequences of sin: destroyed property, spills and stains, overflowing toilets, pests, and building damages. As employees, they are often overlooked, working many hours to maintain an environment with little to no recognition.

Redemption—Jesus was the great janitor/custodian who took on the sicknesses and diseases of the world, cleansing hearts, bodies, and spaces. Janitors/custodians do the hidden work of disinfecting spaces, preventing the spread of millions of germs and diseases. They keep walkways and floors clear of debris and spills so that others might flourish as they walk through them.

Restoration—In the new heaven and new earth, custodians will possibly steward the golden streets of New Jerusalem. The streets will shine from the radiance of God's presence. At every corner and in every place of business, the stories of faithful janitors and custodians will be evident through stories and pictures. The work that was once often invisible and overlooked will be displayed for all to celebrate.

As you and those you lead begin to understand an industry through a biblical lens, the opportunity to challenge broken systems shifts from a desirable goal to a gospel mandate. Alongside attuning with God to imagine what's possible, this perspective provides a solid understanding of daily work as part of God's unfolding plan for the world, catalyzing both you and those you lead to push against brokenness wherever possible.

Helping your congregation to fully adopt this understanding can be life transforming. We have seen people who have embraced the redemptive potential of their industry experience renewed vitality in their work lives. They've gone on to reshape entire workplaces, launch redemptive ventures, and positively change the culture of their organizations.

A FAITH-AND-WORK-INTEGRATED LEADER'S VIEW OF THE WORLD

A faith-and-work-integrated leader views their work as part of God's unfolding plan for the world. This vision infuses every aspect of work with incredible meaning because it arises in response to God's call on one's life. Ideally, this leads to a deep commitment to understanding how their particular industry and workplace operate, recognizing both their innate goodness and brokenness. These persons are committed to pursuing opportunities to be salt and light by seeking to redirect dark processes and systems in their work and industry, all through discerning their role through the work of the Holy Spirit.

A commitment to this unique vision and posture in the world will form faith-and-work-integrated leaders into the type of people who find ways for their workplaces and industries to best represent the goodness of God in the world rather than simply highlighting broken realities. Seeing work as part of God's unfolding plan for the world stokes these leaders' vocational imaginations. This allows them to envision creative new ways to bring goodness into the world through their work, no matter how much—or how little—power and influence they perceive themselves having. They see their responsibility to respond to the particular needs in front of them as directed by the Holy Spirit, and they trust in God's redemptive power to make a difference through their faithful, Spirit-dependent work.

> At the *world* level, a faith-and-work-integrated leader works in a way that
>
> - views their labor as part of God's unfolding plan for the world;
> - understands the innate goodness and brokenness in their industry and workplace;
> - seeks opportunities to shine light on broken processes and systems at work;
> - finds ways for their workplace and industry to best represent the goodness of God; and
> - envisions creative new ways to bring goodness into the world.

A PRACTICE FOR FORMING A FAITH-AND-WORK-INTEGRATED LEADER'S FOCUS ON THE WORLD

You can use the practice below for your own personal growth in the *world* level, as well as to disciple a faith-and-work leadership team. Eventually, you can use it more widely across your congregation.

> ### CREATIONAL GOODNESS AND BROKENNESS ANALYSIS
>
> Consider the industry you work in, along with one or two industries that are critical to the flourishing of your city, and imagine them in their role in God's unfolding plan. Record your thoughts on a chart like the following.

Industry	Creation	Fall	Redemption	Restoration
	How does this industry represent the character of God? How does it bring structure out of chaos? In its best version of itself, why would God have created it? How does it engender fruit of the Spirit?	How is this industry broken? Which part of this industry does not reflect God's character? How does it hurt other people, systems, creations, or structures? How does it detract from flourishing for all? How does this industry create distraction from the fruit of the Spirit (e.g., hate, anger, chaos, impatience, etc.)?	If Jesus came tomorrow, what changes might he make to this industry? What brokenness needs to be solved? What new creation could bring light? How could this industry be part of God's unfolding plan for the new heaven and earth?	How might this industry be expressed in the Holy City described in Revelation? What might it be like as a perfected version of itself? What stories might be told and celebrated in Jesus' restored earth through this industry? As Jesus said, "The last will be first" (Matt. 20:16), what overlooked people in this industry do you believe will be given the highest honor in God's restored creation? What tributes and monuments might be displayed representing this industry in New Jerusalem?

Industry 1
_____

Industry 2
_____

Industry 3
_____

BEGINNING THE VIRTUOUS CYCLE

In summary, the Heart-Community-World framework is an organizing formational structure for helping a leader integrate faith and work within his or her own life. We have covered the framework extensively because integrated leaders are the foundation from which an integrated church and city form and grow. As Solomon declares in Psalm 127:1, "Unless the Lord builds the house, the builders labor in vain." Faith-and-work-integrated leaders undergird the entirety of faith-and-work efforts because they are driven by the power of the Holy Spirit. Though there is a synergistic relationship between leader, church, and city, without at least one faith-and-work-integrated leader somewhere, the virtuous cycle cannot even begin. *Faith-and-work-integrated leaders are the key to building a faith-and-work-integrated church or city.*

REFLECTION QUESTIONS

- In what ways can you personally begin to embody faith and work to model what it means to be a faith-and-work-integrated leader? Consider the categories of *heart, community,* and *world.* (See exercises in the sections above.)
- As you reflect on the Heart-Community-World framework, which aspect does your church naturally emphasize the most?
- What are some of the common idolatries your congregants struggle with at work? (If you aren't sure, ask three or four people from various industries.)
- Do your congregants tend to make work too important (work as a way to self-actualize) or too little (work as a necessary evil for survival)?
- How can you cultivate listening to God's voice about work for yourself and those you serve?
- When you speak of loving your neighbors, do you help congregants see all the people they interact with at work as an expression of their neighbor?
- How do your congregants interact with the *world* part of the triad, paying particular attention to industries and systems? What industries are most broken in your city?

7

THE JOURNEY MAP FOR IMPLEMENTING FAITH AND WORK IN THE CHURCH AND CITY

Your labor is not unknown
though the rocks they cry out and the sea it may groan.
The place of your toil may not seem like a home
but your labor is not unknown.

The houses you labored to build
will finally with laughter and joy be filled.
The serpent that hurts and destroys shall be killed
and all that is broken be healed.

"YOUR LABOR IS NOT IN VAIN,"
THE PORTER'S GATE WORSHIP PROJECT

Having reflected on the intersection of faith and work in your life and the lives of those you lead and having gained clarity on the destinations for and synergy between faith-and-work-integrated leaders, churches, and cities, you are now ready to embark on a journey to build faith and work into your church and/or city. The following chapters provide a journey map, initially focusing on the faith-and-work-integrated church and subsequently the faith-and-work-integrated city. Each chapter includes practical exercises and actionable next steps to guide your implementation journey.

To understand the purpose of this journey map, it is helpful to reflect on the traditional role of a map. Before the prevalence of cell phones, most maps were paper tools, unlocking the path between our starting point and some chosen destination ... or sometimes the unknown. Though people followed paper maps, they also relied on their sense of direction. Digital maps have revolutionized navigation, providing turn-by-turn directions, even for familiar routes. As a result, we are increasingly dependent on them and use our navigational intuition less often. The journey maps in this book offer a strategic overview that relies on your sense of direction—more like paper maps that inform your journey than a digital map that gives you turn-by-turn precision.

> A map does not just chart, it unlocks and formulates meaning; it forms bridges between here and there, between disparate ideas that we did not know were previously connected.[1]

The journey map presented to the right and unpacked in the following chapters is designed to be metaphorically unfolded at your table as you investigate the pros and cons of your next steps based on your context and what you hope to accomplish.

This tool is intended as a launching pad—to stimulate learning and action rather than mandating a rigid process. Although the journey map is primarily focused on implementation within and from a church, with appropriate adjustments its core principles can be applied to nonprofit or city network initiatives as well. (See appendix sixteen for a journey map for city network initiatives.) And, as we have already explored, faith-and-work-integrated leaders attuned to the Holy Spirit are a key foundation to the journey.

As we've supported pastors integrating faith-and-work principles into their churches over the years, we initially refrained from offering an implementation guide. Because we believe strongly in contextualization and the perils of one-size-fits-all models, we were reluctant to provide specific practical steps, fearing they might be interpreted as prescriptive rather than directional. However, the many pastors we have worked with have convinced us of the usefulness of next steps charted out by cartographers who have surveyed the landscape. As such, we have devised the map described in the following chapters based on our work with leaders around the world in various contexts; we hope it can provide a framework across diverse contexts while still encouraging creativity and innovation.

---

[1] Reif Larsen, *The Selected Works of T. S. Spivet* (New York, NY: Penguin Press, 2010), 62.

THE JOURNEY MAP FOR IMPLEMENTING FAITH | 101

Church Journey Map for Faith-and-Work Initiatives

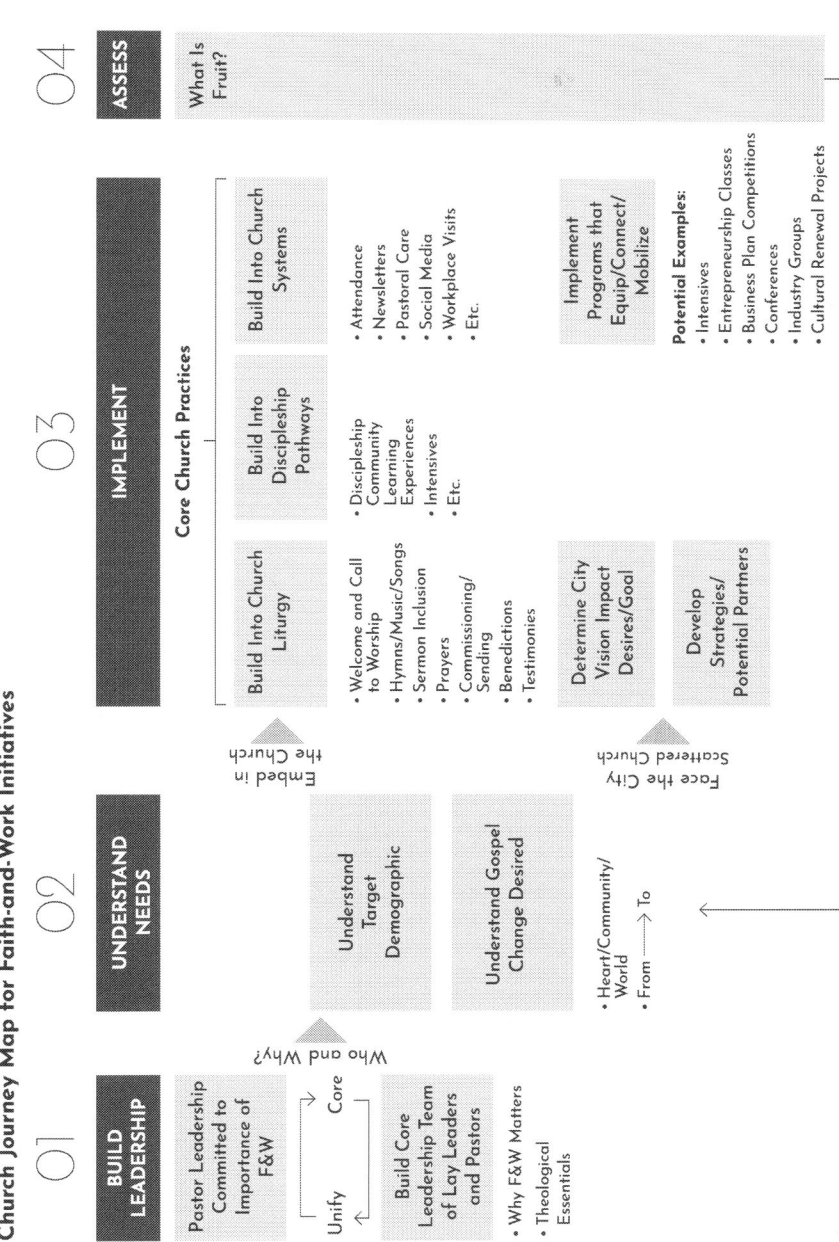

01 BUILD LEADERSHIP

- Pastor Leadership Committed to Importance of F&W
- Build Core Leadership Team of Lay Leaders and Pastors

Unify ← → Core

- Why F&W Matters
- Theological Essentials

Who and Why?

02 UNDERSTAND NEEDS

- Understand Target Demographic
- Understand Gospel Change Desired
  - Heart/Community/World
  - From ——→ To

Embed in the Church
Face the City Scattered Church

03 IMPLEMENT

Core Church Practices

Build Into Church Liturgy
- Welcome and Call to Worship
- Hymns/Music/Songs
- Sermon Inclusion
- Prayers
- Commissioning/Sending
- Benedictions
- Testimonies

Build Into Discipleship Pathways
- Discipleship Community Learning Experiences
- Intensives
- Etc.

Build Into Church Systems
- Attendance
- Newsletters
- Pastoral Care
- Social Media
- Workplace Visits
- Etc.

Determine City Vision Impact Desires/Goal

Develop Strategies/Potential Partners

Implement Programs that Equip/Connect/Mobilize

Potential Examples:
- Intensives
- Entrepreneurship Classes
- Business Plan Competitions
- Conferences
- Industry Groups
- Cultural Renewal Projects

04 ASSESS

What Is Fruit?

8

BECOMING A FAITH-AND-WORK-INTEGRATED CHURCH

AN OVERVIEW

Jesus himself is the map. He invites us into habits of prayer, curious engagement with the Bible, and deep connections with others in the Body of Christ that create further maps. Or perhaps we should say that these practices help us stay on the map that is Jesus, or that these practices are a map that directs toward Jesus. We can pray every day that our maps will become more solid, with richer colors, clearer streets, and highways that lead us where God wants us to go.

DR. LYNNE BAAB

We will first take you through the journey of integrating faith and work into your church, based on our ideal destinations covered in chapter five. If a full implementation process feels overwhelming, there is a Getting Started Guide at the end of this book, which offers practical steps to quickly incorporate faith and work into your existing church activities. Remember, even a small step can have impact and is better than nothing. However, we strongly recommend you also review the entire process highlighted below even if you cannot embark upon it all yet. By focusing on your leadership and deeply understanding your congregant's work experiences and envisioning a faith-and-work-integrated church, you'll create more sustainable and impactful first steps that can lead to greater momentum.

The journey map for integrating faith and work has four distinct stages, which we will explore sequentially. Although these are presented in a linear format, in reality, these steps are inherently cyclical and will repeatedly occur during the life of a church.

104 | FAITH & WORK

Church Journey Map for Faith-and-Work Initiatives

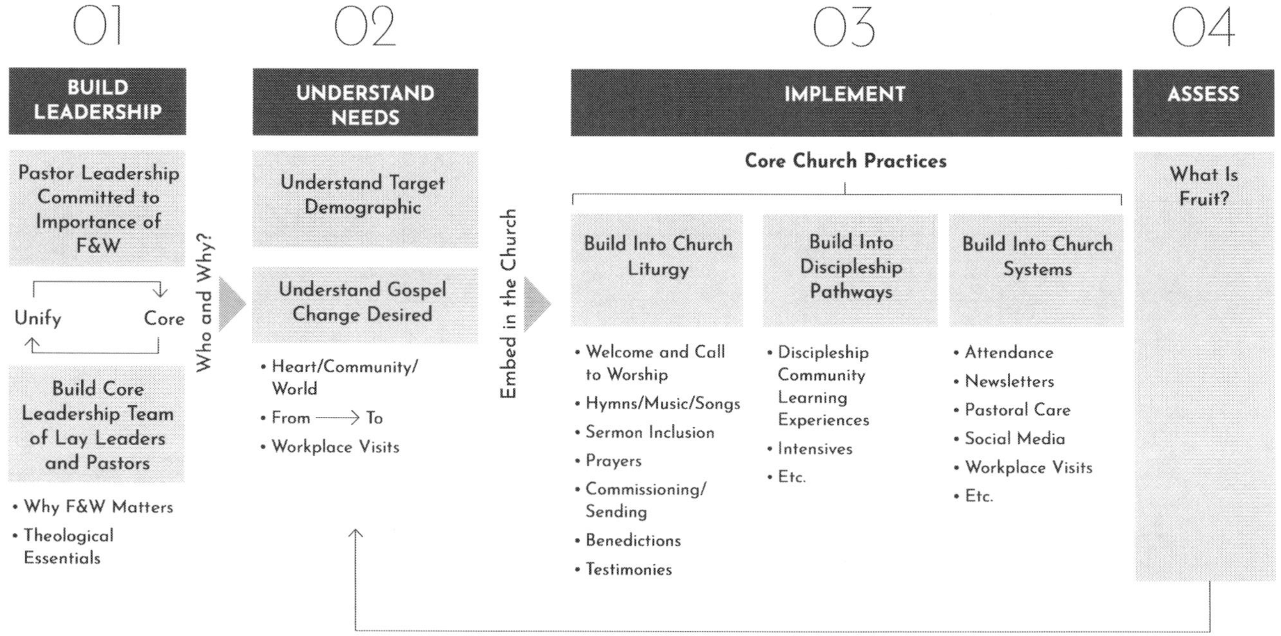

01 BUILD LEADERSHIP

- Pastor Leadership Committed to Importance of F&W
- Build Core Leadership Team of Lay Leaders and Pastors

Unify ↔ Core

- Why F&W Matters
- Theological Essentials

Who and Why?

02 UNDERSTAND NEEDS

- Understand Target Demographic
- Understand Gospel Change Desired
  - Heart/Community/World
  - From → To
  - Workplace Visits

Embed in the Church

03 IMPLEMENT

Core Church Practices

- **Build Into Church Liturgy**
  - Welcome and Call to Worship
  - Hymns/Music/Songs
  - Sermon Inclusion
  - Prayers
  - Commissioning/Sending
  - Benedictions
  - Testimonies

- **Build Into Discipleship Pathways**
  - Discipleship Community Learning Experiences
  - Intensives
  - Etc.

- **Build Into Church Systems**
  - Attendance
  - Newsletters
  - Pastoral Care
  - Social Media
  - Workplace Visits
  - Etc.

04 ASSESS

- What Is Fruit?

Steps 1 and 2 help you to *prepare* well for the journey of faith-and-work integration. Steps 3 and 4 are the *do* steps, where you gain momentum into the effectiveness of various actions and programs through experimenting and then assessing.

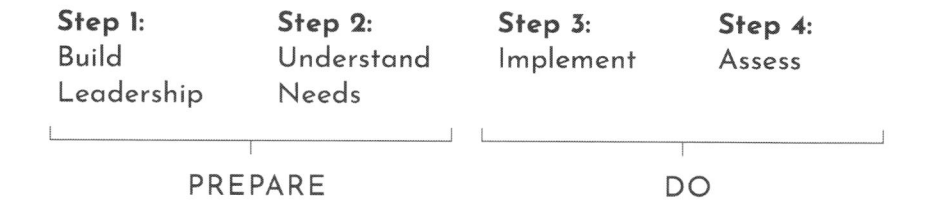

Step 1: Build Leadership	**Step 2:** Understand Needs	**Step 3:** Implement	**Step 4:** Assess
PREPARE		DO	

MISSION: A PRE-STEP CONSIDERATION FACTOR

Before we begin to outline the steps in the map, first a note about the mission of a church, which communicates its core purpose, values, and direction. It articulates a church's purpose and calling and the ways it seeks to serve the local community, as well as how it wants to participate in God's kingdom as it spreads the message of Christ. A church's mission shapes decision-making regarding leadership, focus, and priorities.

We believe faith and work should be a key context for the way you think about defining and executing your mission, but overtly incorporating it into your mission statements *before* you embark on the journey is likely difficult. Still, embedding faith and work into a church's mission should be woven throughout all you are seeking to do—like an invisible thread that weaves through all your church's activities.

Ideally your church's mission would align with faith and work from day one. However, sometimes it is the small faith-and-work efforts implemented in a church that actually begin to inform pastors and elders about its critical role. Adjusting a church's mission is a lengthy, complex task and requires the consensus of many stakeholders. Thus, rather than being stymied by the complications of gaining full mission alignment, we believe it is better to achieve initial momentum with faith and work. Over time, try to build consensus to incorporate faith and work into the church's long-term vision and mission. In the shorter term, we recommend highlighting how work is part of your current mission to disciple people and serve your city. Although in the short term a faith-and-work initiative can operate independently, in the longer term it will falter if it is not aligned with the overall mission of the church. Full alignment sometimes comes *after* implementing faith-and-work initiatives.

As you consider building faith and work into your mission, remember the following:

- Try to include the role of work in your overall mission statements.
- Your church should begin to view work as one of the primary contexts for drawing congregants toward Christ and into heart renewal, and as a place where they can impact their cities and communities—thus positioning it as an essential conduit for mission.
- If loving neighbors is a key component of your mission, make sure that work is highlighted as a key context for congregants to do this.
- If city renewal is part of your mission statement, note that this happens not only through mercy and justice but also through faith and work.
- Incorporate "scattered church" metrics (which include data from people's work as one source of input) when measuring the church's vibrancy. Examples of this are in the Impact Assessment Tool in appendix thirteen.

For helpful reference, below are some examples of missions that are highly aligned with faith and work, as well as one that is not.

Mission Example	Church	Level of Faith-and-Work Alignment	Comment
Our mission is to follow Christ in his mission of loving people, places, and things to life.	Christ Presbyterian Church, Nashville, TN	High	This mission aligns with the heart change and city change possible in faith-and-work-integrated ministries. The workplace is an environment where people can be "loved to life." Work is a place of sanctification and moves hearts toward God, loving them "to life." "Loving places" can include workplaces. "Loving things to life" can include broken systems.
We desire to be a caring family of multiplying disciples, influencing our community and world for Jesus Christ.	Christ Community Church, Kansas City, KS	High	This mission clearly states that "multiplying disciples" (heart change) is a primary objective while also highlighting that a purpose of disciples is to "influence" their "communities" and "world." Community and world impact can happen primarily through work.

Mission Example	Church	Level of Faith-and-Work Alignment	Comment
Reality Church London exists to be a community following Jesus, making him known, seeking the renewal of London. We do this by following Jesus day-by-day, belonging to each other as a church family, bringing our friends to Jesus, and serving London with the whole gospel.	Reality Church, London, UK	High	This mission is aligned with heart change and city change through faith and work. Work is a primary place where congregants can be "making him known." The renewal of London can only be accomplished through involving Christians in their workplaces.
Our main mission is to win souls to Jesus Christ and grow them holistically in mind, body, and Spirit.	Anonymous	Low	The focus on evangelism and discipleship in this mission can take place at work and through work, but this vision statement is not fully aligned with the heart change and city impact that faith-and-work efforts can effect. Further, it does not recognize the potential relevance of work as part of God's unfolding plan for the renewal of all creation.

9

THE INTEGRATED CHURCH

STEP 1: BUILD LEADERSHIP

The work of growing into ourselves, guided by the grace of God, is core to the path of leading well and navigating seasons of disruption, innovation and flux.
MICHAELA O'DONNELL AND LISA PRATT SLAYTON

A unified team with faith-and-work-integrated leaders is the cornerstone of successfully integrating faith and work across your church. Thus, the building of this leadership team is a critical first step. Without ample attention to this step, efforts to integrate faith and work often stall or fail. In fact, in our experience, initiatives that depend on only one leader are the most likely of any to fail.

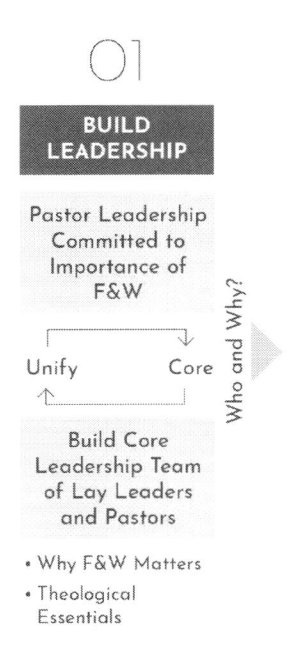

01

BUILD LEADERSHIP

Pastor Leadership Committed to Importance of F&W

Unify ⇄ Core

Build Core Leadership Team of Lay Leaders and Pastors

Who and Why?

- Why F&W Matters
- Theological Essentials

In this step, you will cultivate and unite a core team of pastoral and lay leaders dedicated to integrating faith and work in their own leadership and within your church. The leadership team must be nurtured and led by persons who have an integrated view of faith and work. Your goal is to cultivate a unified team that is committed to this kind of leadership themselves and embraces a holistic view of faith and work, recognizing its importance for heart transformation and city impact.

ELEMENTS OF A UNIFIED FAITH-AND-WORK LEADERSHIP TEAM

A unified faith-and-work leadership team will consist of the following:

Embodiment of faith-and-work integration. As discussed, your leadership team should embody (or at least be seeking to embody) the integration of faith and work as described in the Heart-Community-World framework in chapter six. If an individual (whether pastor or layperson) is on a path of regularly processing their work in prayer and repentance, looking for opportunities to serve others in and through their work, and thinking about the broken areas of their industry and how they can be redeemed, they are likely a strong candidate. Although we can all grow in some of these leadership principles, if an individual has a rigid or truncated view of faith and work, they may not be the right fit. A pastor who cannot comprehend why or how banking can be God-honoring or a lay leader who lacks the theological foundation to challenge broken workplace systems or demonstrate Christlike love toward their colleagues will first need to grow in embodying faith-and-work integration themselves before leading others.

Agreement on definition and scope of faith and work. A primary step in unifying a leadership team is to ensure the group agrees on the definition and scope of faith and work. Building on the discussion of defeaters in chapter three, you may discover some of your team members have limited understandings of faith and work shaped by their denominational upbringing, by restricted exposure to the topic of faith and work, by unsound theological teaching on the topic, and by the influence of mentors with unformed faith-and-work beliefs. The Faith-and-Work Framework for Unleashing the Gospel (see chapter four) highlighted how a limited understanding of the gospel's holistic power leads us to express a truncated version of it in our workplaces. Some of the most common truncated views of faith and work emphasize only one or two of the following in a workplace setting:

- Sharing the gospel
- Working in a distinctly "Christian role" through a helping profession or at a social-impact firm or Christian organization
- Making ethical decisions
- Praying for others
- Serving the poorest worker
- Changing the culture of a company or industry

These are all possible expressions of faith and work. However, considering only one or two as *the* definition of integrating faith and work truncates the gospel. Your church leadership team needs to have and express a holistic understanding of faith and work that includes all of these and more, while also appreciating that an individual may not be called to express *all* these aspects at any one time.

Furthermore, some team members may enter the faith-and-work conversation with alternative views of what the term means. We disagree with one common perspective that stems from what is sometimes referred to as "the prosperity gospel." One aspect of this belief system proposes that God wants financial prosperity for believers and its existence or absence is an indicator of faith. Adherents view wealth as a sign of God's blessing and poverty as a lack of faith suggesting that with enough faith, poverty can be avoided, which does not align with other areas of the Bible regarding money and suffering.

Another truncated view stems from an eschatological view that there is no work in the new heaven and earth. People who hold this view believe that work on this earth has no eternal value other than as a platform to evangelize and fulfill the Great Commission. Although sharing the truth of the good news at work is of course a worthy and biblical focus, when it becomes a singular focus, it fails to incorporate a biblical view of continued work in the new heaven and new earth as informed by Isaiah 60 and Revelation 21.[1]

Given the potential for limited perspectives on faith and work, the leadership formation phase prioritizes cultivating a shared, holistic understanding of faith-and-work theology and its integral context for personal transformation and city impact. There should be strong alignment among your team members on the meaning and expression of "faith and work."

As a note, in a larger church, it is not essential that the senior pastor participate in the faith-and-work leadership team. However, if they do not have a

---

[1] See pages 23–24 of this book for an exploration of this idea.

holistic view of faith and work, in time it will erode progress. We have experienced churches where the senior pastor and the faith-and-work team were not aligned on the holistic nature of faith and work, and, over time, the programs stalled or failed. Thus, while senior pastors are often not driving faith-and-work initiatives, it is helpful that they are aligned with them.

Intentional team size. The ideal size of the initial core leadership team is between three and six members and should include pastoral and lay leadership. As a reminder, Jesus had twelve disciples, and his *core* team consisted of his chosen three disciples: Peter, James, and John.[2] Groups larger than six often struggle with unity, organization, alignment, and coordination as they tend to be less agile and cohesive. Once the core team is unified, expanding the team beyond six to twelve is helpful for longer-term growth and sustainability. Some groups follow the model of three, twelve, seventy-two—meaning three are in the core team, twelve are in the expanded leadership team, and over time, the "seventy-two" become the ministry's key enthusiasts for formally and organically spreading the message out into the church community.[3]

Combined ministry and marketplace leaders. The combination of pastoral and lay leadership allows for a variety of strengths, sensibilities, and wisdom to impact the process. We have both been part of leading church initiatives in New York and Nashville with lay leaders serving alongside pastors. Pastors could exegete and provide spiritual and scriptural wisdom in ways marketplace leaders never could. Likewise, marketplace leaders were able to provide an "in the trenches" perspective, hard won from their years embedded in their industries. This spiritual and theological expertise combined with industry experience brought credibility to the messages that were espoused.

Diversity of perspectives. Your core and expanded leadership team should ideally reflect the diversity of the kingdom of God—but, at a minimum, it should mirror the diversity of your church. It should therefore reflect gender, cultural, ethnic, racial, and age diversity as well as diversity among the types of work

---

[2] Occasionally, Jesus chose to take only Peter, James, and John with him during significant events and moments in his ministry, leaving the other nine disciples behind. For instance, he only took Peter, James, and John to the Transfiguration (Matt. 17:1–13), and to heal the synagogue ruler's daughter (Mark 5:21–43), and to a special area while he was praying in Gethsemane (Mark 14:32–42). Although the exact reasons for this selection are not explicitly stated in the Bible, it is clear that Jesus had specific purposes for these smaller, more intimate gatherings. Overall, while we may never fully understand why Jesus chose these three disciples for these particular events, we can infer that his decisions were intentional and served a greater purpose in his ministry and in the establishment of the early church.

[3] In Luke 10 we see Jesus send out seventy-two (or seventy depending on which original scroll is used) disciples to do broader work in the area for his ministry.

represented. Work challenges and joys for men and women are often different; and the struggles for those in white-collar roles are different from those in blue-collar jobs, which affirms the importance of unity and diversity. Secular research aligns with this concept; it suggests that diversity enhances group decision-making. In his book *The Difference*, Scott E. Page, a professor at the University of Michigan, posits that diverse groups outperform homogeneous ones because they allow for a variety of perspectives and problem-solving approaches.[4] McKinsey points to similar studies that reveal the impact of diversity on organizational performance and growth.[5] As much as possible, try to have your core and expanded leadership team represent the different perspectives that exist within your church and/or city.

BOOSTERS FOR BUILDING A LEADERSHIP TEAM ✓

- Agreeing on a holistic view of faith and work
- Having an intentional core team size (three to six)
- Embodying faith-and-work integration
- Combining ministry and marketplace leadership
- Convening a team of diverse genders, ethnicities, ages, and types of work that reflects the city, your congregation, or both

BLOCKERS FOR BUILDING A LEADERSHIP TEAM ✗

- Failing to ensure that everyone has a unified view of faith and work
- Gathering a team that is too small or too big
- Including persons who are not on a journey to becoming fully integrated faith-and-work leaders themselves
- Forming with a senior pastor who does not support the work
- Convening a homogenous leadership team that does not reflect the diversity of your city, your congregation, or both

---

[4] Scott E. Page, *The Difference: How the Power of Diversity Creates Better Groups, Firms, Schools, and Societies* (Princeton, NJ: Princeton University Press, 2007), 57–60.

[5] "*Diversity Matters Even More: The Case for Holistic Impact,*" McKinsey & Company, 2023, December 5, 2023, https://www.mckinsey.com/featured-insights/diversity-and-inclusion/diversity-matters-even-more-the-case-for-holistic-impact.

DEVELOPING YOUR LEADERSHIP TEAM

Once you have established your core team, it's important to develop them for their role by initiating the following.

COMMIT TO LEARNING

Commit to a unified learning journey that will nurture a holistic understanding of faith and work. Consider one of the following to get started:

- Read a book together which covers a holistic theology of faith and work, such as:
    - *Visions of Vocation: Common Grace for the Common Good*
    - *Every Good Endeavor: Connecting Your Work to God's Work*
    - *The Missional Disciple: Pursuing Mercy & Justice at Work*
    - *Discipleship with Monday in Mind: How Churches Across the Country Are Helping Their People Connect Faith and Work*
    - *Go Forth: God's Purpose for Your Work*[6]
- Participate in an intensive faith-and-work leadership training cohort such as one of the international classes offered at the Global Faith and Work Initiative at Redeemer City to City or the church practicum at Made to Flourish.[7]

ENCOURAGE EACH TEAM MEMBER TO COMMIT TO BECOMING A MORE FAITH-AND-WORK-INTEGRATED LEADER

These church initiatives need to be led by persons with an integrated understanding of faith and work. Therefore, each leader—empowered by the Holy Spirit—should be motivated to increasingly and consciously apply the Heart-Community-World framework to their own experience. (You can use the

---

[6] See the Book Study Recommendations on pages 196–197 in the Getting Started Guide for the full details of these titles, as well as additional resources you can use with your leadership team.

[7] "Designing a Faith & Work Initiative," Global Faith & Work Initiative, accessed December 13, 2024, https://www.globalfaithandwork.com/training; "Church Practicum," Made to Flourish, accessed December 13, 2024, https://www.madetoflourish.org/what-we-do/church-practicum.

Integrated Leadership Assessment in appendix one to help your team identify areas for growth.) Building on our previous exploration of leaders who are integrated at a heart, community, and world level, every member of your leadership team should personally embrace this in the following ways:

Heart

- Participating in healthy daily spiritual rhythms of devotion, prayer, and Bible study focused on all areas of life, including work.
- Consciously seeking the voice of God about work decisions. (See the Attune exercises highlighted in appendix two to help with this.)
- In prayer, regularly analyzing areas of their own workplace brokenness.
- Proactively discussing with people they work with (360 degrees—above, beside, and below them) about how they can work in ways that may be more restorative.

Community

- Actively seeking ways to engage lovingly with all types of people they interact with at work—not just their close coworkers.
- Participating in healthy community-level disciplines, including active involvement in a church community and seeing those in their work context as "neighbors" to love.

World

Participating in actions that develop their awareness of the work issues of their city and beyond. This will include understanding the following:

- ***The story of the city***, including its biggest strengths, its greatest pains, and its "stubborn facts."

    A city's *strengths* can be things that allow it to prosper. For instance, one strength of Singapore is its location in Southeast Asia and port access which has allowed it to become a key transportation hub. One strength of Mexico City is that it is home to a vibrant blend of history, art, and culture, boasting numerous UNESCO World Heritage Sites, museums (like the

National Museum of Anthropology), and a rich tradition of music, literature, and cuisine. New York City is a global center for finance, commerce, and technology; it is home to the headquarters of the United Nations; is a leading job hub for banking, finance, and communication; it is a preeminent arts center; and it has a diverse and international population.

A city's *pains* include wounds that are hard to overcome. For instance, throughout the US in the mid-twentieth century, highways were built through poor neighborhoods; and the impact on these communities was often devastating with displacement of residents, disruption of community, and economic decline. The departure of key industries from a city can often create deep wounds such as has happened in the Rust Belt of the United States.

A city's *stubborn facts* refer to truths or issues that affect a city, country, or region and that are widely acknowledged but difficult to overcome. For instance, when I (Missy) was doing ministry in Nashville, which is famous for the country music industry, it was well known in the music business that the arduous touring schedule of performers is extremely hard on families and often accelerates other problems such as substance abuse. Separately, a "stubborn fact" highlighted by pastors living in one large city in Asia is that the sprawling layout of their city creates lengthy commutes, limiting time for leisure and rest and making it difficult for them to engage in communal and recreational activities beyond their neighborhoods. And in Pretoria, South Africa, frequent power outages disrupt everything, from work schedules to personal lives.

- ***The key industries in the city***, including their history and economic impact. What are the key drivers of the economy in a city? For example, in Nashville, the most significant economic drivers are hospitality (largest bachelorette party destination in the US), music creation and production (earning the nickname "Music City"), higher education, supply chain management, publishing, and health care delivery. Understanding the trends and issues in these industries is helpful, and regional chamber of commerce websites can often be a one-stop shop for all this information.

- ***The areas of greatest marginalization in the city***. Is it homelessness? Racism? A caste system? Unemployment? Drug addiction? Lack of education accessibility? Lack of health care? These issues are often related to and/or impact the main industries that are the economic drivers of the city. Understanding these aspects can provide valuable context for engaging with marketplace leaders and exploring their potential for positive community impact.

> **KEY TOOLS FOR STEP 1**
>
> - Integrated Leadership Assessment—see appendix one.
> - Spiritual Attunement as a Tool for Integrated Leadership—see appendix two.
> - Integrated Leadership Team Assessment—see appendix three.
> - City-Based Learning Tool—see appendix four.

Building the leadership team is the most critical step to the long-term success of implementing faith-and-work efforts in your setting. Although many initiatives have begun with only one person, experience shows that sustained initiatives require a core leadership team. It is critical that the leadership team is united in their understanding of the theology of faith and work and its importance. And of course, each of the team members must be on a path of fully integrated leadership in their own lives.

It's worth taking your time with this step to allow you to find the right people and to cultivate a holistic faith-and-work vision. Once you have your leadership team assembled, you are ready to move to the second step.

REFLECTION QUESTIONS

- Which marketplace leaders would be a good fit for your team and are eager to deepen their personal faith-and-work integration?
- What will be your first steps to cultivate your leadership team to grow in faith-and-work integration collectively? What curriculum or resources could you take them through?
- What are the most common truncated views of faith and work that might exist in your context? How will that impact how you choose leaders?
- How will you ensure diversity of perspectives (vocations, gender, cultural, ethnic, racial, and age diversity) on your team?

10

THE INTEGRATED CHURCH

STEP 2: UNDERSTAND NEEDS

> *Christ says "Give me All. I don't want so much of your time and so much of your money and so much of your work: I want You. I have not come to torment your natural self, but to kill it. No half-measures are any good. I don't want to cut off a branch here and a branch there, I want to have the whole tree down. I don't want to drill the tooth, or crown it, or stop it, but to have it out. Hand over the whole natural self, all the desires which you think innocent as well as the ones you think wicked—the whole outfit. I will give you a new self instead. In fact, I will give you Myself: my own will shall become yours."*
>
> C. S. LEWIS

Once you have gathered your leadership team and begun the learning journey together, momentum should be building. Now you are ready to look at the needs of those you seek to serve.

If you don't take the time for this step, you will reduce the impact of your faith-and-work efforts or, even worse, provide solutions that are detrimental. Understanding needs in this context is not simply a traditional marketing process where a company would seek to assess the needs of a client and attempt to fill them with what the person desires. In this case, you are looking for theological or spiritual gaps in persons' lives and seeking to fill those gaps with gospel truth that leads to heart change and external action.

01 BUILD LEADERSHIP

Pastor Leadership Committed to Importance of F&W

Unify ← Core

Build Core Leadership Team of Lay Leaders and Pastors

- Why F&W Matters
- Theological Essentials

Who and Why?

02 UNDERSTAND NEEDS

Understand Target Demographic

Understand Gospel Change Desired

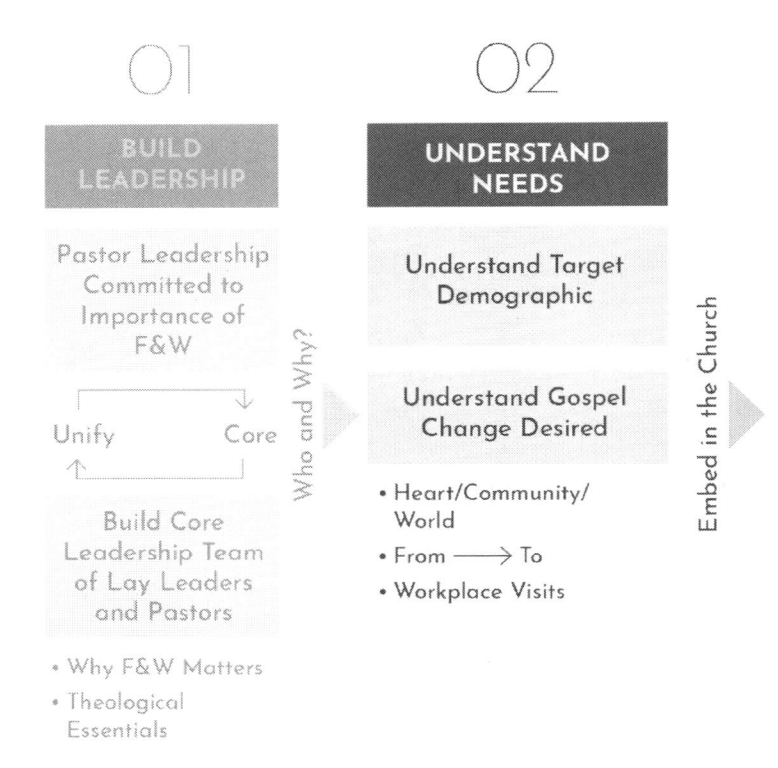

- Heart/Community/World
- From ⟶ To
- Workplace Visits

Embed in the Church

To understand the needs of those you hope to serve, you must explore the following three areas:

- Their demographics
- Their work joys, pain points, and pressures
- The heart change needed to align their perspectives with the gospel

DEMOGRAPHIC ANALYSIS

Start by gathering demographic data: Who do you want to serve, and what is their reality? Do you want to focus on your entire congregation? The neighborhood in which you are located? A portion of your congregation, such as the young professionals, the unemployed, the entrepreneurs, or the working poor?

As part of understanding who you serve (or want to serve), you must research them as individuals and also get to know them as a collective group.

- What are the main professions and work types?
- What are the age groups and work trends in those age groups (e.g., Gen Z, Gen X, Boomers, retirees, etc.)?
- What is their socioeconomic status, and what are the implications of this?
- Where do they live and work, and what are their commute times?
- What is their ethnicity and race?

The following data should be collected, preferably from a statistically significant number of those you hope to serve:

- Age range
- Gender
- Ethnicity
- Years of experience in a paid job
- Years of experience in parenting
- Years of experience in community/volunteer work
- Main place of employment
- Secondary place of employment
- Functional area of employment
- Income range[1]
- Level of employment satisfaction[2]
- Main types of work stress
- Main types of work gratification
- Level of interest in changing jobs

---

[1] If you are asking for income range, the surveys will need to be anonymous to receive accurate data. You may decide it is more meaningful to skip this question in order to have data linked to individuals.

[2] If you are asking for employment satisfaction, the surveys will need to be anonymous to receive accurate data. You may decide it is more meaningful to skip this question in order to have data linked to individuals.

- Hours spent per week in paid work
- Hours spent per week in unpaid work in the home, parenting, or elder care
- Hours spent per week in volunteer work
- Commute time
- Key pain points

> **KEY TOOL FOR STEP 2**
>
> - Congregation Work Survey—see appendix five. This tool can be copied and distributed.

WORKPLACE ANALYSIS

During your formation phase, each person on the leadership team should visit approximately four to eight workplaces to people in industries and jobs that are most representative of your city and of the people you serve. Workplace visits are extremely effective in helping you understand the realities and stresses of various industries, and they also affirm the importance of work to the person(s) you visit. This may well be one of the most significant practices you can do to encourage workers, and this habit is a meaningful practice to repeat on an ongoing basis. When visiting a workplace:

- Ask for as much detail as possible about your congregants' day-to-day work, seeking to understand what is motivating, what is stressful, and what is painful. (For tips, see the Workplace Visit Guide in appendix six.)
- Ask if you can pray for your worker, their colleagues, and the organization/industry as a whole while at their workplace. Of course, be sensitive that this may not be acceptable or comfortable for many in the workplace, especially in secular corporate settings or in industries or countries where Christianity is a risk to profess.

- After each visit, journal about what seems to be creationally good about their workplace and/or industry, what seems broken, and what is most challenging for a Christian in that workplace.

> **KEY TOOL FOR STEP 2**
>
> - Workplace Visit Guide—see appendix six.

Once you have compiled the demographic information and undertaken workplace visits, create a summary document of those you hope to serve that encapsulates their demographics, key work industries, joys and stressors, and main motivations for working. This lays the groundwork for understanding their needs, which you will explore more fully in the process below.

HEART-CHANGE ANALYSIS

Once you know who you hope to serve and have a sense of their demographics and their joys and stressors, it is time to consider the areas for heart change in relation to their work. As such, we recommend viewing their work through a 2x2 matrix (see page 125), which will then lead to what we call a "From→To" model. The From→To will then form the basis of your program development.

Workers' experiences and perceptions of work vary greatly depending on their context and can sometimes create misunderstandings about the true nature of their work. For instance, someone working on the service line in fast food or as a gig grocery-deliverer has little agency over their employment and may be laboring in challenging conditions for little pay in hopes of meeting their needs for survival. In this case, work is likely seen as a means to an end to secure basic necessities. The nature of their work may make it difficult for them to view it positively and as a good gift from God.

Instead, they may see it as a necessary evil—a view that is a distortion of the truth.

In contrast, an executive at a large company with a significant income and extensive team may have meaningful agency and choice in their work. Their relationship with work is likely not just about survival but instead fosters self-actualization through ambition, influence, and comfort. This view—that their work success is core to their identity—is also a distortion.

It is likely that neither of these individuals understands how their work is part of God's unfolding plan for the world. In the first example, the worker probably cares too little about their work and may not see the dignity in cultivating God's creation; and in the second example, the employee may care too much about work, seeing it as critical to their self-worth instead of recognizing that their identity is rooted in Christ. In both cases, there are significant distortions and misunderstandings. Recognizing this will allow you to tailor communication and spiritual guidance for those you serve, which will be critical for lasting heart change.

SPIRITUAL-GAPS ANALYSIS

The following Worker Needs 2x2 Matrix will help you understand the nuance of faith-and-work needs by various constituents. This grid contrasts socioeconomic flexibility and agency with under- or over-employment to identify potential spiritual gaps among different working populations.

The vertical axis indicates the amount of socioeconomic margin an individual has and/or the amount of power or decision-making agency an individual has in the work environment, given education, position, social capital, and so on.

The horizontal axis represents the degree of employment utilization. This refers to how well an individual's skills, income, and time are being used to their full potential. In general, this is intended to represent whether an individual is employed at the highest level of their abilities/experiences.

Worker Needs 2x2 Matrix: Types of Work

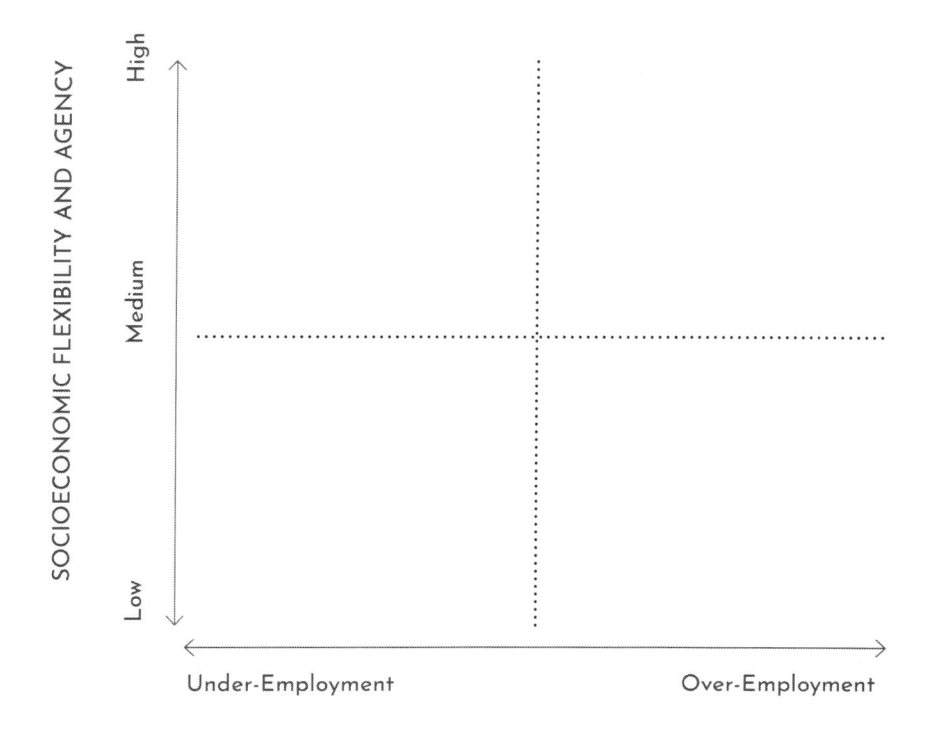

[Chart with y-axis labeled "SOCIOECONOMIC FLEXIBILITY AND AGENCY" (Low, Medium, High) and x-axis from "Under-Employment" to "Over-Employment"]

ROUTINE WORK MODEL

This tool is intended to represent how different types of workers experience work and to suggest general work attitude and thoughts. As a warning, the model is not exhaustive and can lead to unhelpful stereotypes if not used with care. Therefore, test it in your workplace visits; the workplaces you serve may not exactly correlate with the matrix qualities. Cautiously use it only as a tool rather than a prescription, taking what is helpful to sharing the gospel and eliminating what is not.

Looking at the various quadrants of this grid can help reveal what workers' theological needs are and how they may differ.

Worker Needs 2x2 Matrix: Types of Work

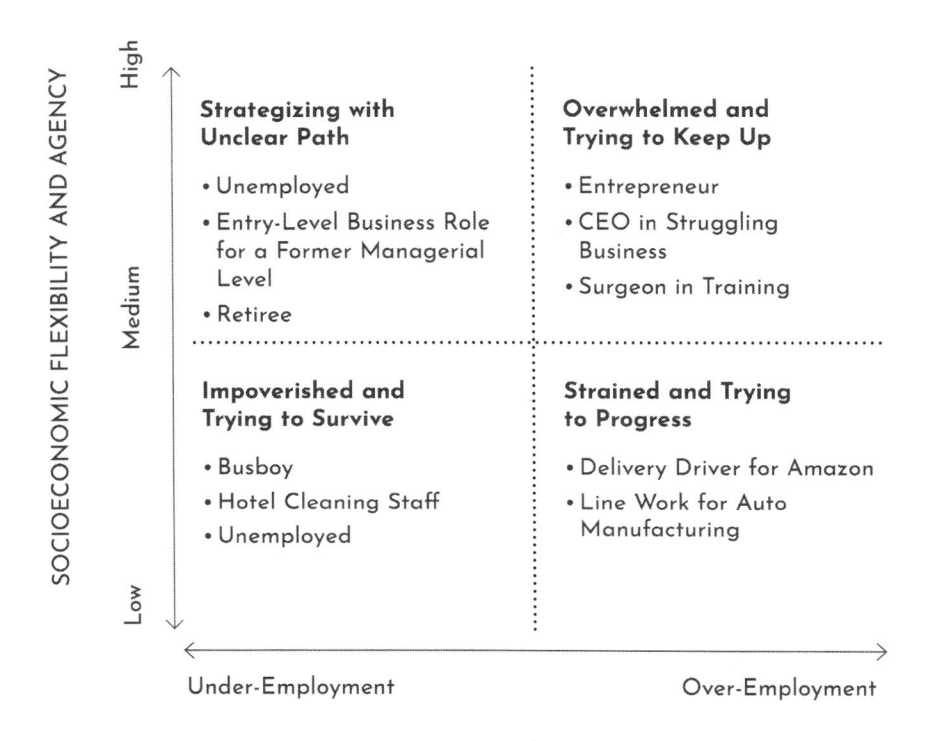

SOCIOECONOMIC FLEXIBILITY AND AGENCY (High / Medium / Low)

	Under-Employment	Over-Employment
High / Medium	**Strategizing with Unclear Path** • Unemployed • Entry-Level Business Role for a Former Managerial Level • Retiree	**Overwhelmed and Trying to Keep Up** • Entrepreneur • CEO in Struggling Business • Surgeon in Training
Medium / Low	**Impoverished and Trying to Survive** • Busboy • Hotel Cleaning Staff • Unemployed	**Strained and Trying to Progress** • Delivery Driver for Amazon • Line Work for Auto Manufacturing

ROUTINE WORK MODEL

The top-right quadrant, for instance, would contain workers such as high-capacity entrepreneurs, surgeons in training, a publicly traded company CEO, a high-ranking political official, and so forth. In general, professionals in the top right can potentially be described as overwhelmed by their roles yet with great agency. As such, their spiritual needs might include shifting from self-reliance to believing God is involved, from anxiety to peace, from an identity found in work to an identity found in Christ, and from overwork to sabbath rest.

In the top-left quadrant, the theological and spiritual issues are likely similar, but the context is different. The top left contains workers with high agency, capacity, education, social networks, and so on; but they are underemployed—either by choice or by force. Examples could include an unemployed person with strong educational credentials, a professional actor between shows or films, or a school principal who was laid off and took an entry-level administration job because they couldn't find alternative employment. The biggest spiritual need in this quadrant centers around identity—knowing they are enough and okay if they fail. But similar to the top right, they likely also have needs around idolatry exploration, anxiety relief, and perhaps sabbath.

The workers in the two quadrants on the bottom half have significantly less socioeconomic flexibility and agency. As such, they may be in jobs that have lower pay and prestige than the jobs in the top quadrants. They likely have very little say over their work type and schedule. They may be in jobs they do not like but are necessary in order to meet their basic needs. Whether they are underemployed and impoverished and trying to survive (bottom left) or strained and trying to progress (bottom right), the spiritual gaps these workers experience in relation to their work likely relate to fairness and God's sense of justice. Understanding that they serve a suffering Savior who completely gave away his agency is an encouragement. They likely need to believe that God sees them and cares about their well-being. Understanding that their work matters in the world could be groundbreaking for them.

Worker Needs 2x2 Matrix: Examples of Spiritual Needs

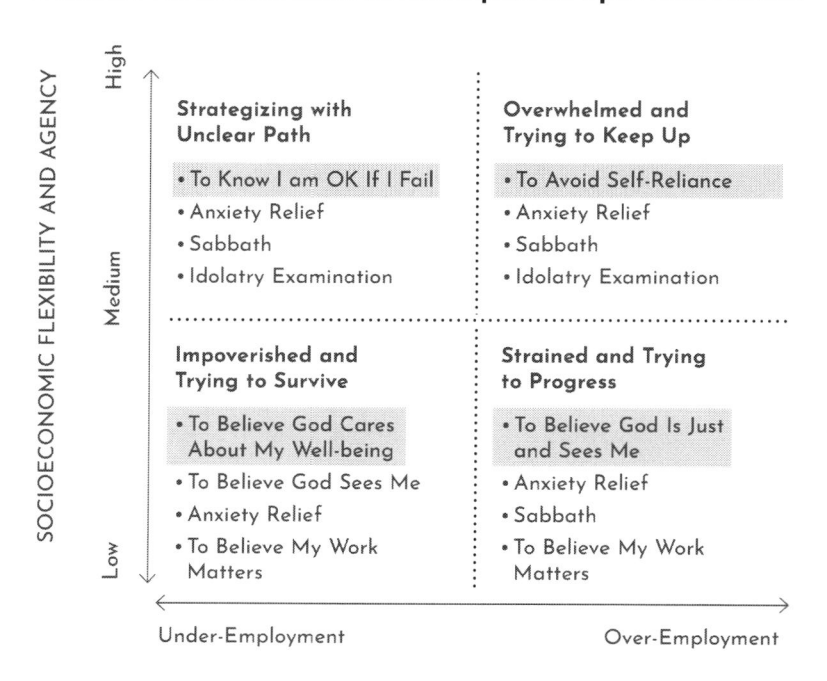

SOCIOECONOMIC FLEXIBILITY AND AGENCY (High → Low)

	Under-Employment	Over-Employment
Medium–High	**Strategizing with Unclear Path** • To Know I am OK If I Fail • Anxiety Relief • Sabbath • Idolatry Examination	**Overwhelmed and Trying to Keep Up** • To Avoid Self-Reliance • Anxiety Relief • Sabbath • Idolatry Examination
Low–Medium	**Impoverished and Trying to Survive** • To Believe God Cares About My Well-being • To Believe God Sees Me • Anxiety Relief • To Believe My Work Matters	**Strained and Trying to Progress** • To Believe God Is Just and Sees Me • Anxiety Relief • Sabbath • To Believe My Work Matters

ROUTINE WORK MODEL

Now that you have a sense of the demographics and high-level needs of your people, as well as the different spiritual gaps that arise for varying types of workers, you will want to build upon what you learned in your workplace visits to determine the most important needs. The goal of this sub-step is to discern people's key work-related beliefs that may need to be re-formed through your faith-and-work efforts. Below are several potential steps that will help this process.

- Host focus groups with key members of your target groups. Listen as the group members engage with each other around topics of faith and work and how your church might help them in this area, so you can make some educated assessments about the messaging and guidance needed. Use the following workplace visit questions to spark conversation:
  o When you hear the phrase "faith and work," what does that mean to you? (*Referring to the Faith-and-Work Framework for Unleashing the Gospel in chapter four, assess whether they lean toward a focus on evangelism, ethics, social impact, or a fuller experience of faith and work.*)
  o What are the most significant stressors in your workplace? What about your industry?
  o Do you see work as mostly good or mostly bad? Why?
  o How is your type of work or industry good for the world?
  o How is your type of work or industry broken?
  o What could your industry be like if it were the best version of itself?
  o What does being a Christian at your workplace mean to you?
  o If your church could do anything to help you with your work, what would that be?

- As you survey congregants, whether formally or informally, you will begin to see a set of needs emerge. However, as mentioned earlier, it is important for you to reflect on the *expressed* need versus the *real* need in light of the truth of the gospel and people's common misunderstandings about work. For instance, when Katherine Leary Alsdorf surveyed church members, she discovered that they were asking for solutions that might alleviate their challenges or discomfort, but these solutions would in fact not fully meet their felt need. Their real need was gospel truth and transformation. The following chart highlights some of her findings.[3]

Expressed Needs Versus Real Needs

Survey Need Expressed	Pain Point the Need Attempts to Solve	Real Need
Influential speakers	"Show me a way to do this!"	The opportunity to reflect with others on biblical truth and process the nuances of decision-making in light of God's Word
List of dos and don'ts—a rule book for work	Answers! "Do I check email on Sunday?" etc.	The ability to know God's truth and hear his voice amidst the cacophony of work voices
A new job	"Get me out of this broken industry/company/team. The grass must be greener somewhere else."	Theological understanding of brokenness at work and the ability to hear God's voice about when to stay and when to leave

---

[3] The From→To chart was developed by the Center for Faith & Work in 2008.

DEVELOP YOUR DESIRED FROM→TO PATH

Now that you have an understanding of your target group's demographics, a nuanced view of their perspectives of work, and an idea of their true needs, it is time for your leadership team to whiteboard the messages most needed, with the aim of creating and implementing programs that, empowered by the Holy Spirit, can create the change you hope to see.

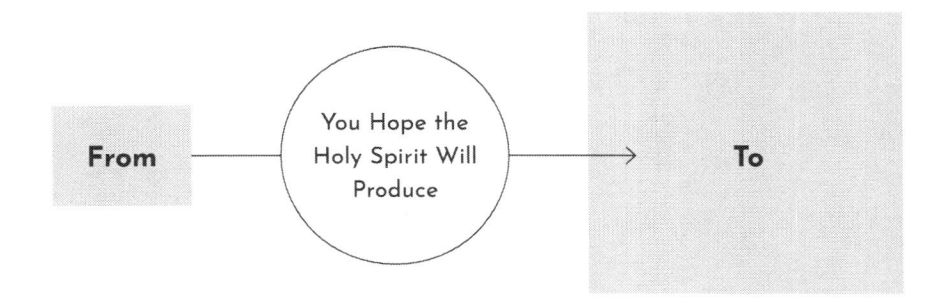

From — (You Hope the Holy Spirit Will Produce) → **To**

Below are a few From→To examples compiled from our work with churches. Although the respondents didn't necessarily use the exact phrases in the "From" side of the chart, we were able to detect common distortions in their approach to work, which allowed us to create the more theologically robust "To" views in the right column. This is a highly contextualized process, and we encourage you to work closely with your leadership team to make your own From→To path. Although you may initially have strong hunches about this, the interviews and surveys provide valuable insights that will either confirm or challenge your assumptions. Going through this process will give you more confidence about what your congregants' actual spiritual needs are regarding work.

Examples of Work-Related Theological Needs

From →	To
I work because I want to be rich and influential.	I am made to work as part of God's story to bring flourishing to this world and glory to him.
Work is miserable, and I only do it in order to survive.	I am made to work as part of God's story to bring flourishing to this world and glory to him.
If my work doesn't make me happy, then I am in the wrong work.	Work is guaranteed to have toil, and we serve a suffering Savior.
I work to have more leisure.	God ordained work and rest as part of his cycle.
Church is on Sunday, and the pastor leads the mission.	The gathered church is on Sunday, and the church sends people out all week as the scattered church on mission for the renewal of the world.
Church work is more sacred than other work.	All work is sacred.
People matter.	People, systems, and institutions matter.
Capitalism is evil.	Businesses bring goods and services into the world in a sustainable way and employ people to use some of their God-given talent—but they are also broken.
Being saved is about going to heaven.	The gospel changes everything, including my day-to-day now.

From →	To
I think I am a pretty good person at work.	I am deeply aware of the depth of my sin at work.
Heaven is "up there," so my work here doesn't matter.	Christ will come again and bring the new heaven and earth; work here matters.
God only does good work through Christians.	God can bring good work into the world through anyone, as the image of God is in all.

> **KEY TOOL FOR STEP 2**
>
> - Blank From→To charts—see appendix seven.

After you examine the demographics and conduct your interviews among your focus groups, you should be able to clearly articulate who you are serving (or want to serve). And after completing this "understand needs" step, you will be able to assimilate the *who* with the *need* in order to articulate the following:

- Who you are serving (or want to serve)
- The variety of work they do and the myriad work issues they face
- The Christ-centered theological movement (From→To) you hope to stimulate in your people (through the work of the Holy Spirit)

Without fully engaging this step of understanding needs, you risk creating messaging and programming that people may find interesting yet don't accomplish the deep and lasting gospel-centered change you envision for their lives and work. For instance, you could bring in a highly successful Christian businesswoman to talk about her business story. And although that might encourage your ambitious congregants, if not carefully vetted, the story may reinforce the idolatry of success instead of focusing on the journey of surrendering that identity. You may organize a "vocational calling workshop" taught by people who perceive missionary work to be more sacred than secular work. (In fact, this kind of messaging often comes from church youth leaders and university ministries to our adolescents at their most formative time as they are considering higher education and jobs.) Let your From→To chart provide a clear guide for your process. It outlines the starting point and the desired outcomes, allowing you to try to measure and evaluate whether your programming is facilitating the intended transformation based on the change that is happening.[4]

BOOSTERS FOR UNDERSTANDING NEEDS	BLOCKERS FOR UNDERSTANDING NEEDS
• Understanding the demographic needs of those you seek to serve • Participating in workplace visits • Determining likely spiritual gaps by understanding where on the Worker Needs 2x2 Matrix your audience typically falls • Developing a From→To table to chart a path for transformation	• Skipping or rushing this step • Focusing on the stated or presenting needs of your people rather than imagining the deeper heart change the gospel requires • Lacking clear alignment on the From→To chart

---

[4] See chapter twelve and appendix thirteen for evaluating impact in your church.

Now that you have identified the change you're seeking, you are ready to move to the next step. It is finally time to stop planning and start doing. The objective of Step 3 is to implement some actions and programs into your church and then, in Step 4, to assess what impact they had.

REFLECTION QUESTIONS

- What process will you use to collect demographic data from your church?
- As you consider the Worker Needs 2x2 Matrix, which quadrant best represents the majority of workers in your context?
- What are some of the expressed needs of your workers that may have deeper underlying needs?
- How would you articulate the greatest changes you want to take your audience From→To?

11

THE INTEGRATED CHURCH

STEP 3: IMPLEMENT

the vision
to see
beauty in wisdom
color in fruit

the space
and time
to linger
for the One

JENNIFER PIRECKI, "ANTHROPOSE"

You've spent significant time laying a great foundation for your faith-and-work ministry. You've assembled a unified leadership team that understands and appreciates the need for a focus on faith and work to create heart change and city impact. You've taken them through a team learning journey to help them become leaders who understand faith and work holistically. And you've also gathered both qualitative and quantitative data about the groups you are hoping to serve. You understand their demographics, you know their primary industries, their pain points, and their vision for their work as Christians in a given industry. You have exegeted their theological gaps and the movement needed in the From→To analysis. The work you've done in the previous two steps has prepared you to start implementing programs with the goal of taking those in your church from a limited knowledge to a deeper understanding and experience of how God is using their work in their hearts, in their communities, and in their world.

BUILDING FAITH AND WORK INTO YOUR CORE CHURCH PRACTICES

The most sustainable way to connect faith with daily life for your congregants is to embed it into your church's core practices. This aligns with the yearning we highlighted in chapter three: People deeply desire to find meaning in their everyday life in light of their faith and want their churches to help them identify this relevance.

Given that you already have a committed group of people attending church, and you are already planning your church rhythms, implementing faith and work into existing activities and programs is a strategic approach that engages everyone and requires minimal effort. More importantly, we believe the church serves as a permanent instrument for teaching and discipling in the ways of Jesus. Therefore, it's crucial to prioritize the integration of faith and work into the church's core practices. As we've discussed, it's essential that work is viewed as a key context in which the church's mission is fulfilled.

We will now explore three key areas in which to integrate faith and work into the church's core practices: church liturgy, discipleship pathways, and systems.

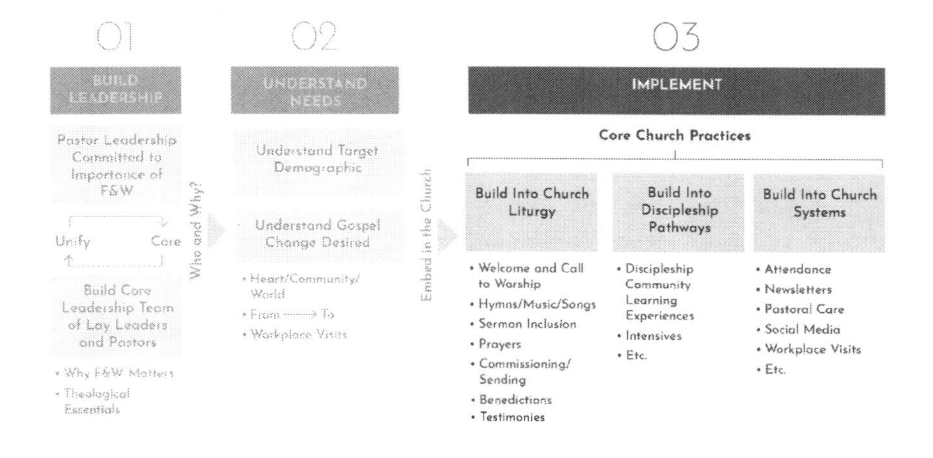

01 BUILD LEADERSHIP	02 UNDERSTAND NEEDS	03 IMPLEMENT
Pastor Leadership Committed to Importance of F&W	Understand Target Demographic	**Core Church Practices**
Unify ↔ Core	Understand Gospel Change Desired	**Build Into Church Liturgy** / **Build Into Discipleship Pathways** / **Build Into Church Systems**
Build Core Leadership Team of Lay Leaders and Pastors	• Heart/Community/ World • From ———→ To • Workplace Visits	• Welcome and Call to Worship • Hymns/Music/Songs • Sermon Inclusion • Prayers • Commissioning/ Sending • Benedictions • Testimonies	• Discipleship Community Learning Experiences • Intensives • Etc.	• Attendance • Newsletters • Pastoral Care • Social Media • Workplace Visits • Etc.
• Why F&W Matters • Theological Essentials		

Who and Why? / *Embed in the Church*

BUILDING FAITH AND WORK INTO YOUR CHURCH LITURGY

One of the key ways to embed faith and work into the core of your church is to build it into the church's liturgical rhythms. Although various denominations have different traditions, the structure of common worship is usually determined by our very best understanding of who God is, what he cares about, and who we are in relationship to him. Since about half of our waking hours are dedicated to work, we must reflect that reality in our church services, enabling people to see their work as a sphere that matters to God. The following suggestions will help you build faith and work into the elements of a worship service. (The Getting Started Guide at the end of this book includes many of the materials and tools listed below.)

WELCOME AND CALL TO WORSHIP[1]

Most churches have some type of opening welcome to define the start of their service. Some denominations have very specific guidelines for how to open a worship service while others have great flexibility. Certainly, a call to worship is a holy act. Worship leader Jarryd Foreman says, "[The call to worship] urges people to turn from worldly distractions and set their minds, hearts, and attention on the glory of God."[2] Yet, have you considered that your words may be passively making statements about people's lives outside of church services? Do your words unintentionally suggest that their day-to-day work is irrelevant at best or undesirable at worst? Can you nuance the wording to encourage the importance of their everyday work as part of God's unfolding story for them and for the world?

- A good call to worship reminds workers that it is God who invites them and draws them to worship, not the other way around. God, who has

---

[1] We'd like to thank Katie Roelofs for her contributions to this section of the book. Katie is part of the Worship for Workers project at Fuller Theological Seminary.
[2] Jarryd Foreman, "The Call to Worship," Doxology & Theology, accessed December 11, 2024, https://www.doxologyandtheology.com/blog/the-call-to-worship.

been present with them all week long in their work and daily living, now calls them to this time of corporate worship with their siblings in Christ. And God will send them back out into the world with the promise of his presence and care.

- If you have an informal call to worship, instead of opening with a phrase such as, "Welcome to worship; we hope it is a respite in your week," consider saying, "We are so thankful you are here to learn more about Jesus and what his life, death, and resurrection mean to our lives outside these doors."
- If you use Scripture as a call to worship, you can sometimes use verses that focus not only on who God is and what he has done for us but also on the relevance for worker's lives outside of church. For instance, Colossians 3:23–24 encourages us to work hard for the Lord, and 1 Corinthians 10:31 broadens the scope of actions that can be done for God's glory.
- Make inclusion of a call to worship a measurable goal. Set your monthly goal and measure your progress. Capture anecdotal and official communication (e.g., emails) about how the inclusion of these comments is impacting your congregants.

For specific examples of calls to worship, see appendix eight (Church Service Inclusion Tools).

HYMNS/MUSIC/SONGS

God's people are found singing throughout Scripture—from a gathering near the Red Sea (Exod. 15:1–18) to the ending celebration before his throne (Rev. 14:3). Thus, music is a key formational element of most church services. Singing not only glorifies God; it also cements his Scripture and our responses into our hearts and minds. Including songs that reflect the realities of work can help congregants understand how their faith applies not just on Sundays but also throughout their working weeks.

- Ensure you have a balanced "song diet" with options that speak to the whole of the worker's experience. When they celebrate a triumph in their work week, what song will they have on their lips to thank God for this gift? When they face a challenge or a loss and need a song to express their grief and lament, what lyrics will they have to sing as they pray? Singing in the sanctuary forms workers as they sing in the city. Form them with words to sing, no matter what Monday might bring.

- Consider rotating at least one work-related song per week (or month) into your repertoire. New sets of worship songs have recently been developed to capture the reality of work and the spiritual struggle within that reality. (Check out The Porter's Gate Worship Project, which has created two albums of worship songs.[3])
- Frame worship songs that you already sing with vocationally conversant introductions. One or two simple sentences can take a song your congregation knows well and allow them to see it, and sing it, through the lens of their daily living.

    Example: *"Great Are You Lord"*[4]
    - Spiritual Reminder: The presence of the Spirit's breath in our lungs prompts us to pour out our praise through our daily living.
    - Sunday morning framing: "The Spirit's breath in our lungs draws us to praise this morning. This is the breath that has been present with us throughout our week, and the same breath that will go with us whatever this next week might hold at work, at home, and in the community. Together, we pour out our praise to our faithful and worthy God—for great is our Lord."

    Example: *"Blessed Assurance"*[5]
    - Spiritual Reminder: God's story is being told in and through us each day.
    - Sunday morning framing: "As we praise God and proclaim in song that 'this is my story' and 'this is my song,' we give God thanks for the ways his story has, and continues to be, told in this world through the work of our hands. We are participants in God's story as

---

[3] The Porter's Gate Worship Project, https://www.portersgateworship.com/.
[4] David Leonard, Jason Ingram, and Leslie Jordan, "Great Are You Lord," 2012 Integrity's Alleluia! Music/Open Hands Music/So Essential Tunes.
[5] Fanny J. Crosby, Phoebe Knapp, "Blessed Assurance," 1873; hymnary.org/text/blessed_assurance_jesus_is_mine.

we bring forth his kingdom here on earth in our vocations and our daily living. Together we join our voices in praise."

- Make inclusion of work-related music a measurable goal. We recommend at least 50 percent of your services contain a work-based song and 100 percent use work-inclusive introductions. Measure the inclusion, and capture anecdotal and official communication (e.g., emails) about how the inclusion is impacting your congregants.

SERMON INCLUSION

If we had to pick only *one* thing in your core church practices to quickly impact your congregation, it would be to build the context of work into your weekly sermons and teachings. We have discovered that sermon inclusion is one of the most effective strategies in affirming the dignity of work to all congregants—which also subsequently makes church feel relevant. As we have mentioned, Jesus used work as a key teaching context. But the parables were not necessarily about *how* to work; often they were the context to teach about the ways of God's kingdom. For instance, Jesus taught lessons about grace, mercy, and obedience through work examples.

- Adding work illustrations into sermons is something you can implement immediately. Here are some examples:
  - *If you are preaching about identity in Christ,* discuss how the desire to be affirmed by one's boss can become the foundation for security rather than being a beloved child of God. Show how that dynamic can reveal the sin of our hearts by exposing jealousy of a colleague's accomplishment or anger about being overlooked for a promotion. Talk about how the desire for leisure can make work a necessary evil instead of something we were created to do.
  - *If you are preaching about the upside-down characteristics of the kingdom,* you can ask the congregation to consider what Jesus would say to them about their job if he returned tomorrow. What changes would he want them to make? Reveal that he is a suffering Savior who comforts those experiencing oppression in jobs where they

are unfairly compensated or have uncaring bosses or unsafe work conditions.
  - *If you are preaching about the Prodigal Son,* work examples can illustrate how we can be either the wayward son or the self-righteous one, both in need of a savior. (See the Sermon Inclusion Tool in appendix nine.)
  - *If you are preaching about the call to live missionally*—by examining both the creational goodness and brokenness within areas such as hospitality, technology, or banking—you can effectively communicate the need to live missionally and embrace the already-but-not-yet of the new heaven and new earth. Can a waitress look for opportunities to show God's love and care to her customers? Can a tech worker think about ways to create more redemptive and less hostile online spaces? Can a banker push against the greed in his industry? (As a pastor, although you may not understand the specific pressures of profit-driven environments, you certainly understand pressure and how it reveals our deepest values and exposes idolatry. If you are uncertain of the work implications of an industry or a passage of Scripture, the Theology of Work website has many useful resources.[6])

- Here are some steps to assist you as you prepare to include faith and work in your sermons.
  - Check the Theology of Work Project's online resources to find work-oriented insights and ensure a well-rounded perspective on work's significance as it relates to your key scriptures.[7]
  - Reflect on the key beliefs you are trying to change or instill—or both—in your congregation through the sermon. How can you include a work-based example as a context in your message?
  - Reach out to a congregant and ask if he or she can help you with an anecdote. This can be a fantastic opportunity to connect with a church member to get some ideas and feedback for a sermon

---

[6] See https://www.theologyofwork.org.
[7] "Theology of Work Bible Commentary," Theology of Work Project, accessed August 14, 2024, https://www.theologyofwork.org/resources/the-theology-of-work-bible-commentary/.

application specific to an industry. One phone call or workplace visit to a congregant is sure to provide an example, and it will also engage a congregant who may be lingering at the edges and wondering about their relevance to the church. Or, if you have already thought of a work illustration, ask a congregant if you can share it with them for affirmation of its relevance and accuracy.
- Consider the professions represented in your congregants each week. What might their greatest challenge be? What brings them joy? How might they need to meet Jesus in the midst of their daily work?
- Remember and recognize significant seasons for particular working professions. Think about your accountants in tax season, your farmers at harvest, your physicians on the anniversary of the COVID-19 pandemic. How might these seasons and milestones shape how your sermon intersects with their current reality?

- Make inclusion of work-related sermons a measurable goal. Aim to include workplace examples in at least 80 percent of sermons and measure it. Capture anecdotal and official communications (e.g., emails) about how the inclusion is impacting your congregants.

KEY TOOLS FOR STEP 3

- Church Service Inclusion Tools—see appendix eight.
- Sermon Inclusion Tool—see appendix nine.

PRAYERS

Most churches include prayers of various types in their services—prayers of confession, prayers of petition, prayers of the people, prayers for peace, and so on. Work as a context can be woven through such prayers, depending on your or your denomination's flexibility. (See also appendix ten, Industry Prayer Examples.)

- In leading a confession, include the work context by simply adding a phrase. For example, you could say, "How have you sinned in thought, word, or deed against God or others at home *or at work*?" or "How have you sinned in thought, word, or deed against God or others in *work*, rest, or play"?
- Include prayers of lament that give voice to the worker's experiences of pain, dissatisfaction, anger, and grief. This will not come naturally. You will need to teach your congregation to speak this language fluently, so it is accessible when they need it for themselves or others.
- Periodically offer "industry prayers"—prayers dedicated to the workers of a particular industry, such as hospitality, finance, construction, students, or even those seeking a job. Such prayers are incredibly impactful when included in the liturgy.

EXAMPLE INDUSTRY PRAYER: A PRAYER FOR FINANCE

We pray today for those in our congregations and city who work in the fields of finance and financial services. In your wisdom, you created this world to be a place where, in order for us to thrive, we would need to cooperate and contribute in the context of our local communities. This collaborative nature means we participate in a range of financial practices including earning, spending, saving, lending, borrowing, and investing. We all use money.

We thank you that you have equipped some with the ability to understand and navigate the stewardship and use of financial resources in a world where the love of money so easily corrupts. Whether they're running spreadsheets, assessing credit, selling services, or orchestrating deals, may their work reflect your beauty and truth and goodness. May they know that their work matters. How else could companies run, or employees get paid, or houses and companies be bought and sold without the order of finance?

You warn us in Scripture that the love of money is the root of all kinds of evil. Finance can be associated with greed and extortion. It can

> be manipulated and opaque. It can serve the rich and leave the poor behind. With all the warnings you give in your Word about the trappings of wealth, we also see many places where your people used wealth for noble, important purposes—from David to Daniel to Joseph of Arimathea. You use finances as a means of stewardship, justice, and love. You use the resources of the many to provide help, create opportunities, and protect the dignity of individuals and families.
>
> Bless those who work in finance and financial services with wisdom, integrity, insight, and prudence. Protect their hearts from greed, unhelpful comparisons to others, and a desire for autonomy from you. Deepen their ability to serve well the people they represent. Let them excel in their work and give them meaningful and helpful relationships within their industry and with their clients. Help them to see their contribution to the economies of this world as an extension of their service to you and your kingdom. And as a result, may their work be to them a source of joy and gratitude to you for your faithful provision to your people.
>
> We pray this in the name of Jesus, your son. Amen.[8]

Below are some tips on how to begin the practice of praying industry prayers.

- Try to include industry prayers relevant to those in your congregations at least once per month. Align them with the calendar and events of your city. For instance, in the US, August and September are a good time to pray for educators returning to school at the beginning of the academic year. February is a good time to pray for the fashion industry as it is fashion week in New York City. Crucial times of prayer may not be obvious for some key industries, but their importance to the context may still warrant designated prayer time. For example, in Argentina, there is

---

[8] Industry prayer written by Missy Wallace.

not a natural time in the annual calendar to pray for oil refineries, but it is a major industry so is important to include at some point in the year.
- Use certain crises or uprisings as opportunities for prayer. If there is a transportation strike, pray for transportation workers and for the industry. If there are tech layoffs, pray for that industry.
- Ask workers in the given industry to assist you in writing or delivering the prayer. We have shared five example industry prayers in appendix ten (Industry Prayer Examples), as well as a guide to help congregants write prayers that are particularly relevant for your context (Guide to Writing an Industry Prayer, appendix eleven). Ideally, the prayers should incorporate focusing on the creation, fall, and restoration aspects of the industry).
- You may or may not want to ask those who work in the highlighted industry to stand during the reading of the prayer. This is an affirming practice, depending on the culture of your city and church.
- Make inclusion of work-related prayers a measurable goal. Aim to include workplace examples in prayers in at least 25 percent of services and measure it. Capture anecdotal and official communications (e.g., emails) about how the inclusion is impacting your congregants. (For example, one Sunday I [Missy] read a prayer about entrepreneurism in my church service, and we received more than twenty requests to send it to individuals.)

> **KEY TOOLS FOR STEP 3**
>
> - Industry Prayer Examples—see appendix ten.
> - Guide to Writing an Industry Prayer—see appendix eleven.

COMMISSIONING OR SENDING

Many churches have traditions and routines about honoring formal ministry workers in church services. How often do you commission or "send out" your formal ministry workers with some kind of ritual? Do you have special times in your service for missionaries? Youth leaders? Short-term service trip members?

Pastoral ordinations? Certainly this practice is warranted and encouraged; but have you considered what this implicitly communicates about other kinds of work? These sending formalities passively suggest that the church cares more about vocational ministry and traditional mission trips than it does about the mission of regular workers in workplaces. And yet, as we've discussed, people need to see their workplaces as places to glorify God. Consider commissioning or sending non-formal ministry workers at some point(s) in your calendar year, as the example below suggests.[9]

> **EXAMPLE FAITH-AND-WORK SENDING**
>
> **Pastor**: In a world filled with brokenness, confusion, darkness, mourning, and loneliness, God has called his people to bring the healing light of the gospel into every sector of our city through every profession, institution, and calling. There is no inch of this city where his gospel cannot redeem.
>
> **Congregants**: We repent of how we have overlooked this great calling we have been given. The Spirit is waking us to see this mission in God's world. We surrender all that we are to serve you, O Lord, our Rock, and King.
>
> We pray for your power, renouncing our selfish pride, to serve our city with excellence in our respective roles, jobs, and professions.
>
> We rest in your unfailing love, which dissolves all bitterness, fear, anxiety, and resentment, so that this world will know we belong to you.
>
> We ask that you would open our eyes to see how the gospel is powerfully at work to transform hearts, communities, and the world.
>
> **Pastor**: And I heard the voice of the Lord saying, "Whom shall I send, and who will go for us?"

---

[9] In some denominations, "commissioning" is very formal and has strict rules. In such denominations using the language of "sending" may be more applicable.

> **Congregants**: Then I said, "Here am I! Send me."
>
> **Pastor**: Go into the world: work, build, design, write, dance, laugh, sing, and create.
>
> **Congregants**: We go with the assurance of God's great commission.
>
> **Pastor**: Go into the world: risk, explore, discover, and love.
>
> **Congregants**: We go with the assurance of God's abundant grace.
>
> **Pastor**: Go into the world: believe, hope, struggle, persevere, and remember.
>
> **Congregants**: We go with the assurance of God's unfailing love.[10]

- To demonstrate the theological truth that all work matters to God and is part of his unfolding plan, try to commission and honor "secular work" in the same way you honor religious work.
  - Can you honor your teachers and other school employees at back-to-school time?
  - Can you highlight health care workers when flu seasons are intense?
  - Can you pray for those in finance to conduct their work with integrity and excellence?

- Make inclusion of work-related commissionings a measurable goal. Aim for at least half of your sendings to be for "secular" work (not formal mercy or ministry work). Capture anecdotal and official communications (e.g., emails) about how the inclusion is impacting your congregants.

---

[10] This commissioning prayer was developed by the Center for Faith & Work and was used in services at Redeemer Presbyterian Church.

BENEDICTIONS

The closing words of your service matter just as much as the opening words. Avoid phrases such as, "Thanks for coming; see you next week" or "It was wonderful to be together worshiping; come back again next week." Instead, consider closing words that contain both a charge and a blessing. A charge sends people out with God's power; a blessing reminds them that they are never sent to do this work alone. The God who sends is the God who goes with them. The God who goes with them is the God who will again welcome them to worship next week.

> **EXAMPLE BENEDICTION**[11]
>
> As you go from this place, back to the place God is calling you, to the place where God has already equipped you to go, may you go with this blessing:
>   God goes before you to lead you;
>   As you go from this place, back to the place God is calling you, to the place where God has already equipped you to go,
>   may you go with this blessing:
>   God goes before you to lead you;
>   God goes behind you to protect you;
>   God goes above you to watch over you, beneath you to support you.
>   God goes beside you to befriend you.
>   Do not be afraid. The blessing of Almighty God goes with you this day and forever. Amen.

For more examples of benedictions, see appendix eight (Church Service Inclusion Tools).

---

[11] Text Source: Anonymous, alt., based on the "Breastplate of St. Patrick."

TESTIMONIES

Do you include testimonies in your services? How often do the testimonies include workplace examples? The challenges of work often lead people to recognize their idolatry and turn to Christ. Work is a context for beautiful justice stories and relationship reconciliation opportunities. Likewise, sharing testimonies of seeing God move at work through common grace is also a huge encouragement.

- Include work-based examples in your testimony rotations. If you have been going on workplace visits, these should emerge organically as you get to know your congregants' work lives. Many people have stories of Christ's work in their hearts through the toils and troubles at work. Caution: be aware of prosperity gospel testimonies as noted in chapter nine.
- Include a video or live Q and A in your service where a trusted congregant talks about what they will be doing "this time on Tuesday." Feature workers with stories of the gospel's impact on their day-to-day life. Ask them what is good about their work, what is broken, and how they need prayer. You can ask them to show how they are pushing against an area of brokenness in their industry or how they are loving competitors in a unique way. You can find examples of this at globalfaithandwork.com/stories.
- Make inclusion of testimonies a measurable goal. Aim for one work-related testimony twice a year if testimonies of other kinds are part of your services. Capture anecdotal and official communications (e.g., emails) about how the inclusion is impacting your congregants.

KEY TOOL FOR STEP 3

- Case Studies of Faith-and-Work Stories—see the case studies section in the Getting Started Guide at the end of this book.

BUILDING FAITH AND WORK INTO YOUR DISCIPLESHIP PATHWAYS

The original Hebrew and Greek words for "disciple" both convey the idea of a "learner"—someone who is committed to growth and development. Thus, a disciple of Jesus is someone who is a learner and specifically one who is learning the ways of Jesus and how to love God with all their heart, mind, and soul. A disciple is someone who seeks gospel transformation in their own heart, in their relationships with others, and in the world around them, including in their sphere of work. Most churches offer some type of activities outside of the weekly church service to assist congregants in learning more about following Jesus. These programs are often referred to as "discipleship pathways." They can include learning intensives, Sunday School classes, one-on-one mentorships, formal curriculums, and more.

Discipleship community learning experiences are a common way for believers to learn to apply the gospel in their day-to-day lives—including family, work, and other spheres. As we have proposed throughout, work is a key context for heart change and gospel impact in the city, and it is therefore natural that classes focusing on the applications of the gospel include work as a context. The focus on work can be embedded into the classes via examples, application, and exercises.

While working together at City to City, we developed or refined different multi-unit curriculums covering a variety of faith-and-work topics that can be easily plugged into discipleship-education rhythms in a variety of contexts—including large and small churches in the US and beyond. These classes are summarized in the Getting Started Guide at the back of this book, and some have been translated into other languages. Other organizations have also produced some excellent faith-and-work resources, which can easily be used in your church's discipleship efforts. New classes are popping up around the world, and thus we encourage you to contact key faith-and-work organizations to stay up to date with new resources. (See appendix seventeen for a recommended list of other faith-and-work organizations.) The key to incorporating faith and work into discipleship lies in creating groups where fellow-believers can process the truths and challenges of work in community, which will hopefully lead to transformed hearts. These changes will gradually ripple outwards, positively impacting workplaces and ultimately cities in subtle and significant ways.

- Build faith and work into your church's discipleship classes. Often this can be accomplished easily by adding contextual examples in lessons or by using faith-and-work specific curriculums.
- Make inclusion of work as a context in your discipleship pathways a measurable goal. Aim for one course each ministry year cycle to be focused on faith and work as a context for mission. Capture anecdotal and official communications (e.g., emails) about how the inclusion is impacting your congregants.

> **KEY TOOL FOR STEP 3**
>
> - Discipleship Courses Chart—see the Getting Started Guide at the end of this book.

BUILDING FAITH AND WORK INTO YOUR CHURCH SYSTEMS

Churches often have many operational systems that can be slightly altered to include faith and work.

- Do you have attendance cards? Add a line to capture vocation.
- Do you have prayer cards? Add work as a category of prayer need.
- Do you have a newsletter that goes out weekly? Add articles about the importance of various industries to God or include a specific industry prayer. The Industry Article Examples in appendix twelve have links to articles about working as a plumber or in finance or in public office, as well as other occupations. You can also find new articles about industries regularly on the Theology of Work website.[12]

---

[12] Theology of Work Project, https://www.theologyofwork.org.

- Do you take your youth on mission trips? Add visits to workplaces on those trips—whether in your city or to other cities or countries. How about also taking them on vocational outings to learn from Christians in various industries, e.g., a Christian architect, a Christian soccer coach, or a Christian trash collector?
- Do you have a care committee that helps those in need (illness, bereavement, mental health issues, and so forth)? Does it include helping unemployed people find work? Start employment assistance groups and have the leader teach faith-and-work theology as they go.
- Do you use social media? Share examples of Christians having an impact at work on your channels.
- Do you have weekly pastor meetings? Talk about the work strains of your people as a topic of context. Talk about your own vocational challenges.
- Do you have worship meetings to plan the service? Ensure the lens of work is included in those meetings.
- Do you have weekly meetings with the church staff (pastor/s, finance, marketing, and so forth)? Make sure your language does not infer that direct ministry roles are superior to other roles.
- Make work as a context in your church systems a measurable goal. Set your key targets and begin to track your success.

The good news is that you don't need a complete overhaul of your core church practices to integrate faith and work. Instead, faith and work simply needs to become a "lens" that your church leadership is looking through when they organize core church practices, including liturgy, discipleship pathways, and systems.

Incorporating faith-and-work principles into existing activities establishes a sustainable foundation for your initiative. Over the years, we have become increasingly convinced of the importance of *embedding* (versus *adding*) faith and work into the church—not just as a *theology* but also as a *context*. For years, we have seen many entrepreneurial church leaders attempt to build faith-and-work programs *at* a church but not build them *within* a church. For instance, instead of taking the time to build faith and work into the discipleship classes already running, they might add a faith-and-work "side class" outside the normal church class rhythms. Or, instead of incorporating faith and work into sermons, they might refer congregants to the "faith-and-work team." In these scenarios, the initiatives are functioning as an adjacent or side ministry of the church. Although these "side efforts" often quickly gain momentum, they are also very susceptible to being cut when budgets are tight ... or abandoned altogether when there is a leadership change. We have seen this happen in many churches. Such initiatives also end up being attractive and accessible to only a small segment of people who can commit the time and possibly finances to that programming, leaving out those who may be in jobs that work in "off hours" or those with significant caretaking obligations. Adjacent ministries thus impact far fewer people than embedded efforts, they are often more time-consuming, and they are susceptible to budget and leadership risks. Although adjacent ministries can be deeply impactful, be mindful of their potential challenges; prioritize embedding faith and work into the primary mission and activities of the church.

Understandably, embedding faith and work into the church can be challenging for different reasons, depending on the church's season. For new church plants, it often feels overwhelming to focus on faith and work amidst all the other priorities. And for more established churches, it is often hard to change systems and processes that have been running for years. However, in both cases, we strongly believe that the effort you put into embedding faith and work will reap significant rewards as it will give your congregants a new vision for how God is using their work for his glory.

Keep in mind that you cannot address every need you have identified on day one. Be encouraged with each small step and be realistic about what you can implement.

As a reminder, *if all you can do at this time is add work-based examples into your sermons, you are making big cultural progress and impacting your entire congregation with minimal incremental effort.* Congregants will be impacted greatly at the heart level and thus are likely to be more committed members of your community and more missional citizens of the city. *Be encouraged!*

BOOSTERS FOR IMPLEMENTATION ✓

- Building work examples and references into your sermons as the most strategic starting point
- Building faith and work into your call to worship, music, prayers, benedictions, and other liturgical rhythms
- Building faith and work into your existing discipleship pathways
- Building faith and work into your other church operational systems and routines

BLOCKERS FOR IMPLEMENTATION ✗

- Assuming faith and work is a separate program
- Assuming faith-and-work efforts require additional staffing, funding, or programming instead of incorporating them into what is already happening at your church
- Taking no action because you feel overwhelmed
- Consistently preaching sermons without work examples

REFLECTION QUESTIONS

- What simple steps can you take as soon as next week to build faith and work into your worship service?
- What larger steps can you take to build faith and work into your worship services over the next three months?
- What simple steps can you take as soon as next week to build faith and work into your discipleship rhythms?
- What larger steps can you take to build faith and work into your discipleship rhythms over the next three months?
- What simple steps can you take as soon as next week to build into your church systems?
- What larger steps can you take to build faith and work into your church systems over the next three months?

12

THE INTEGRATED CHURCH

STEP 4: ASSESS

We cannot skip the way of Jesus in our hurry to get the truth of Jesus as he is worshiped and proclaimed. The way of Jesus is the way that we practice and come to understand the truth of Jesus, living Jesus in our homes and workplaces, with our friends and family.

EUGENE PETERSON

Once you have begun to implement, you will need to think about how you assess the success of the initiatives you have created.

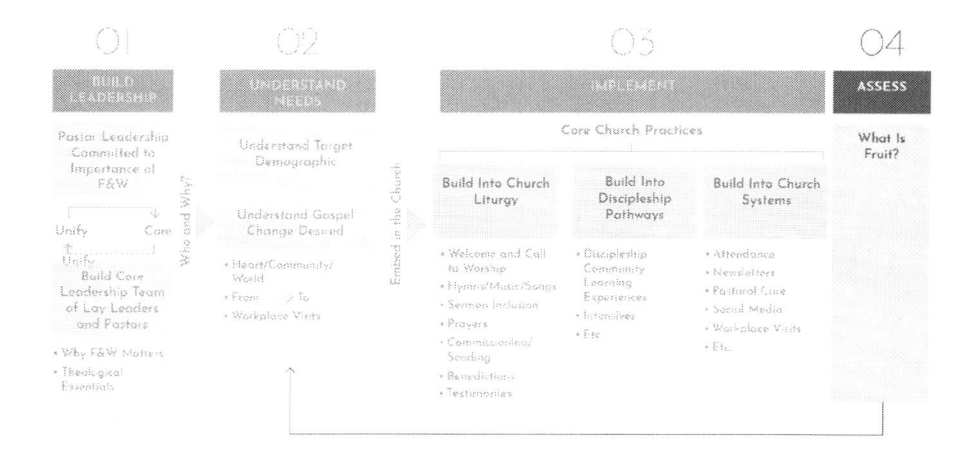

01 BUILD LEADERSHIP	02 UNDERSTAND NEEDS	03 IMPLEMENT	04 ASSESS
Pastor Leadership Committed to Importance of F&W	Understand Target Demographic	**Core Church Practices**	What Is Fruit?
Unify → Core Unify Build Core Leadership Team of Lay Leaders and Pastors	Understand Gospel Change Desired	Build Into Church Liturgy / Build Into Discipleship Pathways / Build Into Church Systems	
• Why F&W Matters • Theological Essentials	• Heart/Community/ World • From → To • Workplace View	• Welcome and Call to Worship • Hymns/Music/Songs • Sermon Inclusion • Prayers • Commissioning/ Sending • Benedictions • Testimonies	• Discipleship Community Learning Experiences • Intensives • Etc.	• Attendance • Newsletters • Pastoral Care • Social Media • Workplace Visits • Etc.

Who and Why? / *Embed in the Church*

You may regularly hear from congregants that they have begun to more effectively integrate their faith into work. You will likely hear stories of how relationships with coworkers or industries are changing because of the paradigm shift that occurs as they begin to see work as a key missional context. People will tell you about staying in jobs they thought they would leave. You will learn of sacrificial efforts at work, as congregants trade ambition for caring for those perceived as "underdogs." You will hear of the downtrodden being encouraged.

But anecdotes, although helpful and indicative, are not enough. You need to attempt to measure your efforts, understanding that heart change and city impact are notoriously difficult to measure. Assessing initiatives and programs has often proven to be one of the most challenging aspects for the individuals and organizations we have worked with. For example, some of your questions might include:

- How do we know if sermon examples make a difference?
- How do we know if someone has a more loving posture in their work?
- How do we know what impact Christian marketplace leaders are having in their industries?
- How do we know if the participants being trained in our programs are changing the ways they interact at the community and industry level in a way that brings light to darkness?
- Most importantly, how do we measure heart change?

These questions are all difficult to answer. Although we can create metric proxies for some of these items, measurements can sometimes have the unintended effect of incentivizing unhelpful progress. Thus, we introduce this assessment section with a word of caution. Yes, you must attempt to assess your initiatives so that you can change, improve, expand, and sometimes stop activities. But it's also important to realize that, when the Holy Spirit is at work, things are often hard to measure.

As you move forward, take each program, initiative, or action plan, and write out the change you hope to see. You may want to look at your From→To chart to determine what specifics you want to measure.

For instance, for five years I (Missy) taught a ten-month faith-and-work discipleship intensive. Our main goals were heart change of the participants and city impact. To gauge heart change, I measured participants' self-reported perception of the presence of the fruit of the Spirit in their lives before the class started and after the class finished. Surprisingly (or not), these self-reports of fruit *declined* over the year. However, alongside this, more than 90 percent affirmed a stronger sense of Jesus' lordship in their lives. I suspect this reported decline was caused by a more accurate reflection of the sin in their lives and their gratitude for the work of Jesus, and thus was evidence of heart change. Like the apostle Paul who declared himself "the worst" of sinners (1 Tim. 1:15), as the participants' knowledge of the gospel increased, so did their awareness of their sin.

Below is a chart with a list of potential measurement proxies and commentary for various programs. This is intended to be illustrative, not exhaustive. Use this as a guide to think about your own measurements.

Example Initiative/ Program	Desired Measurement	Measurable Proxy	Commentary
Embedding work examples in sermons	Does the service feel more relevant? Does it increase church attendance? Are people taking the ideas and living out the gospel more fully?	What percentage of sermons have work examples in them? After one year of including work examples in 80 percent of sermons, has attendance changed? Are archived sermons with work examples shared more often than others?	Impact of sermons using work examples is hard to measure. However, anecdotally, we believe it matters, due to the Barna data about faith-and-work integrators associated with behavior (see chapter three).

Example Initiative/ Program	Desired Measurement	Measurable Proxy	Commentary
Using work-based songs in worship	Does the service feel more relevant? Does it increase church attendance? Are people taking the ideas and living out the gospel more fully?	What percentage of songs are work-based songs?	Music impact is hard to measure. However, anecdotally, we believe it matters, due to the Barna data about faith-and-work integrators associated with behavior (see chapter three).
Building work as a context into discipleship pathways	Are the learnings in the discipleship pathways motivating the participants to more fully live day-to-day in light of the truths of the gospel?	How many people are participating in the faith-and-work training? Are numbers for the discipleship pathways growing? Are disciples motivated to teach and lead others? Track whether individual engagement at church has changed (e.g., attendance, participation, Bible study, or anecdotal fervor).	Tracking individual engagement is not necessarily causal but associatively informative.

Example Initiative/ Program	Desired Measurement	Measurable Proxy	Commentary
Faith-and-work intensives	Are those getting trained in discipleship intensives being impacted at the heart level, the community level, and the world/industry level?	How many people are participating? What is each participant's rating of their fervor of faith (Jesus Christ as Lord of Life)? What is each participant's understanding and application of faith-and-work concepts?	See appendix thirteen for an example of a measurement tool from an intensive.

When we discuss assessment, it's important to note the difference between meaningful activities versus busyness. It is often tempting to fill the calendar with lots of one-hour events without follow-up or pathways for deeper learning. We strongly encourage you to assess your level of activity with a lens as follows: Is this activity leading to heart change, relational change at work, or industry or city impact? If not, is there a pathway from the activities into a more meaningful interface through Sunday services at church, in a faith-and-work learning community, or through directed Bible studies? Often churches err toward non-interactive events that create energy—such as a luncheon, a speaker, or a conference. Though these "taster" events are often great funnels to grow participation in a deeper learning discipleship experience or pathway, they risk becoming mere diversions. Without clear objectives, these events may be engaging but ultimately produce little fruit. At one point in Nashville, I (Missy) plotted all my activities in relation to each other, considering heart change and city impact. Though the plotting used subjectivity over hard quantitative data, it was a helpful way to determine which activities deserved the most focus. This chart—combined with an assessment of each initiative's expense, trajectory toward a more impactful program, and implementation complexity—guided my decisions on which programs to vigorously pursue and which to halt or reduce. In appendix thirteen, you'll find a similar blank chart with instructions to plot your own initiatives.

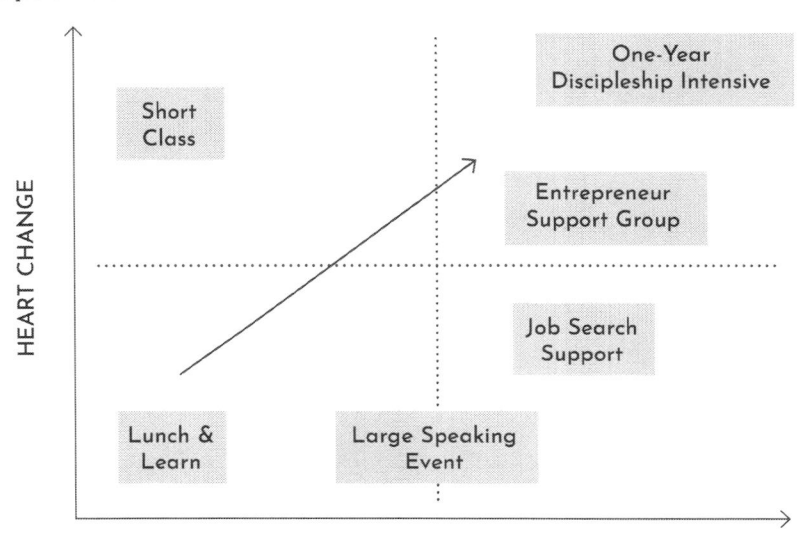

Impact Goal

HEART CHANGE ↑

- Short Class
- One-Year Discipleship Intensive
- Entrepreneur Support Group
- Job Search Support
- Lunch & Learn
- Large Speaking Event

RIPPLE IMPACT ON COMMUNITY/CITY →

[1]

As you assess initial efforts in your programs and activities, refer back to what you know about people who have fully internalized the integration of faith and work. Continue using your understanding of the gospel to identify the real needs beneath the perceived needs. Keep in mind that you are ultimately trying to test programs that change hearts, create opportunities to love neighbors in and through work, and impact cities. You do not just want activity for activity's sake.

Reflect on your efforts: Are people being equipped to serve as ambassadors of the kingdom in and through their vocations? Are they displaying the fruit of the Spirit and articulating and expressing that Jesus Christ is lord in more areas

---

[1] Source: Analysis of activity at Nashville Institute for Faith and Work from 2015–2019.

of their lives? Is your church seeing any fruit from these efforts? Spend time in prayer to hear the Lord's voice.

And although this may take decades to fully develop, consider the change you witness in your cities. Are there any stories of shifts in industries due to the actions of your congregants? Are companies being launched redemptively? Are there new efforts to impact those who are marginalized? Are you able to see real and lasting differences in any area of your city as a result of this work?

There will be moments of frustration when you cannot find a way to measure change or when you have to recalibrate your plans because you do not see an initiative bearing fruit. This is okay; it is part of the process and why the linear nature of the journey map is somewhat misleading. Learning is a continuous loop. Refining your efforts and activities is worth it, as it will equip your people to be more missional in every sector of your city or community, doing their work for God's glory.

BOOSTERS FOR ASSESSING

- Determining how you will measure heart change
- Using your assessments to recalibrate your faith-and-work efforts when needed
- Expecting frustration and surprise in the assessment phase due to both the difficulty of measurement and the results
- Being realistic about the role the Holy Spirit plays in this work and how difficult it is to measure

BLOCKERS FOR ASSESSING

- Avoiding measurement due to its difficulty
- Measuring activity without considering impact
- Assuming one-off attendance equates to heart change

> **KEY TOOL FOR STEP 4**
>
> - Impact Assessment tool—see appendix thirteen.

REFLECTION QUESTIONS

- How will you measure progress while keeping the desired heart change in mind?
- What will your measurement methodology be for your assessment (surveys, interviews, etc.)?
- Once you have assessed your efforts, how will you determine what recalibration is needed to make your initiatives more impactful?

13

BECOMING A FAITH-AND-WORK-INTEGRATED CITY

Joy comes from seeing the complete fulfilment of the specific purpose for which I was created and born again, not from successfully doing something of my own choosing. The joy our Lord experienced came from doing what the Father sent Him to do. And He says to us, "As the Father has sent Me, I also send you."

OSWALD CHAMBERS

Integrating faith and work at both a leader and church level automatically impacts the city. Integrated leaders who oversee integrated churches can't help but make a difference in the community. When work becomes a natural extension of faith, congregants' hearts are changed, and they begin to connect Sunday sermons with everyday actions in every industry they touch. And the collective efforts to address broken systems in every sector across your city inevitably effect positive change.

This momentum often creates a desire for a more coordinated and strategic city impact, and therefore some churches and leaders establish formal initiatives aimed at more fully transforming the city. If you discern this is your call, and you have the necessary resources or volunteers, it's time to consider how to channel your efforts into city-facing initiatives. Although we believe that embedding faith and work in leaders and the activities of the church should be the first implementation priority, we recognize some churches have the capacity to engage in both internal church embedding and city efforts.

This chapter explores high-level approaches for church-led city-facing initiatives. However, appendix sixteen (Church and City Journey Maps) also provides an additional journey map for independent city initiatives. Given the unique challenges of implementing such programs across a city, this guide is a starting point rather than a comprehensive blueprint. It's important to acknowledge that not all churches will implement city-facing initiatives, and that's perfectly acceptable.

164 | FAITH & WORK

Church Journey Map for Faith-and-Work Initiatives

01 BUILD LEADERSHIP

- Pastor Leadership Committed to Importance of F&W
- Build Core Leadership Team of Lay Leaders and Pastors

Unify ↔ Core

- Why F&W Matters
- Theological Essentials

Who and Why?

02 UNDERSTAND NEEDS

- Understand Target Demographic
- Understand Gospel Change Desired

- Heart/Community/World
- From ⟶ To

03 IMPLEMENT

Embed in the Church

Core Church Practices

Build Into Church Liturgy
- Welcome and Call to Worship
- Hymns/Music/Songs
- Sermon Inclusion
- Prayers
- Commissioning/Sending
- Benedictions
- Testimonies

Build Into Discipleship Pathways
- Discipleship Community Learning Experiences
- Intensives
- Etc.

Build Into Church Systems
- Attendance
- Newsletters
- Pastoral Care
- Social Media
- Workplace Visits
- Etc.

Face the City — Scattered Church

- Determine City Vision Impact Desires/Goal
- Develop Strategies/Potential Partners
- Implement Programs that Equip/Connect/Mobilize

Potential Examples:
- Intensives
- Entrepreneurship Classes
- Business Plan Competitions
- Conferences
- Industry Groups
- Cultural Renewal Projects

04 ASSESS

What Is Fruit?

As a reminder from the destination sections in chapter five, an integrated city effort focuses on four crucial aspects to reach its destination: *a leadership team* that begins to address the city's complex challenges holistically, developing a city *vision*, *network*s, and *initiatives*.

Just as there were *prepare* and *do* steps for church implementation, there are similar steps for the city.

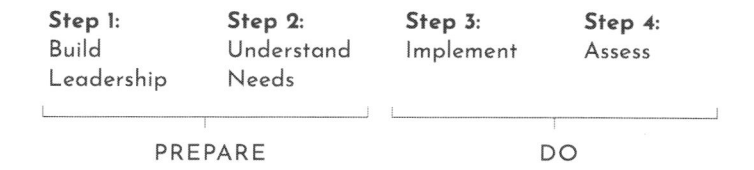

Step 1: Build Leadership	**Step 2:** Understand Needs	**Step 3:** Implement	**Step 4:** Assess
PREPARE		DO	

PREPARE

STEP 1: BUILD LEADERSHIP

01

BUILD LEADERSHIP

Pastor Leadership Committed to Importance of F&W

Unify ↔ Core

Build Core Leadership Team of Lay Leaders and Pastors

Who and Why?

- Why F&W Matters
- Theological Essentials

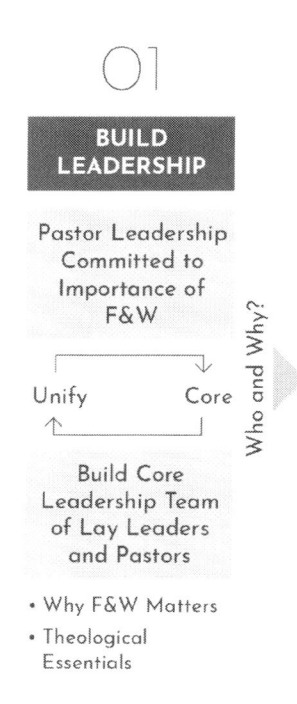

Although you've already built leadership for the church, facing the city will require its own leadership. Building a faith-and-work-integrated city leadership will follow many of the same steps as listed for developing a *leadership team* at the church level (see chapter nine). In both cases, the team size, diversity, alignment on faith-and-work theological essentials, and commitment must be considered. Having key marketplace leaders serving as leaders or volunteers in city-wide initiatives is usually critical. We highly encourage recruiting leaders from your church faith-and-work leadership team to lead the city efforts and involving volunteers who are inculcated in the faith-and-work DNA. However, when considering initiatives on behalf of a city, denominational diversity in leadership—as well as in the effort overall—is critical. Timothy Keller points out that "you will never reach the city unless you are very cooperative with believers across denominational lines."[1]

The faith-and-work sphere offers a unique opportunity for fruitful interdenominational collaboration. Christians scattered in jobs throughout a city don't tend to focus on the denominations of other Christian coworkers. The theology of work itself provides a common ground where denominational distinctions become less relevant. For example, debates about infant versus adult baptism hold little significance in the context of workplace theology. The foundational belief in work as part of our creational design, as well as the call to contribute to the city's common good, are widely shared among many Christian traditions. Nonetheless, potential pitfalls due to diverse beliefs should be considered where possible.

The leadership team should ideally develop a "core values" document that guides behavior and decision-making rather than creating strict rules or membership criteria defining who is "in" or "out." Though not an exhaustive list, the core values for a faith-and-work initiative could include the following.

- **Biblical foundation:** Agreeing to view work through the lens of the biblical narrative.
    - We are created by God to work.
    - Work is broken, due to the fall.

---

[1] "God loves cities and Christians should too, says Tim Keller," *Christianity Today*, October 21, 2010, https://www.christiantoday.com/article/god.loves.cities.and.christians.should.too.says.tim.keller/26938.htm

- Work is part of God's unfolding plan for the world.
- Work may exist in the new heaven and new earth.
- **Holistic framework:** Using the Heart-Community-World triad as a holistic framework.
- **Common grace:** Acknowledging that God's grace extends to all people.
- **Shared Goals:** Committing to heart change and city impact as key objectives.

Additionally, a shared historical creed, such as the Apostles' Creed, can serve as a unifying foundation. Areas of potential conflict should also be considered. These issues often emerge when defining the boundaries of Scripture and historical orthodoxy. We strongly encourage inclusivity wherever possible, as the goal is to unite Christians from various denominations within specific industries and cities, fostering a shared commitment to the common good. As a leadership exercise, the group should study the city, understanding its strengths and weaknesses.

> **KEY TOOL FOR STEP 1**
>
> - City-Based Learning Tool—see appendix four.

STEP 2: UNDERSTAND NEEDS

Although you have probably completed this step as it relates to your church, the needs you will address broaden as you move into city-facing initiatives. Thus, it is important to clarify your vision of *who* you are serving and *what* you want to achieve through your intentional city work.

As you consider your city vision, you will need to refine your "who" and assess whether the needs differ from your church participants' needs. Programs and efforts focusing on broad sets of participants tend to be slower to develop but have a richer cross-city impact and overall acceptance by many because of the variety of people involved. They often create bonds that last well beyond the programs. However, focusing on narrow demographics—for instance, one industry—can result in an accelerated start due to reduced complexity. See the "Target Demographic" table at the bottom of page 168 for more detail.

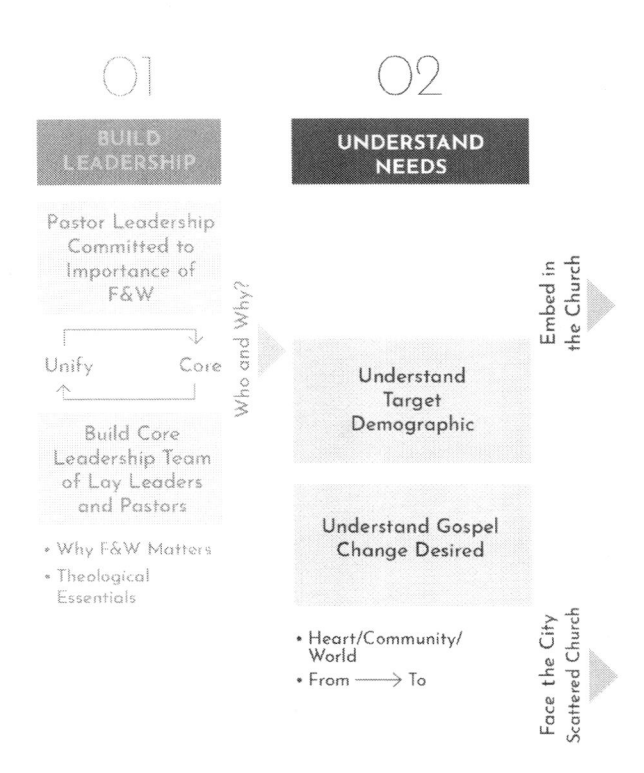

168 | FAITH & WORK

01 BUILD LEADERSHIP

Pastor Leadership Committed to Importance of F&W

Unify ⇄ Core

Build Core Leadership Team of Lay Leaders and Pastors

- Why F&W Matters
- Theological Essentials

Who and Why? →

02 UNDERSTAND NEEDS

Understand Target Demographic

Understand Gospel Change Desired

- Heart/Community/World
- From ⟶ To

Embed in the Church →

Face the City Scattered Church →

Target Demographic

Narrow/Homogenous ←————————————→ Broad/Diverse

	Narrow/Homogenous	Broad/Diverse
PROS	• Comfortable and Easier to Be Vulnerable • Quicker Bonding • Easier to Recruit • Less Theological DNA Navigation	• More City Impact • Growth in Acceptance of Diversity • Mercy and Justice Opportunities
CONS	• City Impact Limited • Growth in Acceptance of Others Limited • Mercy and Justice Opportunities Limited	• Harder to Recruit • More Conflict Resolution • Slower Bonding • Complex Theological DNA Navigation

Below are some questions for your core team to consider as you refine your target and its differences from your church participants:

- What areas of the city do you want to reach?
- What type of worker is your target?
- What are your hopeful outcomes?

Once you consider the breadth of your target group, you will want to clarify your *vision* and hopes for the effort. Below are some example city vision and impact statements. (Though these are hypothetical, they resemble some real city-wide expressions.)

- We aim to equip and unify Christians across the city to focus on key city issues of homelessness and unemployment. (Broad target group with focused impact)
- We hope to cultivate entrepreneurism among the poor in our city over the next ten years with a goal of launching five hundred redemptive small businesses with 70 percent sustainability rates. (Focused target group with broad impact)
- We aim to unite Christians in the arts across the city to focus on pushing against dark systems in their industry as well as creating five large film projects over the next five years. (Focused target group with focused impact)
- We plan to serve those coming out of prison as unemployable, with the goal of increasing employment rates and reducing recidivism. (Focused target group with focused impact)
- We want to train corporate CEOs in a holistic view of faith and work with the aim of creating more loving and just workplaces in our cities. (Focused target group with focused impact)

KEY TOOL FOR STEP 2

- City-Based Learning Tool—see appendix four.

DO

"Do" elements in city-facing efforts can be complex and call for more collaborative partnerships than church efforts, and also require a higher level of personnel and financial resources. They often have interdenominational appeal, bridge denominational divides, and reach unbelievers more quickly, thus providing rich ways to interact with many types of people. Since integrated city efforts are multidenominational, they usually involve partnerships with several churches and parachurch organizations, often leading to *networks* of pastors and key industry leaders on faith-and-work-integration journeys. The first order of action in the city-facing "do" efforts is to determine key partnerships around the city. The primary focus should be on organizing collaborative methods within the networks, followed by implementing initiatives that serve the needs of the target group. Partnering can be complex because those you work with often have different definitions of collaboration. True collaboration requires a common goal with everyone sacrificing, contributing, and reaping the benefits of progress together. However, some organizations confuse true collaboration with truncated versions of communication (no common goal, no sacrifice, no reaping benefits) or cooperation (which may have a common goal but no mutual sacrifice). Having clear understandings with partners about the roles and goals is a critical step.[2]

STEP 3: IMPLEMENT

Based on your city-impact vision statement, you can begin to focus on the *initiatives* you want to try out and *who* you want to partner with for implementation. If we take the wildly varying city impact vision statements from above, you can envision the initiatives and partnerships outlined on pages 172–173. These are intended to be examples rather than fully exhaustive lists.

---

[2] To gain a common understanding of collaboration on your teams, see Liz Weaver, "The Collaboration Spectrum Revisited," Tamarack Institute, accessed October 14, 2024, https://www.tamarackcommunity.ca/hubfs/Resources/Publications/Collaboration%20Spectrum%20Revisited_Liz%20Weaver.pdf.

BECOMING A FAITH-AND-WORK-INTEGRATED CITY | 171

01 BUILD LEADERSHIP

Pastor Leadership Committed to Importance of F&W

Build Core Leadership Team of Lay Leaders and Pastors

Unify ⇄ Core

- Why F&W Matters
- Theological Essentials

Who and Why?

02 UNDERSTAND NEEDS

Understand Target Demographic

Understand Gospel Change Desired
- Heart/Community/World
- From ——→ To

03 IMPLEMENT

Core Church Practices

Embed in the Church

Build Into Church Liturgy
- Welcome and Call to Worship
- Hymns/Music/Songs
- Sermon Inclusion
- Prayers
- Commissioning/ Sending
- Benedictions
- Testimonies

Build Into Discipleship Pathways
- Discipleship Community Learning Experiences
- Intensives
- Etc.

Build Into Church Systems
- Attendance
- Newsletters
- Pastoral Care
- Social Media
- Workplace Visits
- Etc.

Face the City Scattered Church

Determine City Vision Impact Desires/Goal

Develop Strategies/ Potential Partners

Implement Programs that Equip/Connect/ Mobilize

Potential Examples:
- Intensives
- Entrepreneurship Classes
- Business Plan Competitions
- Conferences
- Industry Groups
- Cultural Renewal Projects

City Vision	Initiative	Potential Network Partners	To Determine
We hope to cultivate entrepreneurism among the poor in our city over the next ten years with a goal of launching five hundred redemptive small businesses with 70 percent sustainability rates.	Offer faith-based entrepreneurship classes in the government housing complexes. Have a one-to-one mentor program for each entrepreneur.	Church with predominantly poor members Chamber of commerce City's entrepreneurism center Government aid program University or nonprofit with entrepreneurism curriculum Micro-finance partners with access to capital	Partner roles, including potential participation or representation on the leadership team Implementation timeline with roles and responsibilities Cost of running the program allocated among partners
We aim to unite Christians in the arts across the city to focus on pushing against dark systems in their industry as well as creating five large film projects over the next five years.	Create a faith and arts industry group led by artists. Offer grant funding for redemptive artistic expressions.	Film/art guild and associations University film programs Arts-interested foundations	Partner roles Implementation timeline with roles and responsibilities Cost of running the program allocated among partners

City Vision	Initiative	Potential Network Partners	To Determine
We plan to serve those coming out of prison as unemployable, with the goal of increasing employment rates and reducing recidivism.	Create a job training program with faith-and-work theology and one-to-one mentorship for training, which will continue a year into employment.	Job training curriculum organizations Prison/jail community engagement manager Transitional housing community Companies willing to hire those formerly incarcerated once trained	Partner roles Implementation timeline with roles and responsibilities Cost of running the program allocated among partners
We want to train corporate CEOs in a holistic view of faith and work with the aim of creating more loving and just workplaces in our cities.	Convene CEO small groups with faith-and-work lessons and real peer-to-peer problem-solving.	Chamber of commerce Entrepreneurism centers Other CEO training groups	Partner roles Implementation timeline with roles and responsibilities Cost of running the program allocated among partners

Reaching the target audience effectively in a city environment requires well-developed marketing strategies. Success hinges on the ability to coordinate diverse teams with different skillsets. And the funding, staffing, and technology needs can be substantial for impactful city-facing initiatives. An experienced and committed leadership team with proven implementation and project-management experience is crucial for overseeing such complex initiatives. But, most importantly, the team must be made up of faith-and-work integrated leaders who allow the Holy Spirit to empower and direct their work. This book is intended to *simplify* the process of implementing faith and work, and we appreciate that city-facing programs are *not* simple. Many people inquire about city-facing initiatives, so the following sections will explore various types of initiatives but will not address the intricacies of implementation. Should you wish to consider an independent city-wide initiative, we recommend researching the paths of the Denver Institute for Faith and Work, The Charlotte Institute for Faith and Work, and At Work on Purpose in Cincinnati as potential exemplars. (See appendix seventeen for a list of these and other faith-and-work organizations.) We have also developed a city-specific journey map, which can be found in appendix sixteen (Church and City Journey Maps).

With that in mind, below are descriptions of the types of city-facing initiatives we most frequently encounter.

- **Pastor Cohorts:** A common objective of most intentional city-facing initiatives is to help other churches embed faith and work. Cohorts can be established to train pastors in faith-and-work concepts and provide implementation opportunities in their churches and across city-wide networks. The Global Faith & Work Initiative and Made to Flourish both offer pastor cohorts and curriculums.[3]
- **Entrepreneurism:** Starting a business is essentially an act of great creative energy that brings something out of nothing in hopes of calling it good—mirroring God's work in the Genesis creation account. This creative process is inherently aligned with God's plan to steward creation and foster flourishing. To maximize the positive impact of entrepreneurial initiatives, a deep understanding of the needs of those you are serving is essential, as discussed above. For example, programs designed to bring people out of poverty require a different approach from those supporting high-capacity entrepreneurs tackling global challenges. The former is the focus of Corner to Corner in Nashville, TN,[4] and Paradigm Shift in South Africa.[5] The latter is the focus of Praxis, which serves start-ups out of their base in New York City.[6]
- **Industry Groups:** Some cities have come to be known—at least partially—by their dominant industries. By intentionally gathering like-minded Christians from those professional sectors, it's possible to effect

---

[3] The Global Faith & Work Initiative, https://www.globalfaithandwork.com; Made to Flourish, https://www.madetoflourish.org/.
[4] Corner to Corner, Nashville TN, https://cornertocorner.org.
[5] Paradigm Shift, https://www.shiftingparadigms.org/.
[6] Praxis Labs, https://www.praxislabs.org/.

meaningful change. For example, in New York City, we have seen groups emerge for artists, as well as for those in finance and education. Such groups rapidly attract members seeking connection with like-minded peers. However, the long-term sustainability and impact of these groups often hinges on two key factors: 1) securing an excellent and thoughtful industry leader and 2) the group's ability to coalesce around a clear and actionable goal. Without a purpose that extends beyond social networking, such groups can become insular and ineffectual.

- **Employment-Based Initiatives:** Unemployment can often be a source of great pain. Employment initiatives that are embedded with a holistic faith-and-work understanding can significantly impact the hearts of individuals, increase their income-earning potential, and improve the welfare of their families. Jobs for Life, founded in Raleigh, NC, is a national model empowering the church to help the unemployed.[7] UpRise Nashville exists to alleviate relational, economic, and spiritual poverty through education, the gospel of Jesus Christ, and the power of redemptive relationships.[8]

- **General Learning Intensives:** City-based faith-and-work learning intensives often gather Christians across industries and socioeconomic brackets, fostering unexpected partnerships that drive impactful results. Over several years of teaching such classes, we have seen a remarkable range of cross-sector collaborations. We've witnessed a CEO connecting with marginalized workers while building new manufacturing plants, entrepreneurs launching retraining programs for refugees, real estate agents working together to seek affordable housing solutions, artists partnering with nonprofit workers for impactful storytelling, and even fashion and business leaders collaborating on a new redemptive business for wedding dresses.[9] In diverse learning communities—as people work together and vulnerably confront their own sin in their work sphere and look for areas of redemption—lifelong bonds are formed, and people groups unite across the city for Christ.

Note, one danger with city-wide initiatives is they can begin to fall into the bottom-right quadrant (Social Impact Focus) of the Faith-and-Work-Framework

---

[7] Jobs for Life, https://jobsforlife.org.
[8] UpRise Nashville, https://www.uprisenashville.org.
[9] Videos of cultural renewal stories are available at "How Does the Gospel Change Our Work?" Global Faith & Work Initiative, accessed December 11, 2024, https://www.globalfaithandwork.com.

for Unleashing the Gospel (see chapter four). These efforts must be undergirded with prayer and focus on personal and system brokenness to avoid a savior complex.

> **KEY TOOLS FOR STEP 3**
>
> - Discipleship resources—see the Getting Started Guide at the back of this book.
> - Transformative Learning Experience Guide—see appendix fourteen.

> **EXAMPLES OF CITY-FACING INITIATIVES**
>
> When I (Lauren) worked at the Center for Faith & Work (CFW) in New York City, NY, we had several city-facing initiatives instead of solely focusing on the Redeemer Presbyterian Church congregants.[10] The goal of CFW at that time was to serve Christians throughout the city, without a particular attachment to any one church. Below are some of the initiatives we implemented.
>
> **City Rhythms**
> In a series of events called City Rhythms, we highlighted various sectors during seasons when their work was particularly prominent in the city. For example, during New York Restaurant Week, we focused on the food-and-hospitality industry. A Christian caterer shared how her faith infused her work, followed by a talk on a theology of hospitality and prayer for industry concerns. We similarly held events relating to the finance industry, education, marketing, healthcare, and more. Christians from all churches (and non-Christians in the industry) were invited to

---

[10] In this season of the Center for Faith & Work, I (Lauren) served on a team led by David H. Kim with fellow team members Amilee Watkins, Scott Calgaro, Esther Schissler, Stephanie Cunningham, Jon Seale, and B.W. These initiatives were a collaborative effort of that team.

celebrate the creational goodness of the field highlighted, lament its brokenness, and envision a better future.

Artist-in-Residence Program
For a few years, CFW commissioned artists to create works around a scripture or given theological prompt. Through this program, we saw a photographer's commissioned work featured in the *New York Times*, had a commissioned filmmaker share work at the Metropolitan Museum of Art, and had a Tony-nominated Broadway actress write a new play around a creation-fall-redemption-restoration narrative. These commissions sparked insightful conversations with both Christians and non-Christians about the church's deep-rooted commitment to art and creativity. It proved to be an effective platform for culture-creation and evangelism.

"Pray for Your Work" Evenings
We invited Christians across the city to spend time in conversation, worship, and prayer around the work of our hands. Guest speakers explored topics such as how to bring the Holy Spirit into our professions, praying for our work, and praying for our coworkers.

City-Wide Conferences
We held conferences and large-scale events on imagination and innovation, the wonder and fear of technology, civility in the public square, and more. The goal of these events was to gather Christians from around the city to give "glimpses of glory" of what God was doing in New York. We highlighted innovation and effort amid the broken places of industry by featuring the work of both Christians and non-Christians to demonstrate how God was acting to restore the city. These conferences provided a vision of how God was moving through politicians, transit workers, tech workers, artists, the food-service industry (and many others), and also provided a vision for what the city would look like in the new heavens and the new earth to inspire all of those currently laboring in it.

STEP 4: ASSESS

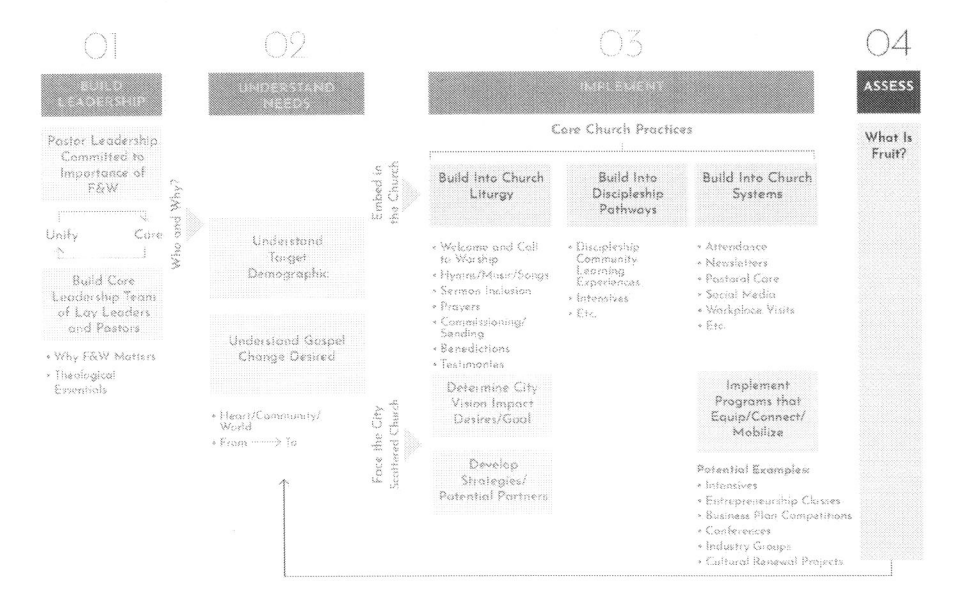

Once you have implemented some test programs, you will need to begin thinking about how you measure the success of your city-facing initiatives. Much of the assessment work for a city has similar opportunities and challenges as those faced by churches, but they are even more complex. For example, some of your questions might include:

- How do we measure city impact?
- How are industries changing due to the impact of Christians?
- What mercy-and-justice efforts are transpiring from workplaces?
- Is entrepreneurship being spurred on by Christians?
- Are work opportunities increasing for marginalized populations?
- How do we avoid triumphalism by properly accounting for others' contributions to change?

Below is a chart with a list of potential measurement proxies and commentary for various programs. This is intended to be illustrative, not exhaustive. Use this as a guide to think about your own measurements.

Example Initiative/ Program	Desired Measurement	Measurable Proxy	Commentary
Entrepreneurship offerings	Are individuals working more fruitfully? Are new businesses creating economic vitality? Are the businesses being run redemptively?	Number of participants Number of businesses started Five-year success rate Revenues into a neighborhood	Measuring the redemptive nature of the operations is difficult.
Employment-based initiatives	How many persons are receiving employment? How long are they remaining in the job? Over time, are we seeing upward mobility in their roles?	Number of participants Number employed Average employment length Wage trajectory by person over time	Measuring whether employment is thriving over the long term can be challenging. To avoid inaccuracies, figures must be screened for helping the same person multiple times.

Example Initiative/Program	Desired Measurement	Measurable Proxy	Commentary
Industry groups	How many industry groups exist? What impact are they making for the individuals participating and in the industry as a whole?	Number of industry groups Number of participants per meeting or activity Number of repeat versus new visitors Impact on the individual's views of work in the industry Actual initiatives undertaken by the industry groups (coalitions, mercy projects, policy changes, etc.)	Industry groups often need a reason to exist beyond learning and working in order to stay active and relevant. It is difficult to measure the impact an industry group actually has in the industry.

Determining how a project impacts a city is complex. Although it's tempting to overclaim credit for specific outcomes, the reality is that impact is often multifaceted and difficult to measure precisely. City work can feel overwhelming, and it can be hard to believe small efforts—which can feel like a drop in the ocean—can create meaningful change. However, Malcolm Gladwell popularized an idea called the "tipping point," which purports that a tiny critical mass can lead to widespread social change.[11] If you apply that concept to your sub-targets, they start to sound more feasible: "Surely, surely we can reach a small percent of the

---

[11] Malcolm Gladwell, *The Tipping Point: How Little Things Can Make a Big Difference* (New York, NY: Little Brown & Company, 2007).

unemployed, or CEOs, or artists in our city! So, what change can we catalyze for the common good?"

A FINAL NOTE ON FAITH-AND-WORK INITIATIVES

Although we have presented this process linearly, it's important to recognize its cyclical nature. Leadership teams will transition, and you will have to rebuild and unify. Trends will evolve, and you will have to reassess needs, listening to and analyzing the desired changes you want to see in your people again. A test program will fail, and you will have to figure out why, as you reflect on your targets. And, as your congregants mature, your From→To charts will need to be refined. This iterative approach isn't unique to faith-and-work integration; it is fundamental to all significant design endeavors. Integrating faith and work is about changing the work, church, and city cultures we find ourselves in, which requires an entrepreneurial spirit, resilient perseverance, and dependence on God.

REFLECTION QUESTIONS

- Do you sense momentum in your community for a city-facing faith-and-work initiative?
- How can you thoughtfully build a leadership team of both ministry and marketplace leaders from diverse backgrounds and perspectives for your initiative?
- Is there a group of churches and parachurch organizations that want to work together?
- What target group are you hoping the city-facing initiative will serve? How can you include language in your vision that will clearly articulate that?
- Are there potential networks or partners that already exist in your city that it might be helpful to connect with?
- What is your vision for an outcome from this initiative that will bless your city?

CONCLUSION

It's worth pausing to again acknowledge that integrating faith and work isn't just a ministry task or program—it's a powerful pathway for church health, city impact, and most importantly, individual heart transformation. Although we know that there are many competing demands for your time, with a variety of obstacles that prevent you from prioritizing faith and work in your church, it is critical to remember that work is one of the most important focuses of an individual's life. Thus, work is the primary context for heart change and galvanizing your church toward community impact. We hope this book has encouraged you to embrace the journey of building faith-and-work integration into your setting—not as a "to-do" list item but rather as a deepening journey with Christ for you and those you serve.

While the theological frameworks and the journey map in this book serve as guides, it's ultimately your personal faith-and-work-integration journey, your unique church context, and your relationships that will bring them to life. By establishing a foundation that marries sound theological insights with practical steps, you'll not only meet the immediate needs of your members but also place them within a broader story—one where the church is known for discipling individuals holistically and for helping them see how God is at work beyond Sunday mornings. Faith-and-work integration reminds them that Jesus is alive in the day-to-day details of their work, resonating through every corner of their industries and communities.

As you thoughtfully apply the theological frameworks and embark on the journey maps, adapting them to your context, we encourage you to do so in a sustainable way—powered by the Holy Spirit and rooted in grace rather than striving. Remember, every act of faith-and-work integration, no matter how small, holds the potential to influence lives far beyond what you may see.

From the first pages of Genesis—where God creates us in his image and invites us to co-labor with him—to the closing pages of Revelation—where we see the arrival of a new heaven and new earth with Christ at the helm—our work is part of his redemptive story, bringing light, healing, and hope to a world in need.

As we write these final words, we pray for you as well as ourselves:

Lord Jesus Christ, through the power of the Holy Spirit, please help each of us to hear you, move toward you, and obey, as we collectively co-labor with you in every good endeavor in the world, and as we long for your will to be done "on earth as it is in heaven."

ACKNOWLEDGMENTS

LAUREN

Writing this book felt like the culmination of pulling together the wisdom and work of the many people who have influenced or poured into me over the years.

There were several people who were foundational to my becoming a Christian and discipling me during my youth: my grandmother (Helen Atkinson), Nancy Glenn, Brother Harry Dooley, Anita Moore, and Peter Trautmann.

I first encountered the faith-and-work sphere at Redeemer Presbyterian Church when I had the pleasure of sitting under Pastor Tim Keller. But the experience that was most formative for me was being part of the Gotham Fellowship at the Center for Faith & Work under David H. Kim, who taught me what true faith-and-work integration means: working for God's glory and not my own. I then had the pleasure of working for David for five years, where he modeled innovation and servant leadership as a real-life example of integrating faith and work. Amilee Watkins was also a vital influence at CFW.

In my time at Redeemer City to City, I have had the honor of being mentored by Katherine Leary Alsdorf and Missy Wallace. I am grateful to Katherine because she always points every issue and teaching to what is going on at a heart level, and I am thankful for her guidance to do that both personally and professionally. Missy Wallace has been a thought partner, collaborator, friend, and champion of me in both the paid faith-and-work sphere of my life and the unpaid work of motherhood.

We have learned so much about how to build faith-and-work initiatives from our international faith-and-work catalysts at Redeemer City to City's Global Faith & Work Initiative: Amma Amegashie, Raphael Anzenberger, Olivier Barrucand, Alistair Chiu, Kimberly Deckel, Bijan Mirtolooi, Christel Ngnambi, Marcelo Robles, and AP and BL.

Our Gotham Network Leaders are a constant source of inspiration, innovation, and commitment: John Worsham, Doug Meikle, Malissa Mackey, Ben Nussbaum, Nick Bannister, Daniel Lee, Jack Carson, Paul Lim, Bernard Zeng, Paul Sohn, Robbie Brown, Julie Silander, Ali Crotts, Luke Boardman,

Case Thorp, Jonathan Ingraham, Karen Bird, and Joel Miles. And thank you to all the Gotham Network Leaders who have served in the past.

Several people helped us make this book possible. We are deeply indebted to our editor, Anna Robinson, who makes order out of chaos with wisdom and grace. Thank you to Charlie Meo for helping us with the case studies in this book and for being a thought partner on so many projects. Thank you to Blake Schwarz and Damein Schitter for their insight into the design pathway. Thank you to Susan Nacorda, Katie Roelofs, and Tracy Mathews for their contributions on various tools and passages.

Thank you to my father and mother, Jim and Ione Hines, who provided examples of hard work throughout my life and sacrificed much time, energy, and support to help me pursue my vocational passions before leaving home.

Thank you to the circle of women who are consistent prayer warriors in my life: Lourine Clark, Ruth Leary, DeWanda Miller, Katrina Miles, Susan Nacorda, and Leslie Talley.

Thank you to my husband, Suneel, who has been a supportive and wonderful partner in every vocational path God has taken me on since we've been married (doing everything from being a driver on film sets to attending lectures to offering up better theology for teaching points). He is my prayer partner, my thought partner, and my partner in pursuing dreams. And to Alexandra and Jason: May you always see your work as part of how God is building his coming kingdom and know how deeply grateful I am that God allowed me to pursue the vocation of motherhood with the two of you.

MISSY

Writing a book was a bigger endeavor than I imagined. There are so many people to thank—from those who informed the content to those who got the book across the finish line, not to mention those who loved and cared for me from the sidelines.

First, it is only in God's kindness that he has pursued me to go deeper and deeper in my faith, which ultimately led to this work; and that pursuit continues to this day. Though my faith germinated early in my childhood church and through Young Life, it was the influence of Tim Keller—starting with his 2009 book *Counterfeit Gods*—that really led me to a new journey of understanding the holistic nature of the gospel and the truth of Jesus as Lord of All. And it was his 2012 book, coauthored with Katherine Leary Alsdorf, *Every Good Endeavor*, that flipped a switch in my understanding of God's role for work. Katherine: Thank you for mentoring me for the last ten years. Meeting you was a fork in the road, which has led to so much goodness.

I thank Professor Earl Lavender, Katherine Leary Alsdorf, David Kim, Amilee Watkins, Scott Sauls, Bob Bradshaw, David Filson, and Paul Lim for helping me launch into the faith-and-work sphere back in 2015. And thank you Gage Arnold for being my sidekick. Without their assistance in starting Nashville Institute for Faith and Work, the foundation for this book would not have been laid. I also want to thank some of my past supervisors and mentors throughout my career in consulting, banking, and education. Without their strong leadership, I would not have such a rich body of experience to write from. Sandra Conway, Jim Andrew, Aliza Knox, Eileen Naughton, David Morgan, Ricky Bowers, and Will Moseley: You all had a deep impact on me; things I learned from you rumble in my mind regularly.

The content of this book was shaped by the hundreds of marketplace leaders and pastors I've worked with over the past decade. You served as faith-and-work "labs." Whether in-person Gotham cohorts or Zoom pastor intensives, in the US or beyond, I am deeply grateful for the insights we learned together as we sought God in and through our work. In recent years, the Gotham leaders around the US and several international church planters helped us pilot the insights and maps in this manuscript. A particular thanks to Andres Garza and Marcelo Robles, who pushed us to refine the maps and teach them to large groups. Katie Roelofs: Thank you for your help with the liturgy and worship section. Damein Schitter and Blake Schwarz: Thank you for helping with the "destinations." Pastors Thomas Hunter and Ronnie Mitchell: Thank you for teaching me more about broken systems.

Leaders need prayer, counsel, and friendship to thrive. To my Warner Park walking buddies: You keep my thoughts safe and my body strong. Thank you. To my Pheebs group—seven incredible women in as many cities who have prayed together monthly since the pandemic: You have been a lifeline. Tracy Mathews: Thank you for teaching me to hear God's voice more clearly and for encouraging all parts of me. To Evie B, my Dutch Camino buddy: Who knew that some iodine on a blister would lead to our journey together? Thank you. To my Deep 8

Connect Group: Thank you for your encouragement and prayer during this writing. Marti Scudder, Lisa Slayton, and Andy Garner: Thank you for guiding me through tough decisions in leadership with compassion, wisdom, and near-constant accessibility. Ken Edwards: Thank you for first teaching me about *Letting Go*. Jennifer Pirecki: I will forever be grateful for how you helped me reexperience the love of Jesus in a tangible, hour-to-hour, day-to-day way while I was writing this book. Because of you, the thread of "constancy" of devotion made its way into the manuscript, and my understanding of God's great love for me has intensified.

As first-time authors, we were incredibly fortunate to have a rockstar editor. Anna Robinson: You are smart, patient, kind, and wise. You are so calm in chaos with crystal-clear communication. Most of all, you give your all to your authors because you want their work to matter. It was a privilege to work with you across continents—I've saved our WhatsApp thread as a souvenir. And thank you to Rich Robinson, who coached us on our outline and gave us the painful push to complete draft one. You have both become dear friends along the way.

Thank you to Redeemer City to City for encouraging and supporting this book and faith and work overall.

To my coauthor, Lauren: When we agreed to this project in 2022, I had no idea how challenging it would be. I'm so thankful for the process of collaboration and appreciate how our strengths complement each other's. (Thank goodness for your knack for deadlines!) You pushed, you produced, and you loved me in the chaos of it all. Our work together is better than our work alone. I'm grateful for the way we ideate, rumble, and, on rare occasions, apologize. I cherish you and this shared journey, which I hope continues beyond what we can imagine.

Finally, my family carried the backpack with me to the finish line. Thank you to my mom and sisters for always cheering for me in my work. My children—Charlotte, William, and Mae: I adore each of you and am full of joy as I watch your own work unfold amidst the gifts you have been given. Charlotte: You are creative, strategic, visionary, and a precise communicator. William: You love the plethora of topics in the world, always trying to figure out how things work. And you think in numbers. Mae: Your abilities to quietly observe a complex situation and quickly understand the nuances of a problem revealed themselves before you could even walk. I hope the truths of God's work and love for you further permeate each of you in time, and that perhaps this book has a role in that. Of all the jobs I have had over the decades, motherhood was always my favorite. Paul: You were the first to say, "You should write a book." You believed more than I did and wouldn't let me ignore the call to write. You have supported all of my work from the get-go, even when it lured us to different continents and compromised yours. Thank you for loving me, believing in me, and reminding me that this work is worthy of the printed page. I am forever thankful and hopeful for the continued work God does in us. I love you and this adventure of our life. *Buen Camino.*

GETTING STARTED GUIDE

HACKS TO INCORPORATE FAITH AND WORK INTO YOUR EXISTING CHURCH ACTIVITIES

We recognize that integrating faith and work into your church or ministry can feel overwhelming. This guide offers *simple, practical steps* to incorporate these elements into your existing activities with minimal additional work. We recommended that you still engage with the fuller process of implementing faith and work as outlined in section two of this book, but the steps included in this Getting Started Guide will provide initial momentum and encouragement.

As a reminder, we believe that work is a critical context for individuals to live out and express their Christian faith. Adopting an integrated view of faith and work impacts an individual's personal relationship with Christ, as well as their relationships and interactions with their working communities, organizations, systems, and industries. *As such, as you embark on implementing faith-and-work initiatives, we encourage you to continually consider the heart change of the individuals and the city impact of their actions as objectives.*

This Getting Started Guide contains suggestions and resources in the following categories:

- ***Worship Service Resources***—simple ways to build faith and work into church services.
- ***Discipleship Resources***—suggested faith-and-work focused courses that are easy to implement in a variety of contexts.
- ***Book Study Recommendations***—a list of faith-and-work books to use as short-term studies.
- ***Case Studies***—a list of faith-and-work stories from various industries.
- ***Workplace Visit Guide***—a guide to assist you with workplace visits of those you serve.

WORSHIP SERVICE RESOURCES

Building faith and work into worship services is an effective way to reach many people with the transformative impact of faith in the workplace. See chapter eleven for a deeper discussion of this concept.

SERMON INCLUSION TOOL

As discussed in chapter eleven, including the context of work in your week-to-week sermons is one of the easiest and perhaps most effective ways to help people understand the gospel in light of how they spend their time each week.

Remember that out of Jesus' roughly thirty-seven unique parables, thirty-two refer to work. Jesus knew the importance of work and its effectiveness as a context to mold hearts. Adding work illustrations into sermons bridges the gap between the sacred and the secular and impacts the hearts of your congregants.

When preparing to incorporate work into your sermons, consider the following:

https://tinyurl.com/yzm2h422

- There are many resources to help you bring work applications into your sermons, including the Theology of Work Bible Commentary and the Faith & Work Bible. Scan the QR code for links to these resources.
- You can ask congregants in advance of your sermon how the text can be applied to their vocations. This affirms the importance and value of their work, invites them to participate in shaping the message, and gives you helpful contextualized examples for your sermon.

Use the chart below to assist you with translating a gospel message into work examples. It could also assist you in preparing a workplace example for a sermon. See appendix nine for blank charts you can use for each sermon.

Questions to Consider	Examples
What types of workers are in your congregation?	Is your audience filled with laborers, finance professionals, artists, etc.? And what percentage? You may want multiple examples to touch varying groups or alternate examples each week.
What is the biblical passage you plan to cover in your upcoming message?	Luke 15:11–32: The Parable of the Lost Son
What are the main points you hope to make in your message?	• God's boundless love • The older brother's need for the gospel (trying to justify his own righteousness) • The younger brother's repentance • The father's forgiveness
Which of your points do you think most lend themselves to a work example?	The older brother's need for the gospel
What are the subpoints you hope to make?	• The older brother reveals an attitude of pride, perhaps believing that he is earning his righteousness through his own behaviors. • The older brother reveals a lack of compassion for others. • The older brother is not aware of the sin in his own heart. • The gospel covers the sins of all—the overt sin of the younger brother and the covert sin of the self-righteous older brother.

Questions to Consider	Examples
How could you use a work example that would be relevant to your congregation?	Can you think of examples when a worker is doing the "right thing" but has a heart posture of feeling superior to others? • Perhaps he is always on time and a colleague is in trouble for being late. • Perhaps she never "plays politics" at work and looks down on those who do as being disingenuous. • Perhaps he always works late when needed and is quick to answer emails after hours, thinking less of coworkers who go home on time. • Maybe she is an actor on a set who is always friendly with the crew and considers herself more of a team player than performers who need more focus to prepare for their roles.

INDUSTRY PRAYERS

As mentioned in chapter eleven, including prayers about work in the flow of regular services can be extremely encouraging to workers.

Redeemer City to City's booklet *Prayers for Work: Industry Prayers for the Church and Its People* includes prayers written by Christians working in eighteen different industries and can serve as a guide for your congregants to write their own industry prayers. Scan the QR code for a link to this booklet.

https://tinyurl.com/4dy2ja2s

Five of the prayers are included in appendix ten of this book as examples.

Welcomes and Benedictions

As discussed in chapter eleven, churches can signal the importance of work or greatly detract from it with welcomes, calls to worship, and benedictions. See appendix eight for work-affirming examples.

Testimonies of Lives Changed by Work

As we explored in chapter eleven, testimonies are a profound way to show God's work in the lives of congregants. Some churches build these life stories into services. Rather than only having testimonies about how someone first came to know God, consider adding testimonies of how the gospel changed the way someone does their work, views their industry, or how they relate to others in the workplace. Showcasing these stories helps bridge the divide between faith and work and sparks people's imaginations for how God might be calling them to work in their own industries.

Songs About Work/Mission

As noted in chapter eleven, God uses songs to plant theological truths into our hearts in ways that spoken words cannot. Music tends to circumvent the cognitive aspect of our being and quickly makes its way to the heart. The Porters Gate Worship Project has created songs about work and mission that can be used for formal congregational worship or anywhere else you want to build in a sense of mission with the music you use. Scan the QR code for links to music recommendations.

https://tinyurl.com/yzm2h422

COMMISSIONING

Many churches have traditions and routines about honoring formal ministry workers in church services. Consider also commissioning your laity in their vocations so they can see their work as an opportunity to be sent out to glorify God.

Below is one example. See appendix eight for further examples.

Pastor: In a world filled with brokenness, confusion, darkness, mourning and loneliness, God has called his people to bring the healing light of the gospel into every sector of our city through every profession, institution, and calling. There is no inch of this city his gospel cannot redeem.

Congregants: We repent of how we have overlooked this great calling we have been given. The Spirit is waking us to see this mission in God's world. We surrender all that we are to serve you, O Lord, our Rock, and King.

We pray for your power, renouncing our selfish pride, to serve our city with excellence in our respective roles, jobs, and professions.

We rest in your unfailing love, which dissolves all bitterness, fear, anxiety, and resentment, so that this world will know we belong to you.

We ask that you would open our eyes to see how the gospel is powerfully at work to transform hearts, communities, and the world.

Pastor: And I heard the voice of the Lord saying, "Whom shall I send, and who will go for us?"

Congregants: Then I said, "Here am I! Send me."

Pastor: Go into the world: work, build, design, write, dance, laugh, sing, and create.

Congregants: We go with the assurance of God's great commission.

Pastor: Go into the world: risk, explore, discover, and love.

Congregants: We go with the assurance of God's abundant grace.

Pastor: Go into the world: believe, hope, struggle, persevere, and remember.

Congregants: We go with the assurance of God's unfailing love.[1]

DISCIPLESHIP RESOURCES

https://tinyurl.com/42mm6y7n

If you are looking for courses you can easily plug into a Bible study or community group curriculum, we recommend the following faith-and-work resources. Scan the QR code to discover the resources recommended in the table below.

---

[1] This commissioning prayer was developed by the Center for Faith & Work and used in services at Redeemer Presbyterian Church.

Resource	Description	Level
Go Forth: God's Purpose for Your Work: An 8-Week Bible Study	An eight-week Bible study in workbook format that uses a biblical lens to examine how God is using our work. Authored by The Global Faith & Work Initiative at Redeemer City to City.	Introductory
Why Your Work Matters	A four-module online course to help deepen participants' understanding of why and how God is using their work to bring about his glory. Through biblical teaching, theological reflection, and practical exercises, this course establishes a foundation for integrating faith and work.	Introductory
Faith & Work Bible Study	This course uses six different Bible passages to provide insight concerning God's intention for our work and can be used in a group format. Leader's and participant's guides are provided with weekly teachings, spiritual practices, discussion points, and optional daily devotionals.	Introductory
Faith & Work Immersion	A robust eight-module online faith-and-work course that provides an intensive look at the basic theology of faith and work, calling, heart renewal, ethics, relationships at work, excellence at work, and city vision. Teaching includes videos, readings, worksheets, and extensive tools for bringing faith into vocational life. Students will see that their work matters to God—from the actual work that they do, to the way they conduct themselves and their relationships at work, to the hope they can have for their vocations and our industries.	Intermediate Significant outside work required for students

Resource	Description	Level
The Missional Disciple: Pursuing Mercy & Justice at Work	Designed around short videos presented by leading practitioners and theologians, this is a six-week course exploring how mercy and justice are not only central to the biblical story but are also at the heart of God's character. Created for group use and packed with case studies, community discussion questions, simple practices, and prayer prompts, this interactive course will help participants discover a holistic paradigm and equip them to become a restorative presence in their everyday workplaces.	Intermediate
The Praxis Course	Free video-based course by Praxis about faith and entrepreneurship. Content and discussion focused on what it means to be a faith-based entrepreneur.	Specific for entrepreneurs
Faith Driven Entrepreneur Foundation Series	Two six-week video-based courses (with facilitator guides) developed by the Faith Driven team with particular emphasis on biblical entrepreneurship and investing.	Specific for entrepreneurs and investors of any experience

BOOK STUDY RECOMMENDATIONS

One easy way to gain faith-and-work momentum is to host a discussion group focused on a book that articulates a holistic vision of faith and work. At the time of publication, here are some books we suggest.

- Timothy Keller with Katherine Leary Alsdorf, *Every Good Endeavor: Connecting Your Work to God's Work* (New York City, NY: Penguin Publishing Group, 2014)

- Jim Mullins and Michael Goheen, *The Symphony of Mission: Playing Your Part in God's Work in the World* (Grand Rapids, MI: Baker Academic, 2019)
- Makoto Fujimura, *Culture Care: Reconnecting with Beauty for Our Common Life* (Downers Grove, IL: InterVarsity Press, 2017)
- Andy Crouch, *Culture Making: Recovering Our Creative Calling* (Downers Grove, IL: InterVarsity Press, 2017)
- Steve Garber, *Visions of Vocation: Common Grace for the Common Good* (Downers Grove, IL: InterVarsity Press, 2014)
- Denise Daniels and Shannon Vandewarker, *Working in the Presence of God: Spiritual Practices for Everyday Work* (Peabody, MA: Hendrickson Publishers, 2019)
- Michaela O'Donnell, *Make Work Matter: Your Guide to Meaningful Work in a Changing World* (Grand Rapids, MI: Baker Books, 2021)
- Kara Martin, *Workship: How to Use Your Work to Worship God* (Midview City, Singapore: Graceworks, 2017)
- Joanna Meyer, *Women, Work, and Calling: Step Into Your Place in God's World* (Downers Grove, IL: InterVarsity Press, 2023)
- Skye Jethani and Luke Bobo, *Discipleship with Monday in Mind: How Churches Across the Country Are Helping Their People Connect Faith and Work* (Kansas City, MO: Made to Flourish, 2017)
- Jordan Raynor, *The Sacredness of Secular Work: Four Ways Your Job Matters for Eternity (Even When You're Not Sharing the Gospel)* (Colorado Springs, CO: WaterBrook, 2024)
- Redeemer City to City, *The Missional Disciple: Pursuing Mercy & Justice at Work*, ed. Lauren Gill (New York City, NY: Redeemer City to City, 2022)
- Charlie Meo and Redeemer City to City, *Go Forth: God's Purpose for Your Work*, ed. Lauren Gill (New York City, NY: Redeemer City to City, 2024)

Scan the QR code for purchase links for all the books listed above.

https://tinyurl.com/yzm2h422

CASE STUDIES

Often, it is hard to really comprehend the myriad of ways the gospel can impact an individual's life and the systems and organizations in which they work. In order to help expand your congregants' imaginations of what is possible, we have collected video interviews and stories of people who have experienced the love of God and henceforth brought renewal—in ways large and small—to their work in the following industries:

- Commercial Arts
- Criminal Justice
- Education
- Fashion
- Film
- Finance
- Healthcare Compliance
- Hospitality
- Legal
- Travel

Scan the QR below to access these videos.

https://tinyurl.com/e9ws6y59

We recommend using these stories in courses or worship services to inspire your congregants by showing everyday examples of how God is using the day-to-day work of others for his kingdom.

WORKPLACE VISIT GUIDE

Visiting church members is a wonderful way for you to affirm their work while at the same time giving you invaluable experience of the culture, joys, and challenges of various types of workplaces and industries. Whenever you would normally hold a meeting with a congregant at the church building, in a local eatery, or in the home—whether that be to address faith questions, for pastoral support, or for anything else—we highly encourage you to offer to hold such meetings at the congregant's place of work. Sometimes they will not be able to accommodate this request, but often they will. Visiting their workplace affirms their work by showing them that what they are doing is seen by you as their pastor. Your presence gives their work a sense of inherent dignity, even if the meeting is not about work itself. Often, just by being in their place of work, they will be much more forthcoming about their vocation. We also encourage you to visit workplaces for the sole purpose of learning about your congregant's occupation. The more workplaces you visit, the more you will learn about the commonalities and differences in many types of work, and thus the better you will be equipped to engage with people at the heart level around their work.

EXAMPLE QUESTIONS TO ASK

- What circumstances brought you to this job?
- What motivates you to work here?
- What aspects of your work are challenging or stressful?
- What changes would you like to make in your work?
- What brings you joy in your work?
- How is conflict handled in your workplace?
- Does your faith impact your work? If so, how?
- What would God say is good about your industry?
- What would God think is broken in your industry?
- What support might you want from a church or ministry to help you with your faith-and-work journey?
- If you would want your pastor to know one thing about your work, what would it be?

THINGS TO LISTEN FOR

- Why are they doing the work they do, and what is motivating them on a daily basis? Listen for their sense of giftedness for their work, any idolatries that may be driving them, and any sense of God's calling to their specific work. Discern whether there is any sense of work for survival or work being a source of misery for them—or of work being a source of self-actualization. Do they have a sense of being created to work?

- What aspects of their work bring them joy? What aspects of their work give them frustration and struggle, interfere with their success, and/or are fruitless? Are they able to reframe the toils of work? Do they understand that all work has toil?
- In what ways does their relationship with God and their understanding of the gospel have bearing on their work life (e.g., prayer, character and virtue, leadership and followership, work/life/rest pacing, sense of God's calling, vision for reform or service, witness to others in the workplace, etc.)? Are there areas in which you can encourage them to expand this vision?

The stories you hear will reveal a lot about the culture of their workplace and their deeply held beliefs about the way the world is. Over time you will become more adept at understanding the pains and joys of various workplaces, empathizing with people rather than just listening to their stories. As you absorb more stories, you will naturally begin building these sensibilities into sermons and conversations, informing and encouraging workers along the way.

AFTER THE MEETING

Write down what you have learned from the conversation. As you increasingly engage with congregants in their workplaces, look for common themes and narratives about how God is using their work.

Workplace Visit Questions	Answers	Potential Gospel or Sermon Application
What circumstances brought you to this job?		
What motivates you to work here?		

Workplace Visit Questions	Answers	Potential Gospel or Sermon Application
What aspects of your work are challenging or stressful?		
What changes would you like to make in your work?		
What brings you joy in your work?		
How is conflict handled in your workplace?		
Does your faith impact your work? If so, how?		
What would God say is good about your industry?		
What would God think is broken in your industry?		
What support might you want from a church or ministry to help you with your faith-and-work journey?		
If you would want your pastor to know one thing about your work, what would it be?		

Post-Visit Questions	Reflections	Potential Gospel or Sermon Application
What did I learn about this industry or company?		
What might this worker not be believing about God and work?		
What idolatries exist?		
What is creationally good about this work?		
How could the church encourage this worker?		
How could something I learned here be relevant to a sermon?		

Scan the QR code for a downloadable blank Workplace Visit chart.

https://tinyurl.com/ 2w4s7z68

APPENDIX 1

INTEGRATED LEADERSHIP ASSESSMENT

Use this tool to establish a baseline for assessing where you need to focus your leadership development to more seamlessly integrate your faith and work.

HEART

- Articulate what you think God says about the importance of your work.
- What are your core idolatries related to your work? What deep-seated needs or desires are you looking to fulfill through your work (e.g., comfort, approval, control, power, etc.)? What specific actions can you take to address these issues and reorient your heart toward God?
- What are your rhythms of convening with the Holy Spirit *throughout* your work, not just in the morning or at the beginning of a meeting? Do you seek the Lord's guidance around the large and small issues in your work? What are some next steps you can take to deepen this connection? (See the Attune exercises in appendix two for assistance.)

COMMUNITY

- Who are the primary groups of people you interact with in your job (e.g., clients, congregants, suppliers, direct reports, etc.)?
- If Jesus were to come tomorrow and join you at work for the day, what suggestions might he make about how you and your organization treat people?
- With whom do you interact who has little agency or power? How could you empower these individuals?
- Who do you believe God calls you to better care for at work? Do you consider this on a regular basis?

WORLD

- What industry are you part of?
- How is it good?
- How is it broken?
- How can you shine light on the broken parts of your industry?
- Do you recognize the creational goodness and brokenness of other industries?
- Do you have a vision of how industries can impact city flourishing?
- What systems in your city are you part of? In what ways are they good or broken, and what can you do to push toward more goodness?

Based on your responses, we encourage you to review the heart, community, and world section in chapter six for next steps toward integration.

APPENDIX 2

SPIRITUAL ATTUNEMENT AS A TOOL FOR INTEGRATED LEADERSHIP

As mentioned in the integrated leader section of this book (chapter six), the most foundational principle of all faith and work, and discipleship in general, is learning to discern the voice of God. As such, we strongly believe in centering discernment activities in your personal leadership journey, your leadership teams, your church rhythms, and all faith-and-work initiatives.

The following was written by Tracy Mathews at Attune:

"Come to me, all you who are weary and burdened, and I will give you rest. Take my yoke upon you and learn from me, for I am gentle and humble in heart, and you will find rest for your souls. For my yoke is easy and my burden is light" (Matt. 11:28–30).

As Christian leaders of churches, businesses, and other organizations, we all know this passage. And yet, most of the leaders I come into contact with, despite being genuinely devoted to Jesus, wouldn't describe their work as "easy" or "light." The words "weary" and "burdened" are much more readily used.

How do we actually take Jesus up on this very attractive offer?

Well, at Attune, we've come to understand that most Christian leaders, including pastors and others operating in explicitly Christian organizations, have yet to develop their abilities to hear from Jesus in their day-to-day work and leadership. Yet, the ability to hear Jesus is a critical part of taking on his yoke. When we learn to hear his direct, personal communication with us, we gain a felt sense of his nearness, his love, and his power. We experience at a heart level the deep knowledge that he is with us and is bearing the bulk of the load. We also hear his step-by-step guidance, so we know how to navigate our daily work with his wisdom, heart, passion, and supernatural effectiveness.

Through our work at Attune, we've witnessed leaders and teams grow in their ability to hear God's voice in their daily leadership. We've seen God give people a strong sense of peace, strength, freedom, motivation, and play, even when nothing in their very difficult circumstances seems to be changing. We've also seen God guide people into brilliant new approaches and solutions to everything from strategic direction for their organizations, to how to approach a contentious sermon topic, to how to navigate a complex and high-stakes conversation.

If we learn to hear and follow God's voice, we not only become more creative, effective, impactful leaders for the kingdom, but we also carry less of the burden ourselves and learn to live freely and lightly.

The "easy yoke" really is possible. But it takes learning to hear and listen to God's voice. There are many, many ways to learn. We encourage you to try out a number of different approaches and do more of what works for you. Better yet, find at least one other person who wants to go on a learning journey with you and explore, learn, and grow together.

Learning to listen to God's voice in your daily work and life truly is a path toward the "easy yoke" of Jesus.

If you want to learn more, Attune regularly runs learning cohorts for groups and individuals. Attune has also partnered with Fuller Seminary's De Pree Center for Leadership and The Theology of Work Project to develop a devotional called *Wisdom From Above*. With biblically based insights, this five-day devotion highlights the importance and goodness of spiritual attunement for your everyday work and leadership, inviting you into daily practice with Attune's *Wisdom from Above* Attunement Exercise.

Scan the QR code for the link to the *Wisdom From Above* devotional.

https://tinyurl.com/42mm6y7n

APPENDIX 3

INTEGRATED LEADERSHIP TEAM ASSESSMENT

Does your leadership team have a holistic view of faith and work? Check the boxes below that apply and identify any areas that are missing. Read pages 110–113 as a reminder of the ideal leadership team.

- ☐ We are created to work.
- ☐ Work is fallen; individuals and systems are broken.
- ☐ Jesus came to reconcile the world to himself, and work is part of reconciling people and broken systems to himself.
- ☐ We work to bring "on earth as it is in heaven" in our relationships, systems, and organizations.
- ☐ All good work is of God whether the person believes it or not.
- ☐ All good work matters to God, not just the work of those who believe in Christ.
- ☐ Most industries have a creational goodness and a reason to be in the world, and they are all also broken.

- What size is your leadership team? Is the core between three and six members?
- Are there ministry and business/market/art leaders involved in your team?
- If you are part of a church, to what extent is the senior pastor aligned with faith-and-work efforts?
- Pray about the next steps for your own individual leadership integration.
  - What steps do you need to take immediately?
  - What steps do you need to take in the next three months?
  - Who will help you stay on track?

- Pray about the next steps for your leadership team.
    - What steps do you need to take immediately?
    - What steps do you need to take in the next three months?
    - Who needs to agree to this with you?
    - Who will help you stay on track?

APPENDIX 4

CITY-BASED LEARNING TOOL

Below is an exercise for you to complete with your leadership team to assess your city. You can share it with your faith-and-work team as you begin to process the needs of your city. We often say that to love *your city is to* know *your city. Thus, you want to develop a clear understanding of your city in terms of who God might be calling you to serve and how he is moving your city in a particular direction over a twenty-year period.*

We recommend working through this worksheet with your key leaders and then spending some intentional time processing the discussion questions.

INTRODUCTION

As you consider how to impact your city, you may view the process with great optimism or feel overwhelmed by the city's brokenness and thus view it through a more cynical lens. As the people of God, we are called to seek the prosperity of the cities where we are planted.

Based on World Urbanization data, as of 2017, over half the world's population lived in cities; by 2050, it is projected to be close to 66 percent.[1] The importance of cities in God's unfolding story is paramount. And, as discussed below, loving our cities is key. But in order to *love* our city, we must *know* our city.

Consider the following excerpt to understand the importance of ministry *in* cities, and then complete the following analysis about your own city in order to gain deep context for your work.

In Jeremiah 29, God told the Israelites who had been taken into Babylonian captivity, "Build houses and settle down; plant gardens and eat what they

---

[1] "Urbanization," Our World in Data, September 2018 (rev. February 2024), https://ourworldindata.org/urbanization.

produce. Marry and have sons and daughters; find wives for your sons and give your daughters in marriage, so that they too may have sons and daughters. Increase in number there; do not decrease. Also, seek the peace and prosperity of the city to which I have carried you into exile. Pray to the Lord for it, because if it prospers, you too will prosper" (Jer. 29:5–7).

While the Jews were living in that place, they were to engage fully in life, even in the life of a city that was ostensibly opposed to God. Even though the Lord gives them a self-oriented reason for doing so—"if it prospers, you too will prosper"—the fact remains that he is telling them to seek, work for, pursue, and be concerned for the peace and prosperity of that place.

It was a pretty radical idea—that God's people should work for the good of people who are not living in right relationship to him. That, however, is what he tells the Israelites. This may sound radical to us today, but it is very much in accord with what Jesus deemed to be the second greatest commandment, "Love your neighbor as yourself" (Matt. 22:39). It is right in line with the idea that Israel, God's people at that time, was to be a "blessing for the nations" (Gen. 12:3). And it is right in line with John 3:16, "For God so loved the world ..."

Repeatedly throughout the Scriptures, we see God's concern for cities and the people within them, both those inhabited and dominated by his people, like Jerusalem, and those that were not, such as Nineveh and Babylon. God is just as concerned today about cities as he was back then, and therefore so should we.

There are many reasons why we ought to be concerned about the city, not the least of which are the following:

1. The cities are where people are and increasingly will be.
2. The cities are the key centers of influence culturally, spiritually, and in nearly every other way.
3. The city is God's invention, part of God's plan and purpose, and as such should not be regarded as evil. Life in a city is our eventual destiny—or at least our eternal destiny will revolve around a city.[2]

---

[2] Al Barth, "A Vision for Our Cities," Redeemer City to City, January 1, 2009, https://redeemercitytocity.com/articles-stories/a-vision-for-our-cities.

EXERCISE

To love a city requires us to *know* it—to know its beauty and its brokenness, its systems, its people and its trajectory. Seeing a city holistically allows us to move toward what is creationally good and to push against the brokenness through our work.

Most cities have a chamber of commerce or city association which collects a city's data. However, online searches and interviews with city leaders may help populate your analysis as well.

LEARNING EXERCISE

Name of Team Completing Worksheet: _____

City name	10 years ago	Current	10 years from now—projected or possible (imagine the positive and negative)	Comment/ areas of change/ drivers of change/ detail about change, etc.

City population

Average age

Ethnicity Breakdown

---

214 | FAITH & WORK

| City name | 10 years ago | Current | 10 years from now—projected or possible (imagine the positive and negative) | Comment/ areas of change/ drivers of change/ detail about change, etc. |

% of marginalized populations

Average family income

Biggest economic drivers (industries)

Largest employers

Goodness of key industries

CITY-BASED LEARNING TOOL | 215

City name	10 years ago	Current	10 years from now—projected or possible (imagine the positive and negative)	Comment/areas of change/drivers of change/detail about change, etc.
Brokenness of key industries				
Strengths of the city				
Weaknesses of the city				
Wounds/stubborn facts of the city				
The city stereotype narrative is: "Our city is _____"				

- What most surprises you about your city, now that you have viewed it holistically?

  _____

  _____

- What visits, tours, or meetings do you feel would help bring this data to life?

  _____

  _____

- Sit in prayer and ask God to illuminate to you the key areas of the city you should focus upon.

  _____

  _____

- Are there any obvious next steps?

  _____

  _____

Scan the QR code for a downloadable blank City-Based Learning Tool worksheet.

https://tinyurl.com/2w4s7z68

APPENDIX 5
CONGREGATION WORK SURVEY

Note: As you consider faith-and-work initiatives for your constituents, it is important that you understand their current types and areas of work, their needs, and their struggles. Below is a sample survey which we recommend you customize for your purposes and send out as an online survey. We advise using an electronic survey platform such as Google Forms, Survey Monkey, or whatever is most common for your church or in your geographical region. Scan the QR code for a sample Google survey, which you can copy and adapt for your context.

https://tinyurl.com/32h2tu3a

SURVEY

Thank you for taking time to complete this survey. As an organization, we want to better help you connect your Christian faith to your day-to-day life. Thus, we would like to understand how you spend your time outside of church activities. This survey is completely anonymous and will be used only to assist us with efforts to better equip you. Please know that we believe that all good work is part of God's unfolding plan for the world, not just church and missionary work. As we type, we pray for your work.

1. **What best describes your relationship to this church/organization?**
   - Member
   - Frequent attender
   - Observer from afar (social media, etc.)
   - No relationship

2. **What is your age?**
   - Under 18
   - 18–22

- ○ 23–30
- ○ 31–40
- ○ 41–55
- ○ 56–70
- ○ Over 71

3. **What best describes your ethnicity?**
   - ○ [*Leader note: Insert comment field for an answer.*]

4. **What is your marital status?**
   - ○ Single and never married
   - ○ Married
   - ○ Divorced
   - ○ Widowed
   - ○ Other

5. **Do you have children under age 18 in the home?**
   - ○ Yes
   - ○ No

6. **How many years of full-time work experience do you have outside of the home?**
   - ○ Less than 5
   - ○ 6–10
   - ○ 11–20
   - ○ 21–30
   - ○ Over 31

7. **Which industry best describes your main area of current work? (based on NAICS classification codes)**
   - ○ Agriculture, Forestry, Fishing, and Hunting
   - ○ Mining, Quarrying, and Oil and Gas Extraction
   - ○ Utilities
   - ○ Construction
   - ○ Manufacturing

- Wholesale Trade
- Retail Trade
- Transportation and Warehousing
- Information
- Finance and Insurance
- Real Estate and Rental and Leasing
- Professional, Scientific, and Technical Services
- Management of Companies and Enterprises
- Administrative and Support and Waste Management and Remediation Services
- Educational Services
- Health Care and Social Assistance
- Arts, Entertainment, and Recreation
- Accommodation and Food Services
- Other Services (except Public Administration)
- Public Administration
- Volunteer work
- Parenting

8. **How much time do you spend working outside the home in a paid role?**
   - 0–15 hours
   - 16–40 hours
   - 41–50 hours
   - Over 51 hours

9. **What is the name of the company or organization where you currently work?**
   Note "self" if you are self-employed; note 'home" if you work full time in the home; note "unemployed" if you desire paid work but currently do not have it.
   - [*Leader note: Insert comment field for an answer.*]

10. **What are your top two motivations for work? (check two)**
    - Survival

- Financial accumulation
- Status
- Power
- Enjoyment
- Social interaction
- Contributing to society
- Structured routine
- Mental stimulation
- Pursuit of passion
- Legacy and impact

11. **How much choice do you feel you have about the kind of job you can do?**
    - No choice at all
    - Very limited choice
    - I am not sure
    - A fair amount of choice
    - Unlimited amount of choice

12. **How engaged or connected are you in your day-to-day work?**
    - I am not engaged at all. I would leave as soon as possible if I could.
    - I am not really engaged, but I am not actively seeking to leave.
    - I am neither engaged nor disengaged.
    - I am engaged in my work.
    - I am extremely engaged.

13. **What two significant work problems cause you the most stress? (check one or two)**
    - Logistics of the work (commute, coordinating schedule, etc.)
    - Hours/workload (too much or not enough)
    - Pay
    - Organizational issues
    - Interpersonal conflict
    - Job satisfaction and engagement/sense of meaning

- Performance and development of myself and/or my coworkers
- Ethical and legal concerns
- Workplace safety and health
- Technology and innovation
- Communication and collaboration
- Financial and resource management (budget constraints, etc.)
- Other

14. **What are the most gratifying areas of your job? (check one or two)**
    - Helping others: I find fulfillment in helping and making a positive impact on others' lives.
    - Creativity and expression: I enjoy expressing my creativity and seeing my ideas come to life.
    - Learning and discovery: I find satisfaction in learning new things and making discoveries.
    - Leadership and achievement: I enjoy leading teams and achieving goals.
    - Social impact: I am gratified by the social impact and contributions of my work.
    - Teaching and mentoring: I find fulfillment in teaching, mentoring, or coaching others.
    - Problem-solving: I enjoy solving complex problems and finding innovative solutions.
    - Contributing to society: I can see how my work is helping my company, industry, the community, and/or the world.
    - Relationships: I enjoy the people I work with.
    - Other
    - I do not find anything gratifying at my work.

15. **Optional: What is your level of annual income?**
    - [Leader note: Insert levels applicable for your country. Make wide bands with "less than" at the beginning of the range and "more than" at the top of the range. Make sure this question is optional, or you may lose survey respondents.]

16. **If someone asked you what belief in Jesus Christ means to your day-to-day work, how would you answer?**
    ○ [*Leader note: Insert comment field for an answer.*]

17. **What would most help you in a journey to understanding what being a Christian means to your day-to-day work life?**
    ○ [*Leader note: Insert comment field for an answer.*]

18. **Optional: If you would like to stay informed about our progress and plans to help equip and support you in your faith-and-work journey, please leave your email here**
    ○ [*Leader note: Insert comment field for an answer*]

APPENDIX 6

WORKPLACE VISIT GUIDE

Visiting church members is a wonderful way for you to affirm their work while at the same time giving you invaluable experience of the culture, joys, and challenges of various types of workplaces and industries. Whenever you would normally hold a meeting with a congregant at the church building, in a local eatery, or in the home—whether that be to address faith questions, for pastoral support, or for anything else—we highly encourage you to offer to hold such meetings at the congregant's place of work. Sometimes they will not be able to accommodate this request, but often they will. Visiting their workplace affirms their work by showing them that what they are doing is seen by you as their pastor. Your presence gives their work a sense of inherent dignity, even if the meeting is not about work itself. Often, just by being in their place of work, they will be much more forthcoming about their vocation. We also encourage you to visit workplaces for the sole purpose of learning about your congregant's occupation. The more workplaces you visit, the more you will learn about the commonalities and differences in many types of work, and thus the better you will be equipped to engage with people at the heart level around their work.

EXAMPLE QUESTIONS TO ASK

- What circumstances brought you to this job?
- What motivates you to work here?
- What aspects of your work are challenging or stressful?
- What changes would you like to make in your work?
- What brings you joy in your work?
- How is conflict handled in your workplace?
- Does your faith impact your work? If so, how?
- What would God say is good about your industry?
- What would God think is broken in your industry?

- What support might you want from a church or ministry to help you with your faith-and-work journey?
- If you would want your pastor to know one thing about your work, what would it be?

THINGS TO LISTEN FOR

- Why are they doing the work they do, and what is motivating them on a daily basis? Listen for their sense of giftedness for their work, any idolatries that may be driving them, and any sense of God's calling to their specific work. Discern whether there is any sense of work for survival or work being a source of misery for them—or of work being a source of self-actualization. Do they have a sense of being created to work?
- What aspects of their work bring them joy? What aspects of their work give them frustration and struggle, interfere with their success, and/or are fruitless? Are they able to reframe the toils of work? Do they understand that all work has toil?
- In what ways does their relationship with God and their understanding of the gospel have bearing on their work life (e.g., prayer, character and virtue, leadership and followership, work/life/rest pacing, sense of God's calling, vision for reform or service, witness to others in the workplace, etc.)? Are there areas in which you can encourage them to expand this vision?

The stories you hear will reveal a lot about the culture of their workplace and their deeply held beliefs about the way the world is. Over time you will become more adept at understanding the pains and joys of various workplaces, empathizing with people rather than just listening to their stories. As you absorb more stories, you will naturally begin building these sensibilities into sermons and conversations, informing and encouraging workers along the way.

AFTER THE MEETING

Write down what you have learned from the conversation. As you increasingly engage with congregants in their workplaces, look for common themes and narratives about how God is using their work.

Workplace Visit Questions	Answers	Potential Gospel or Sermon Application
What circumstances brought you to this job?		
What motivates you to work here?		
What aspects of your work are challenging or stressful?		
What changes would you like to make in your work?		
What brings you joy in your work?		
How is conflict handled in your workplace?		
Does your faith impact your work? If so, how?		
What would God say is good about your industry?		
What would God think is broken in your industry?		
What support might you want from a church or ministry to help you with your faith-and-work journey?		
If you would want your pastor to know one thing about your work, what would it be?		

Post-Visit Questions	Reflections	Potential Gospel or Sermon Application
What did I learn about this industry or company?		
What might this worker not be believing about God and work?		
What idolatries exist?		
What is creationally good about this work?		
How could the church encourage this worker?		
How could something I learned here be relevant to a sermon?		

Scan the QR code for a downloadable blank Workplace Visit chart.

https://tinyurl.com/2w4s7z68

APPENDIX 7

FROM→TO CHART

The following worksheets support the development of certain theological truths you hope to impart in those you serve in the "Understand Needs" step of the journey map as discussed in chapter ten.

Combine your many observations from your interviews and surveys into a coherent whole and discern the changes you seek through the programs you will create. Sometimes the perceived or articulated needs of your community are only scratching the surface of their actual needs. For example, a person may state that what they really need to be happy in their work is a new boss when, from a gospel perspective, they may actually need to grow in their ability to work with a difficult boss. A gospel-centered approach to ministry design enables us to get closer to the "heart of the matter," which usually involves gospel change in our beliefs, desires, and actions.

Consider the following questions when creating your From→To chart.

- Who is the target worker you hope to serve?
- What is the change you hope to see in your workers' hearts, minds, and hands?
- What is the scope of impact you hope to have on individuals in the context of your institution (e.g., disciple the congregants of your church)? And/or what is the scope of impact you hope to have on your city (e.g., cultivate entrepreneurship in your city)?

Examples of Theological Needs Around Work

From →	To
I work because I want to be rich and influential.	I am made to work as part of God's story to bring flourishing to this world and glory to him.
Work is miserable and I only do it in order to survive.	I am made to work as part of God's story to bring flourishing to this world and glory to him.
If my work doesn't make me happy, then I am in the wrong work.	Work is guaranteed to have toil, and we serve a suffering Savior.
I work to have more leisure.	God ordained work and rest as part of his cycle.
Church is on Sunday, and the pastor leads the mission.	The gathered church is on Sunday, and the church sends people out all week as the scattered church on mission for the renewal of the world.
Church work is more sacred than other work.	All work is sacred.
People matter.	People, systems, and institutions matter.
Capitalism is evil.	Business brings goods and services into the world in a sustainable way and serves to employ people to use some of their God-given talent but is also broken.
Being saved is about going to heaven.	The gospel changes everything, including my day-to-day now.
I think I am a pretty good person at work.	I am deeply aware of the depth of my sin at work.
Heaven is "up there" so my work here doesn't matter.	Christ will come again and bring the new heaven and new earth. Work here matters.
God only does good work through Christians.	God can bring good work into the world through anyone, as the image of God is in all.

Blank From → To Chart

From →	To

Scan the QR code for a downloadable blank From→To chart.

https://tinyurl.com/2w4s7z68

APPENDIX 8

CHURCH SERVICE INCLUSION TOOLS

The majority of this appendix was authored and compiled by Katie Roelofs of the Worship for Workers Project at Fuller Theological Seminary

WEEKLY WORSHIP TEMPLATES FOR GATHERING AND SCATTERING WORKERS

Two of the elements you can use to build faith-and-work focus into your services involve how you gather and scatter workers.

Below you will find examples and templates for some key service elements that can be focused on faith and work, including a call to worship; a template and examples of gathering words; and a template and example to use for sending words at the conclusion of service. These will help you gather and scatter workers, incorporating worker testimonies and stories.

A CALL TO WORSHIP

>Children of God,
>Come to the altar.
>Come as you are.
>Bring your whole selves, your whole week,
>Your sorrows and your joys.
>Don't hide that which preoccupies you.
>Don't ignore that which burdens.
>Bring your whole self to the altar,
>Your work and your responsibilities,
>Your victories and your triumphs.
>God desires that you enter here with fullness of heart.
>Bring your stories of salvation and sadness.
>Come and give them to the Lord.

Invite several workers to reflect on the examples and ask them to fill in the templates with their own voices. This not only allows workers to bring their work to God in worship but also to share their experiences with their community for prayer. Consider using this basic structure for several weeks in a row, asking workers to share and be blessed. How might the voices of a few encourage the voices of many?

TEMPLATE FOR GATHERING

- I bring my week of service and labor as a _____.
- In this week, God equipped me to _____.
- I felt God's presence when _____.
- God calls me now to worship because _____.

EXAMPLES FOR GATHERING

These are meant to be examples (although they could be used in worship as well). As you invite your workers to participate and fill in their own gathering words from their own experiences, these might help them see how to use the template above.

Example 1: Delivery Driver

- I bring my week of service and labor as an Amazon driver.
- In this week, God equipped me to complete my routes safely, ensuring people received everything from books to bar soap, medical supplies to matcha tea.
- I felt God's presence when I delivered a birthday package to a child and completed a route for a colleague who went home for a family emergency.
- God calls me now to worship because in the midst of dealing with goods and services, I worship the One who is the giver of all good gifts—always on time, always ready to receive, always riding with me, blessing my work.

Example 2: Drug Regulator

- I bring my week of service and labor as a drug regulator for the Food and Drug Administration.
- In this week, God equipped me to analyze a clinical trial drug with the layers of scientific and medical knowledge he has given me. I approved this drug with my team, and new medical options will be available to cure disease.
- I felt God's presence when I read through the case studies of the hundreds of people who have responded positively to this medical miracle, giving them a chance of many more years of living.
- God calls me now to worship because my incomplete knowledge is met and received by God who is above all, through all, and in all. To God be the glory in and through my work.

SENDING WORDS

Friends, this is not the end of our worship but its beginning.

We go now into the city to continue lives of worship and service,

In the marketplace and the storeroom,

In the medical facility and the classroom,

In the quietness of retirement and the hustle of household.

And so we go to extend our worship into the world.

We go, to extend these songs of grace and mercy to our coworkers and classmates.

We go, to extend this table of hospitality to our neighbors and family members.

We go, trusting that God is at work in this world, using us and our gifts for his glory.

We go, equipped with the power and presence of the Spirit who goes out before us and lights our path so that we might love and serve.

SENDING TEMPLATE

- God sends me out to my work as a _____.
- In this week, may God equip me to _____
- I pray for God's presence in _____.
- May God bless the work of my hands and yours as we together serve God's kingdom.

EXAMPLES FOR SENDING

These are meant to be examples (although they could be used in worship as well). As you invite your workers to participate and fill in their own scattering words from their own experiences, these might help them see how to use the template above.

Example 1: Pediatrician

- God sends me out to my work as a pediatrician.
- In this week, may God equip me to care for the health and well-being of all God's children—strengthening bodies and engaging young minds. May God equip me to swiftly treat the minor and discern the potential major. May God keep me healthy that I might continue to serve.
- I pray for God's presence when treating patients and families who suffer. When I see signs of abuse or neglect, let me act with loving care. When I know the diagnosis and am too scared to say it, soften my heart and my tongue to speak truth in love. When I am tired of treating colds and administering injections, remind me, Great Physician, of what it means to be an agent of healing in your broken world.
- May God bless the work of my hands and yours as we together serve God's kingdom.

Example 2: Architect

- God sends me out to my work as an architect.
- In this week, may God equip me to create that which is beautiful, that which is useful, and that which is safe. May God equip me to collaborate

well with urban planners and permit offices, recognizing that a building never stands alone.
- I pray for God's creativity when I have an empty blueprint in front of me and I don't know where to start. I pray for God's wisdom when I'm making final adjustments and tweaks. I pray for kindness when the builders change their minds. I pray for satisfaction in my work, recognizing I am always an important part of a larger process.
- May God bless the work of my hands and yours as we together serve God's kingdom.

MORE BENEDICTION EXAMPLES

Example 1: A Charge and Benediction for Workers

Leader: We have assembled together in this place as the gathered body of Christ, lifting our voices to proclaim Christ to the world through our worship.

People: We prepare to leave now as the scattered body of Christ, lifting our voices, for Christ is with us in our work in the world.

Leader: As lab techs and lawyers, as firefighters and farmers,

People: Christ is with us in our work in the world.

Leader: As tellers and teachers, as accountants and auto mechanics,

People: Christ is with us in our work in the world.

Leader: As managers and marketers, as nurses and nannies,

People: Christ is with us in our work in the world.

Leader: As engineers and event planners, as postal workers and production managers,

People: Christ is with us in our work in the world.

Leader: As salespeople and social workers, as cashiers and construction workers,

People: Christ is with us in our work in the world.

Leader: And as you go, know that you do not go alone. Your work is held in the power and covered in the blessing of the Triune God. May the love of God the Father, the grace of the Lord Jesus Christ, and the fellowship of the Holy Spirit rest, rule, and abide with you all as you carry Christ in your work in the world.
—*Written for the Worship for Workers Project of Fuller Seminary by Anthony Bolkema from South Holland, Illinoi*

Example 2: "This Time Tomorrow" Sending Prayer

Picture with me
where you will be tomorrow,
what you will be doing
and whom you will meet.
And pray with me
for the place you will be,
for the work you've been given to do
and for the people you will serve.
(Pause for silent prayer of the congregation.)
May you find God
there before you,
working alongside you,
blessing those around you.
And go in the name of
the Father,
the Son,
and the Holy Spirit.
Amen.
—*Written for the Worship for Workers Project of Fuller Seminary by Uli Chi from Seattle, Washington*

Example 3: "Go Forth" Sending Prayer

Go Forth!
May God's presence comfort you.
May the Son's work empower you.

May the Spirit's presence encourage and propel you.
May your mind be enlightened.
May your hands be crafty.
May your feet be steady.
May your radar be sensitive to the kingdom.
May your spirit be generous.
Go forth to join God's work.
Go forth to plant seeds.
Go forth to be good news.
In the office,
In the meeting rooms,
In the classroom,
In our words written,
In our word spoken.
Go forth as the aroma of God.
Amen

—Written for the Worship for Workers Project of Fuller Seminary by Vincent Bacote from Wheaton, Illinois

APPENDIX 9
SERMON INCLUSION TOOL

As discussed in chapter eleven, including the context of work in your week-to-week sermons is one of the easiest and perhaps most effective ways to help people understand the gospel in light of how they spend their time each week.

Remember that out of Jesus' roughly thirty-seven unique parables, thirty-two refer to work. Jesus knew the importance of work and its effectiveness as a context to mold hearts. Adding work illustrations into sermons bridges the gap between the sacred and the secular and impacts the hearts of your congregants.

When preparing to incorporate work into your sermons, consider the following:

- There are many resources to help you bring work applications into your sermons, including the Theology of Work Bible Commentary and the Faith and Work Bible. Scan the QR code for links to these resources.

    https://tinyurl.com/yzm2h422

- You can ask congregants in advance of your sermon how the text can be applied to their vocations. This affirms the importance and value of their work, invites them to participate in shaping the message, and gives you helpful contextualized examples for your sermon.

Use the chart below to assist you with translating a gospel message into work examples. It could also assist you in preparing a workplace example for a sermon.

Questions to Consider	Examples
What types of workers are in your congregation?	Is your audience filled with laborers, finance professionals, artists, etc.? And what percentage? You may want multiple examples to touch varying groups or alternate examples each week.
What is the biblical passage you plan to cover in your upcoming message?	Luke 15:11–32: The Parable of the Lost Son
What are the main points you hope to make in your message?	<ul><li>God's boundless love</li><li>The older brother's need for the gospel (trying to justify his own righteousness)</li><li>The younger brother's repentance</li><li>The father's forgiveness</li></ul>
Which of your points do you think most lend themselves to a work example?	The older brother's need for the gospel
What are the subpoints you hope to make?	<ul><li>The older brother reveals an attitude of pride, perhaps believing that he is earning his righteousness through his own behaviors.</li><li>The older brother reveals a lack of compassion for others.</li><li>The older brother is not aware of the sin in his own heart.</li><li>The gospel covers the sins of all—the overt sin of the younger brother and the covert sin of the self-righteous older brother.</li></ul>

Questions to Consider	Examples
How could you use a work example that would be relevant to your congregation?	Can you think of examples when a worker is doing the "right thing" but has a heart posture of feeling superior to others? • Perhaps he is always on time and a colleague is in trouble for being late. • Perhaps she never "plays politics" at work and looks down on those who do as being disingenuous. • Perhaps he always works late when needed and is quick to answer emails after hours, thinking less of coworkers who go home on time. • Maybe she is an actor on a set who is always friendly with the crew and considers herself more of a team player than performers who need more focus to prepare for their roles.

Blank Sermon Inclusion Chart

Questions to Consider	Examples
What types of workers are in your congregation?	
What is the biblical passage you plan to cover in your upcoming message?	
What are the main points you hope to make in your message?	
Which of your points do you think most lend themselves to a work example?	
What are the subpoints you hope to make?	
How could you use a work example that would be relevant to your congregation?	

Scan the QR code for a downloadable blank Sermon Inclusion chart.

https://tinyurl.com/2w4s7z68

APPENDIX 10

INDUSTRY PRAYER EXAMPLES

Below are five examples of industry prayers in the fields of hospitality, finance, construction and architecture, government, and creative industries. These prayers are part of Redeemer City to City's booklet *Prayers for Work: Industry Prayers for the Church and Its People*, which includes prayers written by Christians working in eighteen different industries and serves as a guide for your congregants to write their own industry prayers. Scan the QR code for a link to this booklet.

https://tinyurl.com/ 4dy2ja2s

HOSPITALITY

Father, Giver of every good gift,

Thank you for welcoming us with your extraordinary hospitality. In the beginning, you created a space for humanity to dwell—brimming with beauty, order, and diversity, providing for our every need. You fashioned our hearts to find great joy in what you made. You formed our hands to cultivate and extend hospitality to others. And then, when we turned our backs on you, you came close, taking on flesh and serving us in the most intimate of ways.

Would you help us see how sacred this work is that we've been called into? Dispel the idolatrous lies that our work is somehow "less than." Instead, help us see the ways we bear your image as we welcome strangers and serve them in a way that puts your goodness and love on display. People are desperate for connection, to be seen, and genuinely cared for. We thank you that we get to participate in that work with you!

Jesus, when guests treat us poorly, meet us with your humility. Remind us that you lavish grace upon us, even when we are among your mockers. Also, redeem us from the evil spirit of the age that values people according to their wealth and extends hospitality with partiality. We confess that this is not the way of your kingdom.

Protect those who work in the "shadows" of the hospitality industry. Bring fair wages and provide for their every need, Lord. May our whole industry, and especially those of us who follow you, love these vulnerable workers well. May we all value their work as you do.

Our work is centered around the table; may it always be sustained by coming back to your table. As we partake of the bread and wine of the new covenant, feasting on your unfathomable grace, we also look ahead to our future destiny ... for blessed are those who are invited to the marriage supper of the Lamb.

May the joy and creativity of our daily service offer our guests a small taste of your coming kingdom, inviting them to know the good and gracious King.

In Jesus' name, Amen.

FINANCIAL SERVICES

Lord, you are the supplier of all of the resources that we have. You have made us stewards, cultivators, and administrators of your creation. We pray for all the professionals in the financial services industry. May they use their capacities and gifts to faithfully administer the resources they are given to serve their community through economic activity.

May those in the industry be honest, truthful, and transparent in their business interactions and have wisdom in all of their deals and decisions. May they reflect your image as Creator and Sustainer of all things as they work to contribute toward the sustenance of your creation. Help them avoid the temptation to engage in dishonest practices or selfish tendencies which would exploit instead of serve others. We pray love would guide their relationships with their coworkers, clients, and customers.

We pray that in their work they would see their calling to be responsible fiduciaries. Help them to see that their work contributes to the economic stability of families, the generosity of the saints, the education of children, the retirement accounts of the elderly, and so much more. That people are behind these numbers, and you are using them to love and serve those people well.

God, we pray you will strengthen their sense of vision in their vocation to see how their work contributes to the economic sustainability of this community and blesses the lives of its people.

In Jesus' name, Amen.

CONSTRUCTION AND ARCHITECTURE

Dear Father, Maker of heaven and earth,

We praise you for the gift of beauty and order here on earth. Thank you, Lord, for all forms of material expressions you've inspired in our architects and our construction workers. We praise you for glimpses of heaven in our midst, which inspire visions of flourishing for our built environment. Thank you, Lord, for the gift of Christ and the Holy Spirit that helps us to understand and imagine light and hope in our broken world.

Father, we ask for your grace and blessing for all those involved with refining our built environment here on earth. We pray for elected government officials, policy makers, developers, and investors who manage the needs of our cities. We pray that they would have a vision that is greater than return-on-investment. We pray that their hearts would be for the powerless and the marginalized.

Lord, we pray for the architects and engineers who address the needs of our cities. We pray that they would use the gift of imagination to design a built environment where people can rest, heal, learn, praise, and find inspiration. We pray that their desire will not only be for the favor of developers and clients, but also for provision of dignity and equality, where class barriers are broken and not reinforced. We boldly pray for ideas that can help democratize our cities.

We pray for safety on construction sites across our city and that builders would work with integrity and pride in their work.

Lord, we remember how you blessed Nehemiah and Israelites from every background to unite and rebuild the wall of Jerusalem. We pray for boldness, joy, creativity, and vision to glorify you in collaborations between developers, investors, architects, engineers, contractors, tradesmen, and elected officials. Father, inspire and equip all those who are tasked with building our cities. Give us reverence for all of your creation so that we would serve those in need and use resources rightly.

In Jesus' name, Amen.

GOVERNMENT

Father God, we recognize there is no authority on earth that has not been provided by you—our local authorities among them. We want to pray for those who work in our local government. We know you have entrusted them with great responsibility and pray that you will help us honor and respect them. We pray you give them guidance and wisdom to lead our city into flourishing that is more reflective of your kingdom.

We pray these leaders will look to you and that you would protect them from the temptation to engage in behavior that may be dishonoring of the responsibility you have given them. May every decision they make contribute to the well-being of our citizens and our city.

We pray you would protect those in government from falling into fear. Our authorities need you; please make them aware that they are in your service for the good of society. We pray you would protect those in government from danger and animosity, that they would be open to listening to perspectives that are different from their own, and that you would grant them wisdom to make decisions in the best interest of those they serve. We pray you will use every government official for your glory.

In Jesus' name, Amen.

CREATIVE INDUSTRIES

Father, we come before you to pray for the artists in our city.

You are the original Creator. All truth, all beauty, comes from you. You brought forth the heavens and the earth as your medium to serve humankind.

Father, you first poured out your Spirit of creativity for the sake of honoring beauty and truth—for the sake of worship, for the sake of celebrating all that is good and just.

We thank you for those who take part in this sacred dance of creativity, a process of surrendering and creating. The Spirit is revealing your true nature through their work. May their hearts and hands always be aligned with authenticity and honesty. We pray that these artists can be the cultivators and storytellers of the richness of this life, drawing inspiration from the joys and the sorrows of our communities, to create an honest reflection of truth and beauty.

Let them continually awaken to your greater calling and continually shed the weight of selfish ambition and pride which the world tries to put on them. Help them to surrender, for the sake of what is good and just, to the stories you want them to tell.

In Jesus' name, Amen.

APPENDIX 11

GUIDE TO WRITING AN INDUSTRY PRAYER

As noted in chapter eleven, including work in the rhythms of prayers in your church services is an integral and rather simple way to build faith-and-work theological truths into the hearts and lives of your congregants.

We highly recommend using the Writing an Industry Prayer *guide below with people in your own church or context so that you can create prayers that are specific to your city and to give people in your ministry a sense of inclusion in the creation of these materials. That being said, feel free to use those we have already curated in any way that they are helpful to you (see appendix ten).*

Writing a prayer for your industry allows you to view that industry through the lens of the biblical narrative and helps you identify and articulate the areas of goodness and brokenness that need prayer and consideration. In prayer, you can celebrate the creational goodness of the industry and also ask God to enter into its fractured areas to bring a full flourishing of your work for its intended purposes.

THE PURPOSE OF THE "PRAYERS OF THE PEOPLE"

"Pastoral prayer" or "prayers of the people" is a time-honored tradition used in some churches and denominations, inviting the congregation to intercede for the needs of the church and the world. This adaptation of focusing on industries allows churches to cultivate a deeper awareness of the needs of particular work contexts. Such prayers affirm individuals' work and are meant to remind us that we are sent as the "priesthood of all believers" (1 Pet. 2:9) into our places of work.

PREPARING YOUR PRAYER

Biblical prayers and the prayers of great Christians through the centuries are poetic and heartfelt. They are richly textured with God's truth and promises, bathed in humility, and grounded in confidence that they will be answered. Let your prayer flow out of your private communion with God. Your industry, personality, and passion for God should be evident in your prayer. You have been called as a child of God and a part of the body of Christ, bringing a unique distinctiveness in the calling you've received.

Celebrate the richness of the names and metaphors God has given us by which we may know and address him. Use "we" rather than "I" as you are praying on behalf of the church.

WHAT TO PRAY FOR

As you think about praying for your industry, consider the following:

- What is the biblical narrative of your industry? What is creationally good that should be celebrated? What is deeply broken that should be lamented? What could this industry be in its best version of itself?
- Pray using language familiar to those in your industry, and try to be specific without being dated or exclusive.
- Pray against specific areas of brokenness you've seen (injustice, discrimination, inequity).
- Pray for those who work in your industry, that they (both Christian and non-Christian) might be used by God to bring about his glory on earth as it is in heaven.
- Pray against the temptations and common areas of brokenness that entice the individuals who work in the industry.
- Pray for those affected by your area of work, that the work might bring about greater human flourishing.
- Affirm where you sense God's Spirit is at work, offering hope and igniting a desire to change, bringing heaven on earth.

Your prayer does not have to cover every issue in your industry. Prayerfully choose what is most relevant to include in your prayer. Trust the Holy Spirit in directing your words.

APPENDIX 12

INDUSTRY ARTICLE EXAMPLES TO INCLUDE IN COMMUNICATIONS

Including articles about faith and work into your routine communication tools is helpful reinforcement. Here are some examples. You can repost the work of others and/or commission and write your own.

- Nathaniel Marshall, "Instead of Becoming a Pastor, I Minister as a Plumber," *Christianity Today*, September 1, 2022, https://www.christianitytoday.com/2022/09/i-wanted-to-be-pastor-now-im-plumber/.

  https://tinyurl.com/yc3zrnnz

- Bill Haslam, "Public Office as a Spiritual Discipline," *Comment*, January 11, 2018, https://comment.org/public-office-as-a-spiritual-discipline/.

  https://tinyurl.com/5btd4v3p

- "What Does the Bible Say About Finance?" Theology of Work Project, accessed April 4, 2023, https://theologyofwork.org/key-topics/finance.

  https://tinyurl.com/7585wh6j

- "Discuss Work in Common Occupations" (various videos), Theology of Work Project, accessed April 4, 2023, https://www.theologyofwork.org/resources/view-all/discuss-work-in-common-occupations.

  https://tinyurl.com/3r4whb8z

APPENDIX 13

IMPACT ASSESSMENT TOOL

Most faith-and-work efforts exist to have Holy-Spirit-empowered impact—impact on the individual and impact on the community/city. Although impact can be hard to measure, we must pay attention to it.

When first starting faith-and-work activities, it is easy to measure things such as number of efforts, attendance, participation rates, growth, and even survey results. However, over time, it is important to assess heart change as well as city change.

Heart change and city change are long, slow processes. Small efforts such as luncheons, conferences, or even a one-off sermon series, are unlikely to create profound heart change. Likewise, city transformation is slow and requires shifts across many sectors before it results in a tipping point.

Thus, though heart change and city impact are not easily measurable, they must still be intuited.

If you have the budget and can embark on a full measurement process, investigate the work of Steve Patty and Dialogues in Action. He has developed a unique qualitative tool to assess heart change in the work of nonprofits. Scan the QR code to go to the Dialogues in Action website:

https://tinyurl.com/yzpuyz8t

It is helpful to answer the following questions about each program/gathering stream/event that you offer. You may do this survey work in a qualitative fashion or a quantitative fashion. If qualitative, ask open-ended questions; if quantitative, ask closed questions (multiple choice, rank, or yes/no/maybe).

ASSESSING HEART CHANGE

Ask individuals who participate in your programs the following kinds of questions.

(Note: The first two questions are phrased in both qualitative and quantitative ways as examples.)

- In what ways do you better understand the role of work in God's plan to redeem the world? [*Qualitative/Open*]

  or
- Do you better understand the role of work in God's plan to redeem the world? [*Quantitative/Closed*]
- How is Jesus more lord of your life after this program? [*Qualitative/Open*]

  or
- Is Jesus more Lord of your life after this program? [*Quantitative/Closed*]
- What changes have you experienced around the role of work in your life?
- Are you more aware of the fruit of the Spirit in your life (or its lack)?
- Have you learned to hear God's voice in regard to your day-to-day work?
- How is your industry creationally good? Where is it broken?
- What types of sacrifice can you make day to day for those with less power and agency in your work setting?
- How has noticing broken systems changed you?

ASSESSING CITY IMPACT

Ask individuals who participate in programs the following kinds of questions:

- Which projects that you are working on in your company/industry/city push against broken systems?
- What outcomes have happened since your view of faith and work has broadened?
- What holes are you able to fill that bring about more goodness in your community, industry, or city?
- How do you see work as a place to impact your city?

ORGANIZER QUESTION

Ask yourself and others who organized the program the following kinds of question:

- How are the fruits of the program visible in the community through projects or partnerships or addressing areas of brokenness?

After assessing your programs, create a chart of each type of activity, project, or program and its effectiveness.

Assessment Chart Example

Program/ Project	Description	Heart Change	City Impact
Intensive	A year-long faith-and-work cohort with thirty participants covering an in-depth curriculum as well as exercises around heart issues and projects in your place of work	High	High
Lunch-and-Learns	An open invitation series of ten luncheons in the city center focused on issues of faith and vocation	Low	Low
Entrepreneur Support	A six-month project to help entrepreneurs understand their call in light of the gospel and assist them in bringing ideas to life	High	High
Sermon inclusion	Work with pastors to ensure each Sunday has a faith-and-work example	High	Medium

Once you have analyzed each program/project, you can create an assessment of the level of change they brought about, which can affect the programs you keep. You can map the programs into the following boxes in a relative fashion.

Example Subjective Qualitative Mapping 2x2

Impact Goal

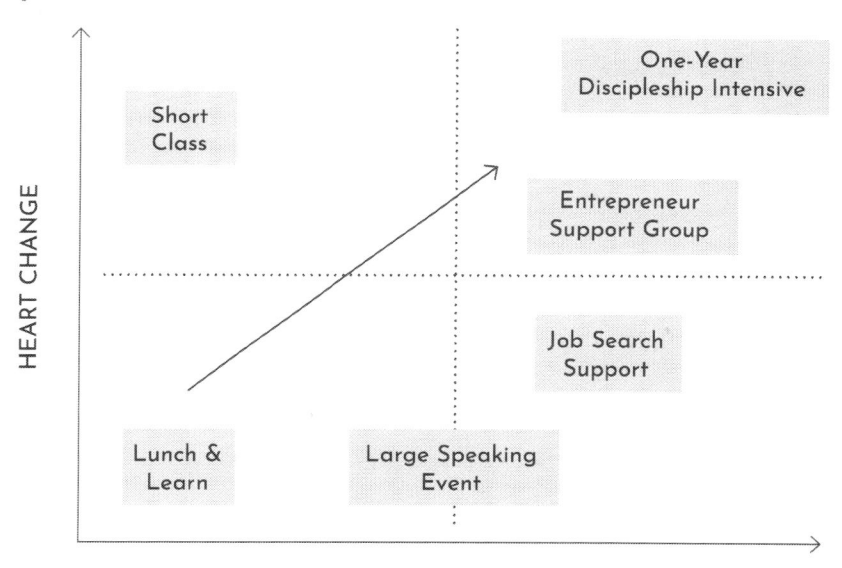

```
HEART CHANGE ↑
             |
             |    Short                    One-Year
             |    Class                    Discipleship Intensive
             |
             |                             Entrepreneur
             |                             Support Group
             |----------------------------
             |                             Job Search
             |                             Support
             |
             |    Lunch &    Large Speaking
             |    Learn      Event
             |_____→
                     RIPPLE IMPACT ON COMMUNITY/CITY
```

Once they are mapped, it is easy to have an objective discussion about where to expand, enhance, or eliminate efforts.

High Heart Change and Low City Impact	High Heart Change and High City Impact
• Programs here should be continued with enhanced emphasis on moving people to action out of gratitude for the Savior's work in their lives. This program may need more focus on broken systems.	• Efforts or programs mapped here are *winners* and should be cultivated. • These are likely to be labor- and time- intensive programs, so fewer offerings with higher focus may be warranted.
Low Heart Change and Low City Impact	**Low Heart Change and High City Impact**
• Efforts or programs mapped here should be eliminated *unless* they are an easy pipeline to move someone into another square.	• Efforts or programs here should be continued with emphasis on slowing people down to focus on the heart-level issues. These programs may need to focus on understanding personal brokenness in order that actions arise from the fruit of the Holy Spirit.

Blank Evaluation Chart

Program/ Project	Description	Heart Change	City Impact

Scan the QR code for a downloadable blank Evaluation chart.

https://tinyurl.com/ 2w4s7z68

Blank 2x2

High Heart Change and Low City Impact	High Heart Change and High City Impact
Low Heart Change and Low City Impact	Low Heart Change and High City Impact

Scan the QR code for a downloadable blank 2x2 chart.

https://tinyurl.com/2w4s7z68

APPENDIX 14
TRANSFORMATIVE LEARNING EXPERIENCE GUIDE

Faith-and-work learning experiences can take many forms—from book studies to online classes to in-person classes. They can be large or small, short or long term. Whatever the specifics, based on ten years of teaching intensive discipleship courses—as well as drawing from Damein Schitter's dissertation, "Wholly Forming: The Formative Experience of Whole-Life Discipleship Among Participants of Non-Formal Learning Communities"[1]—we have identified five essential components for transformative discipleship initiatives:

- **Community:** The initiative includes a group of people learning together. Social learning theory suggests that adults learn better with others, particularly when collaboration is involved. The ideal cohort size is from six to fifteen, which enables a plethora of views and full participation by all involved.

- **Difficulty:** Doing something hard together fosters bonding and produces transformation as evidenced by the use of the concept in medical and military training and the rise of fitness programs such as CrossFit. Note: Difficulty can be a barrier to entry for some, but the payoff of transformational impact is worth it. An initiative can be challenging due to its time commitment, homework requirements, complex material—or all three.

---

[1] Damein Schitter, "Wholly Forming: The Formative Experience of Whole-Life Discipleship Among Participants of Non-Formal Learning Communities," unpublished PhD diss., Trinity Evangelical Divinity School, 2018.

- **Vulnerability:** In order to be known, we must be willing to share our hearts. Brené Brown has written extensively about vulnerability and posits that it is a gateway to change. By embracing vulnerability, participants can learn to see themselves more fully—flaws and all—and through the power of the gospel, develop a greater sense of gratitude, compassion, worth, and other-centeredness. Additionally, vulnerability allows the participants to connect more deeply with others, which ultimately furthers their learning about God, themselves, and the world—leading to transformation.

- **Commitment to daily convening with God:** Part of transformation is learning to hear God's voice, which is best accomplished by stilling oneself before God in Scripture reading, prayer, and silence. We often advise people in our discipleship programs to make daily time with the Lord a top priority, and to sacrifice their coursework if needed to make time for this discipline.

- **Hands-on projects:** Intellectual learning is important, but it's the application of knowledge that truly transforms individuals. Those who apply their learnings in their work environment, powered and guided by the Holy Spirit, often experience the most significant changes in their work and in their hearts. In the words of one former participant of an intensive: "I came here thinking I needed to change jobs because there is so much greed and corruption in mine. However, what I gained is a new perspective and [I] realize God is encouraging me to be a light in the darkness as part of his story to redeem the world."

    Over the last ten years, we have seen countless examples of students participating in large and small projects in their work contexts, which have significantly impacted their jobs, companies, and even industries; but, equally importantly, their own relationship with the Lord has been impacted as well. We have captured some of these stories as video case studies, which can be viewed by scanning the QR code.

https://tinyurl.com/e9ws6y59

Although you can find one or two of these learning components in other experiences that aspire to bring transformation (e.g., other Bible studies, small groups, CrossFit exercise programs, secular leadership programs), we believe that the combination of these five factors creates a transformative experience for participants.

APPENDIX 15

TRANSFORMATIVE LEARNING EXPERIENCE SAMPLE SURVEY

Below is an example of a survey that we use for the Gotham Fellowship program, which is an intensive nine-month transformative learning experience.[1] It is included here for your reference as you think about assessment for your programming. If you are attempting to measure impact, it is helpful to administer this survey at the beginning of a learning experience and again at the end.

INFORMATION

- Name:
- Industry:

BELIEFS

Answer the following questions with one of these responses:

- ○ *Strongly disagree*
- ○ *Disagree*
- ○ *Somewhat disagree*
- ○ *Somewhat agree*
- ○ *Agree*
- ○ *Strongly agree*

- I view my work as a major context to live out my faith.

---

[1] https://faithandwork.com/gotham-fellowship/. Thank you to Susan Nacorda for her help with this survey.

- My knowledge of the biblical narrative informs how I view my work and purpose.

- I view my vocation as a ministry.

- I view my work as a context to live out God's calling to do mercy and justice.

- I have spiritual friendships with people who encourage me in how I live out my faith at work.

- My identity as a child of God informs my day-to-day decisions, hopes, and challenges.

- It is important to consider how I can support and include those on the margins in my workplace and industry.

- I believe I should make a difference in my community.

- My understanding of common grace informs how I view and engage with colleagues who don't share my beliefs.

- I am able to identify areas of brokenness in my workplace or industry and imagine ways to bring practical gospel-centered renewal.

- My faith enables me to see God's purposes for and appreciate different industries and spheres of our society.

- I view creating culture as an important expression of Christian faith.

BEHAVIORS

Answer the following questions with one of these responses:

- Little/none

- o *Monthly*
- o *Weekly*
- o *Daily*

- How often do you spend time with God in Scripture/devotional reading?

- How often do you connect with God in prayer?

- How often do you practice self-reflection and repentance?

- How often do you pray for your workplace and colleagues?

- How often do you participate in gospel community (e.g., Bible studies or discipleship/mentoring relationships)?

- How often do you share vulnerably in gospel community?

- How often do you share your time, treasure, or talent with those on the margins of your community?

- How often do you counsel yourself with the gospel when you struggle with sin and experience challenges at work?

- How often does your faith inform your work decisions as it relates to your job responsibilities (e.g., making ethical decisions, whether or not to work with excellence, considering the impact of your decisions on the community you serve)?

- How often does your faith inform your work decisions as it relates to how you treat your colleagues and clients?

PROGRAM FEEDBACK

- Please rate the following program elements in terms of helpfulness
  [*Leader note: Insert fields with program elements for an answer.*]
    - Not Helpful
    - Somewhat Helpful
    - Helpful
    - Very Helpful

- Do you believe this experience has helped you to better understand the purpose of your work? Why or why not?
  [*Leader note: Insert an open-ended answer field.*]

- Has this program impacted the way you interact with clients, coworkers or colleagues? Please explain.

- How likely are you to recommend this program to a colleague?
  [*Leader note: Insert a scale of 1 to 10, with 10 being most likely.*]

- Is Jesus Christ more Lord of your life than he was before this program?
  [*Leader note: Insert a scale of 1 to 10, with 10 being absolutely yes.*]

APPENDIX 16
CHURCH AND CITY JOURNEY MAPS

In chapters seven through thirteen, we shared the church journey map on page 263, along with detailed steps for each point in the design process for your church or ministry.

Remember: This map is meant to provide a strategic overview that helps inform the journey for your initiative rather than being a step-by-step guide you should rigidly follow.

On page 264 is an additional journey map for independent city initiatives. Given the unique challenges of implementing such programs across a city, this guide is a starting point rather than a comprehensive blueprint.

CHURCH AND CITY JOURNEY MAPS | 263

Church Journey Map for Faith-and-Work Initiatives

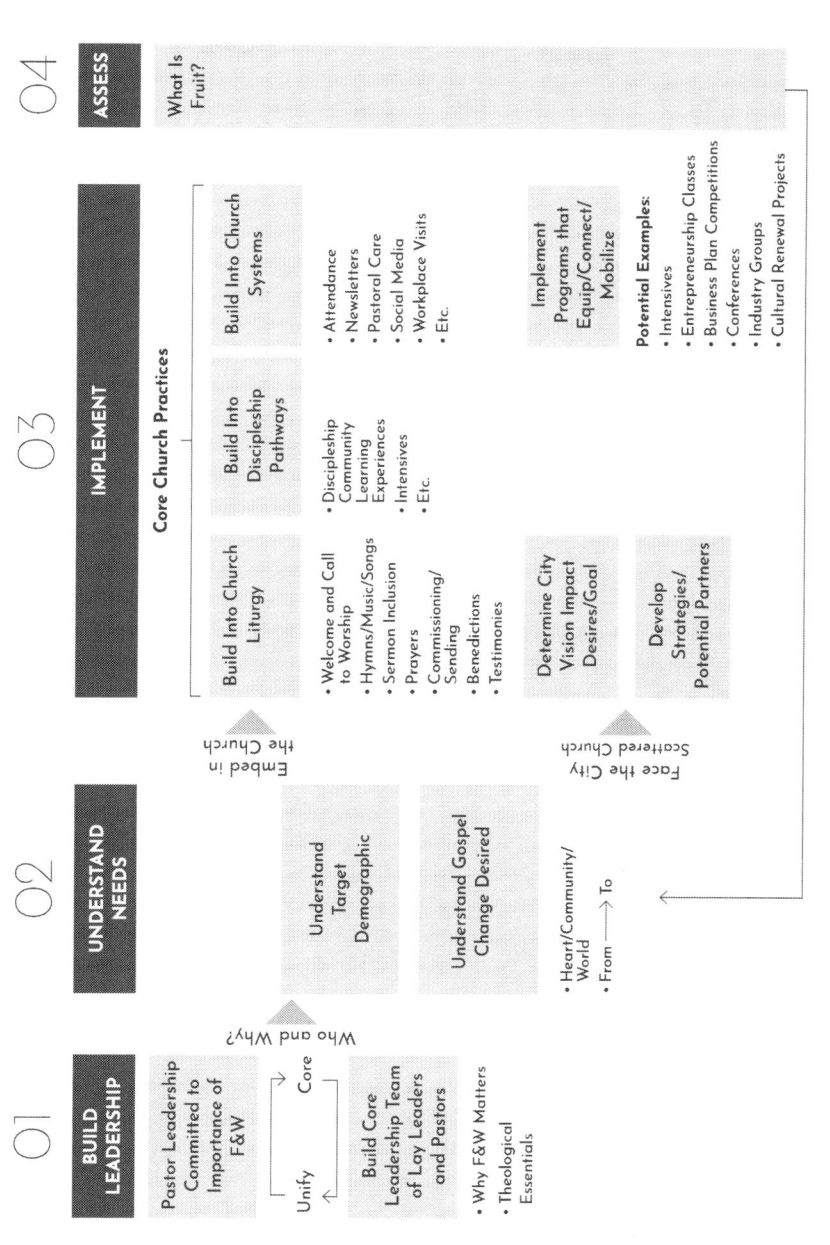

01 BUILD LEADERSHIP

- Pastor Leadership Committed to Importance of F&W
- Build Core Leadership Team of Lay Leaders and Pastors

Unify ↔ Core

- Why F&W Matters
- Theological Essentials

Who and Why? →

02 UNDERSTAND NEEDS

- Understand Target Demographic
- Understand Gospel Change Desired
  - Heart/Community/World
  - From → To

Embed in the Church →

Face the City Scattered Church →

03 IMPLEMENT

Core Church Practices

- **Build Into Church Liturgy**
  - Welcome and Call to Worship
  - Hymns/Music/Songs
  - Sermon Inclusion
  - Prayers
  - Commissioning/Sending
  - Benedictions
  - Testimonies

- **Build Into Discipleship Pathways**
  - Discipleship Community Learning Experiences
  - Intensives
  - Etc.

- **Build Into Church Systems**
  - Attendance
  - Newsletters
  - Pastoral Care
  - Social Media
  - Workplace Visits
  - Etc.

- Determine City Vision Impact Desires/Goal
- Develop Strategies/Potential Partners

Implement Programs that Equip/Connect/Mobilize

Potential Examples:
- Intensives
- Entrepreneurship Classes
- Business Plan Competitions
- Conferences
- Industry Groups
- Cultural Renewal Projects

04 ASSESS

- What Is Fruit?

264 | FAITH & WORK

City Journey Map for Collaborative Faith-And-Work Initiatives

01 BUILD LEADERSHIP

- City-Wide Dedicated Leader Committed to Importance of F&W
- Build Core Leadership Team of Committed Church Pastors and Key Lay Leaders

Unify ↔ Core

- Why F&W Matters
- Theological Essentials

02 UNDERSTAND NEEDS

Understand The City

- Understand Target Demographic
- Understand City Impact Desired

Embed in Churches ↑

Collaborate for City Impact ↑

03 IMPLEMENT

Core Church Practices

- **TRAIN PASTORS Together with a Core Lay Leader**
  - Integrated Leaders, Churches, and City
  - F&W Intensives
  - F&W Monthly Trainings
  - Cohort Development

- **COACH PASTORS to Make Plans for Church Journey Map**
  - Church Maps Demographic
  - Heart Change Desire
  - City Change Desire
  - Build into Core Church Practices

- **PROVIDE Tools, Resources, and Processes**
  - Curriculums
  - Sermon Prep
  - Resources

- Determine Organizational Model
  - Shared F&W Theological Vision
  - Partnership Structure
  - Funding Model
  - Leadership
- Determine Partnerships
- Generate Funds
- Implement Concepts
- Plan Programming
- Launch Program ← Assess

Examples:
- Intensives
- Entrepreneurship Classes
- Business Plan Competitions
- Conferences
- Industry Groups
- Cultural Renewal Projects

04 ASSESS

- What Is Fruit?
- What Is Fruit?
- Convene and Learn ⇄

APPENDIX 17

RECOMMENDED FAITH-AND-WORK ORGANIZATIONS

Below is a list of faith-and-work organizations for your further research. Links to all their websites can be viewed by scanning the QR code.

https://tinyurl.com/mpkdyjmx

- Center for Faith & Work (https://faithandwork.com/)
- Center for Public Christianity (https://centerforpublicchristianity.org/)
- Charlotte Institute for Faith & Work (https://www.charlottefaithwork.org/)
- The Collaborative Orlando (https://collaborativeorlando.com)
- Denver Institute (https://www.denverinstitute.org)
- Faith and Work Chicago (https://faithandworkchicago.com/)
- Faith Co-Op (https://faithcoop.org/)
- Faith Driven Entrepreneur (https://www.faithdrivenentrepreneur.org)
- Fuller De Pree Center (https://depree.org/)
- Goldenwood (https://goldenwoodnyc.org/)
- Imago Dei (France) (https://www.imagodei.fr/)
- Iniciativa Fe & Trabajo (America Latina) (https://www.feytrabajo-latam.com)
- Made to Flourish (https://www.madetoflourish.org/)
- Nashville Institute for Faith & Work (https://www.nifw.org/)
- Praxis (https://www.praxislabs.org/)
- Resource Global (https://www.resourceglobal.org/)
- The Surge Network (https://www.surgenetwork.com/)
- Theology of Work (https://www.theologyofwork.org/)
- Triangle Fellows (https://www.trianglefellows.org/)

- TrueWorks Houston (https://www.trueworkshouston.org/)
- Wheaton College Center for Faith and Innovation: Innovation Lab (https://www.centerforfaithandinnovation.org/about-ilab)
- Women, Work, & Calling (https://www.womenworkandcalling.com/)
- Worship for Workers at Fuller Theological Seminary (https://worship-forworkers.com/)

ABOUT THE AUTHORS

MISSY WALLACE has over thirty-five years of experience in business, education, and ministry and trains global marketplace and church leaders to better integrate faith and work. As former managing director at Redeemer City to City, she trained hundreds of leaders worldwide. Founder of the Nashville Institute of Faith and Work, her career also includes Boston Consulting Group, Time Warner, and Bank of America. Deeply influenced by her Camino de Santiago pilgrimage, she's passionate about helping others connect with Jesus. Missy holds a BA in Economics from Vanderbilt and an MBA from Kellogg at Northwestern. She enjoys hiking with her husband, three adult children, and dogs.

LAUREN GILL is the senior director of the Global Faith & Work Initiative at Redeemer City to City, where she helps leaders around the world equip their laity in faith and work. Previously, she worked at the Center for Faith & Work at Redeemer Presbyterian Church and as a vocational counselor. She is a coauthor and the general editor of *The Missional Disciple: Pursuing Mercy and Justice at Work* and editor of *Go Forth: God's Purpose for Your Work*. A New York University and Columbia University MA graduate, she lives in New York City with her husband, Suneel, and their two children, Alexandra and Jason.

Made in the USA
Middletown, DE
14 March 2025